States of Fantasy

The Clarendon Lectures in English Literature 1994

States of Fantasy

JACQUELINE ROSE

CLARENDON PRESS · OXFORD

Oxford University Press, Great Clarendon Street, Oxford OX2 6DP

Oxford New York

Athens Auckland Bangkok Bogota Buenos Aires Calcutta
Cape Town Chennai Dar es Salaam Delhi Florence Hong Kong Istanbul
Karachi Kuala Lumpur Madrid Melbourne Mexico City Mumbai
Nairobi Paris São Paolo Singapore Taipei Tokyo Toronto Warsaw
and associated companies in
Berlin Ibadan

Oxford is a registered trade mark of Oxford University Press

Published in the United States by
Oxford University Press Inc., New York

First published in paperback 1998

British Library Cataloguing in Publication Data
Data available

Library of Congress Cataloging in Publication Data
Rose, Jacqueline.
States of fantasy / Jacqueline Rose.
(The Clarendon lectures in English literature)
1. English literature—History and criticism—Theory, etc.
2. English literature—Study and teaching.   3. Psychoanalysis and
literature.   4. Canon (Literature)   I. Title.   II. Series.
PR21.R67   1996   820.9—dc20   95-40672
ISBN 0-19-818280-5 (hbk)
ISBN 0-19-818327-5 (pbk)

1 3 5 7 9 10 8 6 4 2

Typeset by Graphicraft Typesetters Ltd.,
Printed in Great Britain
on acid-free paper by
Bookcraft Ltd.,
Midsomer Norton, Bath

For Mia
and Adam

Acknowledgements

THE central chapters of this book were delivered in their original form as the Clarendon Lectures in Oxford in May 1994. Two further chapters on writers whose works are fundamentally connected to the argument have been added. I have also included as an Afterword the inaugural lecture delivered at Queen Mary and Westfield College in October 1993 which was very much the kernel from which the subsequent ideas grew. Since an inaugural lecture is an address to a specific institutional occasion, I have chosen to include it unamended despite a slight overlap of material with one or two other points in the book.

'On the "Universality" of Madness: Bessie Head's *A Question of Power*' first appeared in *Critical Inquiry*, 20 (Spring 1994); 'Dorothy Richardson and the Jew' in *Between 'Race' and Culture: Representations of 'the Jew' in English and American Literature*, edited by Bryan Cheyette (Stanford University Press, 1996); and 'Freud and the Crisis of our Culture' in *Critical Quarterly*, 37/1 (Spring 1995).

My thanks to the Oxford English Faculty for the invitation to deliver the Clarendon Lectures, and to Oxford University Press, especially to Kim Scott Walwyn for encouragement of all kinds. My time in Oxford was made especially enjoyable by Marilyn Butler, to whom I owe a long-standing debt stretching back to my years as an undergraduate, and to Jeri Johnson. Special thanks to Queen Mary and Westfield College English Department who gave me time to prepare the lectures and who have provided such a supportive and stimulating intellectual environment. I have benefited much from the comments of many colleagues, in particular Lisa Jardine, Bryan Cheyette, Richard Bourke, and Lorna Hutson, and from the presence of Pat

Hamilton and Andrew Penman. The final research and writing up of the lectures was made possible by a Senior Research Fellowship awarded by the British Academy/Leverhulme Trust. Personal thanks to Gillian Rose, Diana Stone, Sally Alexander (again), Laura Mulvey, and Hugh Haughton, all of whom have made their crucial and distinctive contribution. Lauren Azuolay was my main Jerusalem informant; she never tired of sending me articles, cuttings, poems, and everything she thought would be helpful, all of which made a huge difference. My thanks to Edward Said for heated discussion at the Conference organized in tribute to his work at Warwick University in March 1994. Finally, thanks to Adam Phillips, whose presence and writing have been a constant source of provocation, in the best sense, and pleasure.

Contents

States of Fantasy

Fantasies moved within her like ghosts [. . .] dark rays doing their
work invisibly in broad light.

George Eliot, *Daniel Deronda*, 1876

[Pathological phenomena] are, one might say, a State within a State,
an inaccessible party, with which co-operation is impossible, but
which may succeed in overcoming what is known as the normal
party and forcing it into its service.

Sigmund Freud, *Moses and Monotheism*, 1934–8

During those terrible nights of the June war, Arab men flocked there
to fish . . . they were searching in the sea for the reassurance that
there was something stronger than our state.

Emil Habiby, *The Secret Life of Saeed, the Ill-Fated Pessoptimist:—A Palestinian
Who Became A Citizen of Israel*, 1974

> . . . feelings heard,
> But every time articulate
> Scarcely a word.
> But you have too long deferred
> Your visit to the modern state.

Muriel Spark, *The Mandelbaum Gate*, 1963

THIS book begins in 1980, during a visit to Israel. I was visiting a
sister who was living at the time with a Bedouin community in
occupied Sinai—land which, on the terms of the 1979 Camp David
treaty, was to be returned to Egypt the following year. I had never been to

Israel before. Until this sister's personal journey spared me the need for a justification which I had been unable to find, it had felt impossible.

There is something bizarre about travelling to a country where you do not belong, in the sense of having no lived connection, not for me, not in my family's past, a country to which I was not therefore returning, but where to say that much is already, in the eyes of the country itself, grounds for reproach. Not to return as a Jewish woman to Israel, not to feel a sense of belonging, not to recognize the very fact and existence of Israel as in itself a historic return, is to break on each count the symbolic parameters of the nation. It is a willed refusal, a rejection of profferred desire. Going to Israel is to enter a country in yearning, one whose passions flow not only from people to homeland but also and just as powerfully the other way. This is a nation which desires its potential citizens—exiled, diaspora Jewry— to come home, with as much fervour as it banishes the former occupants of its land from their own dream of statehood.

I think it is for this reason that talk of the postmodern predicament— belonging everywhere and nowhere at the same time—has never felt quite right. There is something about this vision of free-wheeling identity which seems bereft of history and of passion. As if the anxiety of belonging, itself the product of stories which stretch back in time, could be redeemed in the present by dispersal, the heart miming, shadowing, beating to the tune of a world whose contours can no longer confidently be drawn. Loss of confidence may be welcome, especially where it was misplaced, coercive, or oppressive (you might want to argue that confidence is always one of these three). But it is far from clear that the mind leaps from here into freedom. Hearts can retrench; the body which feels weak rearms itself. The carapace of selfhood and nations cannot be willed—does not fall so easily—away.

At first glance, the title of this book—'States of Fantasy'—no doubt conjures up a more salacious vision of the mind (it will not be the first time for me that the title of a book—*Feminine Sexuality* was another—can be so surely guaranteed to lead to disappointment for some of its readers). In common parlance, fantasy is what you get up to when the surveying mind and surveying society are both looking the other way. Fantasy is supremely asocial. Doubly licentious, it creates a world of pleasure without obligation to what it is either permissible or possible, outside the realm of fantasy, to do. You might think, however, that these two forms of profit cancel each other out. If fantasy is private only, revelling in its own intimacy out of bounds, then however outrageous its contents, it will be powerless to affect or alter the surrounding world.

Although psychoanalysis is often associated with this version of fantasy (the dirty tricks of the mind), it in fact begins somewhere else. In his earliest correspondence with Wilhelm Fliess, Freud distinguished fantasies (*Phantasien*) from dreams on the grounds that unlike the latter, which travel back from perception to unconscious, disintegrating and reordering themselves as they go, fantasy is always progressive.[1] Never completely losing its grip, fantasy is always heading for the world it only appears to have left behind. For some, it is only when Freud credited fantasy with its own unique, psychic reality that psychoanalysis proper could begin (for others this was his grossest act of betrayal, as he shifted his focus from the accounts of real seduction of his female patients which he had seen as the cause of their disorder up to then).

But this moment, while crucial to the history of psychoanalysis, is one step to the side of the aspect of fantasy which interests me here. In the quarrel over Freud's relinquishment of the 'seduction theory of neurosis', almost no attention has been paid to what Freud was saying about fantasy *before* his famous theoretical turn. Continuing his discussion with Fliess, Freud turns from fantasy to morality: 'Another presentiment, too, tells me, as I knew already—though in fact I know nothing at all—that I shall very soon discover the source of morality.'[2] Tentatively (both sure and unknowing), Freud passes from fantasy to the question of how subjects tie themselves ethically to each other and enter a socially viable world.

What he came up with was guilt for crimes not committed, unconscious wishes, troubled identifications which—although it would take him a quarter of a century to formulate it—formed the basis, the emotive binding, of social groups. Mourning was the key. No other experience captures the ambivalence of love and recrimination, allegiance and triumph, exoneration and guilt; no other condition reveals in the same way a tie which binds most powerfully at the very moment when, objectively speaking at least, it has set you free. As early as 1897, therefore, Freud links fantasy to what makes group identifications possible and impossible at one and the same time (only in 1915, in the middle of the war, will he return to this link between mourning and ethics). Fantasy is not therefore antagonistic to social reality; it is its precondition or psychic glue. But fantasy surely ceases to be a private matter if it fuels, or at least plays its part in, the forging of the collective will. More simply, you don't have to buy into Freud's account of hidden guilt to recognize the force in the real world of the unconscious dreams of nations.

Once it is seen in these terms, fantasy sheds its private, illicit nature and goes to work in the world at large. 'For a revolution not to latch onto an inner cycle,' writes Ammiel Alcalay, 'is to remain forever removed from every turn.'³ He is writing about the Palestinian *intafadah*, but his comment can be stretched beyond its immediate context to take in all those moments when a historical desire, drawing its energy from the legacy of ages, emboldens and actualizes itself. Although, as the target of the *intafadah*, Israel was on the opposite side of this conflict, it could itself be seen as one such desire, a nation built by its own account out of sand and dreams. In the words of the twenty-ninth Zionist Congress of 1982, 'Zionism is the uniquely Jewish movement for national liberation and redemption based upon our messianic dreams and upon practical action for self-realisation.'⁴ Israel, as Amos Oz put it in a 1992 lecture, is 'a dream come true'.⁵ Perhaps one reason why Israel is often felt to be so awkward politically for both supporters and critics is that it wears its heart so transparently on its sleeve.

It is central to the argument of this book that there is no way of understanding political identities and destinies without letting fantasy into the frame. More, that fantasy—far from being the antagonist of public, social, being—plays a central, constitutive role in the modern world of states and nations, in which Israel since 1948 (longer if you include the *idea* of Israel) has played such an important and difficult part. Israel is not the only modern state that will appear in what follows. South Africa up to April 1994 also figures, since one of the threads of the argument is the connection between the two and then the link that binds England, historically and culturally, to both (we have, I will be arguing, been very selective in the ways the literary map of the world has recently been redrawn). But Israel has a special status because the fierce and traumatized intensity of longing that went into its creation seems so recalcitrant, so unable or unwilling—for those in power at least—to soften or modulate itself. Not all Israelis feel this, of course; there is a significant minority who for some time now have supported the idea of a bipartite state (some of them will also appear in the pages to come). But if you listen to one dominant rhetoric, it seems as if Israel cannot grant statehood to the Palestinians, not just because of felt real and present danger, but also because so great is the charge of fantasy against such a possibility that, were it to be granted, the nation would lose all inner rationale and psychically collapse in on itself.

One of the objectives of this book, then, is to place fantasy at the heart of our political vocabulary, but with a qualification. If fantasy can be grounds for license and pleasure (the popular meaning is not of course completely out), it can just as well surface as fierce blockading protectiveness, walls up all around our inner and outer, psychic and historical, selves. Political passion might take on the colours of resistance—Ammiel Alcaley's quote—but there is no guarantee that it will travel that way. In fact in psychoanalytic

language, resistance as a concept is far closer to defensiveness than to freedom; you resist when you don't want to budge. There is a common assumption that fantasy has tended to be excluded from the political rhetoric
of the left because it is not serious, not material, too flighty and hence not
worth bothering about. My starting premise works the other way round.
Like blood, fantasy is thicker than water, all too solid—*contra* another of
fantasy's more familiar glosses as ungrounded supposition, lacking in foundation, not solid *enough*.

For one line of thinking, the concepts of state and fantasy are more or
less antagonists, back to back, facing in opposite directions towards public
and private worlds. But fantasy, even on its own psychic terms, is never
only inward-turning; it always contains a historical reference in so far as it
involves, alongside the attempt to arrest the present, a journey through the
past. In the opening epigraph from *Daniel Deronda*, Gwendolen Harleth is
struggling to shed her knowledge of her husband's guilty secret, his past
mistress and children who—in the chapter called 'Revelations' from which
the quote is taken—appear along the railings to stare at her as she rides
with him in the park. Rejoining the Greek meaning of fantasy as 'spectral
apparition' or 'phantom', Lydia Glasher stands witness for a history which
might have been Gwendolen's (might have been any woman's), and for the
most tangible of claims—her felt right to a legacy of which Gwendolen, by
marrying, has deprived her. Shake the cobwebs from your vision, look the
apparition straight in the eye (twice this moment is recalled as a 'Medusa-
apparition'). What petrifies is an age-old story of the unequal and punishing
sexual-cum-legal history of women: 'As if some ghastly vision had come to
her in a dream and said "I am a woman's life".'[6]

Behind any fantasy, there is likely to be some such potential narrative.
'Fantasies', Freud writes to Fliess, are *'protective fictions'*, 'psychical façades
which bar the way to memories' (this is fantasy as pure defence and the
version Freud is considered to have left behind).[7] But fantasy is also a way
of re-elaborating and therefore of partly recognizing the memory which is
struggling, against the psychic odds, to be heard. In 1897, the examples Freud
gives could all be grouped under what has come to be known today as
'trans-generational haunting', forms of remembrance—most often of hidden
and shameful family secrets—which hover in the space between social and
psychic history, forcing and making it impossible for the one who unconsciously carries them to make the link.[8] (Contrary to the normal argument,
therefore, in this early account Freud was theoretically way ahead of himself.) Like the young woman afraid of becoming a prostitute who was, without knowing it, reliving in fantasy her father's seduction of serving-girls

(unconscious solidarity we might say); or the agoraphobic woman whose refusal to go out was her way of asserting her mother's unfaithfulness (an unconscious bid for freedom so unacceptable that it could only be experienced as terror).[9]

Go back to *Daniel Deronda*, and trans-generational haunting would also be the appropriate term to describe the other strand of fantasy coursing through the text: Zion, whose possible actualization is the only way for the hero to redeem his Jewishness in the face of the concerted denials of those around him, and of his absent mother behind them. Like the hysterical patient whom Freud described as 'in the peculiar situation of knowing and at the same time not knowing—a situation, that is, in which a psychical group [is] cut off', Deronda finds himself enacting a history which exceeds his conscious grasp.[10] Hence one might argue Deronda's grandiosity, his wild and omnipotent belief in himself as the saviour of his people. To argue that George Eliot simply concurs with the Zionist vision is to ignore the extent to which she represents Deronda's passion as his symptom (states of conviction tend to be involved in an invisible quarrel with themselves). Israel willing itself into being sounds solipsistic and a bit crazed. There are moments when Deronda's zeal could be put alongside this comment of Moshe Dayan's reported after the 1967 Six-Day War: 'If we believe [in it] and want it, the map of Israel can be determined by ourselves.'[11]

In Eliot's novel, Gwendolen Harleth and Daniel Deronda are haunted in very different ways and with very different consequences; only Deronda is allowed to settle his ghosts by giving historical substance to his dreams (Gwendolen returns to her mother). But both of their inner landscapes, hers no less than his, are peopled with the burdens of history. For both of them a history not of their choosing unfolds in the deepest recesses of the mind.

If fantasy reaches out to the unspoken components of social belonging, 'state' also has a set of meanings which move back from public being into the heart. Most likely, it is this connotation which my title—'States of Fantasy'—will immediately evoke. If the expression 'states of fantasy' does not appear to yoke opposites together, it is because state—in thrall to fantasy, one might say—has gone over to the private side of its semantic history and shed its public face. In fact the word 'state' has a psychological meaning long before its modern-day sense of polity, or rather one which trails beneath the shifting public and political face of the word. To take a relatively modern instance: in his 1854 psychology book, *Unsoundness of Mind*, J. C. Bucknill commented of one insane: 'he was *fully conscious of his state*, and had great hopes of being cured in an asylum' (my emphasis).[12] Here 'state' is almost a synonym for 'insanity'. Thus idiotism and madness were 'states of mind' distinguished by their passivity from other mental acts and operations in which the mind was assumed to retain a grip on itself. It would therefore be pointless to ask of Bucknill's example: if he is fully conscious, exactly how far gone, or indeed partly redeemed, is his state?

Think of the modern expression 'in a state'; it has the same feel—you never have to spell out, especially if you are the sufferer, what exactly it means. As if to be 'in a state' is precisely to lose the capacity to travel with any clarity through the world of words. 'States of confusion', 'states of panic', 'state of dissociation': they could all be seen as tautologies. In each case, the mind simply falls apart, lets go of itself. To describe 'a state' as involving a *relinquishment* of authority would not in this context be a contradiction in terms. But in this, the word state, unexpectedly perhaps, exactly rejoins that of fantasy in one of its modern, psychoanalytic, definitions: 'The intrusion of fantasy causes the ego to give up its own self-government for a moment [. . .] While remaining the seat of its actions, the ego momentarily refuses to be its author.'[13] It is because fantasy arrogates an authority which properly belongs to the ego alone, threatens the ego's supremacy, and forces it to step down, that—like Freud's pathological phenomena in the second epigraph above—it could be described as a 'State within a State' (*ein Staat im Staat*).[14]

One of the reasons the idea of fantasy has a hard time getting into the political argument is, I believe, because it is seen as threatening political composure. In politics, at least, we can be sure of our psychic ground, shedding if only for the brief moment of our political being all tortuous vagaries of the inner life. For some time now, feminism has reproached politics as he is fought for precisely such an imaginatively restrictive vision. Thus Olive Schreiner, whose 1883 *Story of an African Farm* was the first novel to bring South Africa home to the British, argued in her later feminist tract, *Woman and Labour*, that a politics which gave due place to women would not feel threatened by being fragmentary, provisional, but would precisely carve out an agenda closer to the shape of the mind (the feminist manifesto, *Beyond the Fragments*, would reproduce this argument almost verbatim in 1979).[15] Although none of them were alluding to the unconscious, what Schreiner and the authors of the later text were getting at was that politics cannot divest itself of its affective colours, it cannot step free of its subjective undercurrents—its psychic states. As Beatrix Campbell once famously commented, the difference between male left politics and feminism is that men tend to enter the former armed with the truth, whereas women are more likely to become feminists when everything, starting with truth itself, has collapsed. But it is a form of redemptive fantasy in itself to believe that, in the world of publicly engaged action, you can step forth free of mental embarassment (enter the grown-up world). This is, note, a point distinct from the recent argument that modernism's aesthetic project, also pseudo-redemptive, was to repair the horrors of the real world with words.

Look a little more closely at the word 'state' in its political significance as polity, commonweal, commonwealth. Place it alongside that other meaning of 'state' (and of 'fantasy') as loss of authority, and it appears that the private and public attributes of the concept 'state' are not opposites but shadows—outer and inner faces precisely—of each other. In a sense this is obvious, since wherever there is authority there is always the possibility of its demise. Hence Machiavelli's famous assertion, which some see as the beginnings of modern statehood, that the prince must set about 'conquering *and maintaining* his state' (my emphasis).[16] The prince's state was a front; it relied on deceiving the people and on cowing them into submission (far better for a prince to be feared than to be loved).

Likewise Max Weber, listing the factors which secure allegiance to the modern state—tradition, charisma, legality—ends by commenting that '*in reality*' (his words, my emphasis), the obedience of the people rests on hope and fear: 'fear of the vengeance of magical powers or of the power-holder, hope for reward in this world or in the world beyond'.[17] A state may be sovereign (in this context 'sovereign state' is the tautology), but that doesn't dispense with, it intensifies, the requirement to make *sure* of itself. Over and above its monopoly of legitimate violence, the modern state's authority passes straight off the edge of the graspable, immediately knowable world. 'When and why do men obey? Upon what inner justifications and upon what external means does this domination rest?' (the first being the question Freud was led to in his consideration of fantasy in that early correspondence with Fliess).[18]

In fact, as the first pages of *Economy and Society* make clear, it is particularly difficult for the state, as a collective entity, to get into Weber's basic frame of rationally purposive action (actions which the individual himself can explain). It can do so only in terms of the inner meaning it holds for its subjects or the subjective belief they attach to it. But these are factors which, precisely because of their intangible, speculative component, cannot be held to reason. They immediately threaten to run into the arms of all the other 'borderline' factors which Weber lays out as most recalcitrant to sociological explanation of the type being proposed: ends which defy intellectual grasp, hidden 'motives' and 'repressions', mystical experience which cannot be fully communicated with words. If the state has meaning only 'partly as something existing', if it rests on the belief of individuals that it 'exists or should exist', then it starts to look uncannily like what psycho-analysis would call an 'as if' phenonomenon.[19] You mould your acts and gestures to a persona that deep down you know isn't really there.

Something irrational—not as in unreasonable, but as in relying on a power no reason can fully account for—has entered the polity. For social theory, the decisive shift occurs at the point where the ruler, instead of 'maintaining his state', serves a separate constitutional and legal state which it is his 'duty to maintain'. Once real authority is no longer invested in the prince and his trappings, it loses its face and disembodies itself: 'With this analysis of the state as an omnipotent yet impersonal power,' Quentin Skinner concludes his study of the foundations of modern political thought, 'we may be said to enter the modern world.'[20] The modern state enacts its authority as ghostly, fantasmatic, authority. But it would be wrong to de-duce from this—like those who misread Freud's attention to fantasy as essentially trivializing—that the state is any the less real for that.

In fact there is a paradox here, for it is this transmutation—the impersonal-ity of the modern state—which guarantees the possibility of freedom (a democratic order into which everyone formally can enter) even if in reality the state has more and more been reduced to serving ruthless competition in the modern world. In this split between state and civil society, the individual's collective being is unrealized—in Marx's words, 'abstract', 'artificial'; detached from the ideal, it becomes no less fantasmagoric, the mere shadow of itself.[21] Pure phantom—'Individuals are only phantoms like the spectrum' (Schelling)—the individual yearns for true embodiment in the state. 'I want,' writes Fichte in Foundations of Natural Law, 'to be a human being . . . it is the aim of the state fully to procure this right for man' (Deronda could be seen as enacting the frantic, willed, form of such self-incarnation).[22]

It should perhaps then come as no surprise to notice the curious but striking proximity between this account of modern statehood and the su-perego, that part of the mind which Freud eventually theorized as the site of social law. For Freud, the superego exerts an authority beyond all rea-son, implacable to the precise extent that it draws on all the unconscious energies it is meant to tame (it therefore endlessly punishes *and* recycles the crime). Which is why inside the head, the law always feels a bit crazy and why, although it never stops trying, it can never quite justify itself. Like the state, the superego is both ferocious and a bit of a fraud. Seen in this light, the corruption of government, widely recognized today as the predominant characteristic of this Conservative administration—the most salubrious details hit the British press daily as I write—would be no news (or rather only news).[23]

It has often been argued that Freud's concepts owe more to the society surrounding him than he allowed, but it has not been suggested, as far as I know, that it is not the contents of social being that Freud imported into the psyche so much as its *form*. This ruthless superego looks very much like Weber's vision of the modern state, binding its subjects to a violence which— Weber makes this central to his definition—is pure *means* without end (there is no way of defining the state in terms of its ends given that there is no end which '*some* political organization has not at some time pursued').[24] It also borrows something of Weber's account of charismatic authority which he invites us into via the image of heroic frenzy, manic seizure, and mad dogs.[25] But it is not only Weber who has analysed this punishing, alien component of the state's putative reason. 'It seems to me,' writes Gramsci, 'that one cannot start from the point of view that the State does not "punish" [. . .] the State must be conceived as an "educator", in as much as it tends precisely to create a new type or level of civilisation.'[26] It is because the state has become so alien and distant from the people it is meant to represent that, according to Engels, it has to rely, more and more desperately, on the sacredness and inviolability of its own laws.[27]

I would like to suggest that the terrifying fragility and intransigence of modern statehood can be illuminated by placing it into this dialogue with Freud: not just in so far as his concept of the superego tracks the modern theorization of statehood; nor just to the extent that psychoanalysis might help to elucidate the subjective component of political being (extending Benedict Anderson's famous 'imagined community' of nations); but in this further sense, that psychoanalysis can help us to understand the symptom of statehood, why there is something inside the very process upholding the state as a reality which threatens and exceeds it. As Weber lays it out so clearly in that opening chapter of *Economy and Society*, you cannot call up the subjective dimension and expect to keep it in place. For while it may be in the unconscious that you most profoundly submit to the law, the unconscious is also, according to psychoanalysis, the place where all your other and better ideas can be found. If the modern state is a fantasy—if it relies on fantasy for an authority it can ultimately neither secure nor justify—then fantasy will always be there to one side of it, like Emil Habiby's fishermen of the third epigraph, calling its bluff, knowing better, wanting something more, something else: 'During those terrible nights of the June war, Arab men flocked there to fish . . . they were searching in the sea for the reassurance that there was something stronger than our state.'[28]

As 'A Palestinian Who Became A Citizen of Israel', Saeed Pessoptimist does not in fact, other than purely formally, have a state in the full meaning of the term. In response to this dilemma, he moves liminally through his political world. He hails the narrator and reader on the first page from outer space and starts the chapter of this quotation from deep within the catacombs of Acre (in a crucial later scene, the freedom-fighter Walaa walks into the sea with his mother). In this novel it is at least an open question whether you should ever take the risk, politically or psychically, of *grounding* yourself.

When Freud took his metaphor for pathological phenomena from the state—'a State within a State'—he was a stateless person (it would be wrong to see psychoanalysis in its first generation as untouched by these historic concerns). Not for the first time, one might say, he was unconsciously analysing himself. Living in England, Freud was working on *Moses and Monotheism*, his great 'Jewish' work completed in the shadow of the impending war and written across his own passage into exile. It would not appear until after his death in 1939, but he had started it in Vienna in 1934, four years before he had been forced to leave. The living—and dying—representative of the crisis which would eventually lead to the creation of the state of Israel, Freud did not offer a heroic account of Jewish history (for that reason many saw it as not only inaccurate, which it was, but inopportune). Instead he told the story of a people violently willing themselves into a nation. Freud believed that Moses was an Egyptian, that there was not one Moses but two, and that the first had been murdered by his followers. It was the stubborn persistence and later re-emergence of that trauma in the form of deferred obedience to the first dead Moses that led to Freud's analogy with the symptom ('a State within a State')—something defiant and potentially destabilizing that will not go away.

If there is something wild about Freud's story then its form of extravagance is of special pertinence to what I am trying to evoke here. Slowly and through the passage of his own history, Freud makes his way back to the traumatic theory of neurosis which, according to the dominant account, he had definitively relinquished in 1897. In terms of *history*, trauma reappears; the journey of the concept through Freud's opus thus beautifully imitates its content (trauma always returns). The story, and the analogy, are there to remind us of that part of historical being, passionate and traumatized, which runs backwards and forwards, never completely in the grasp of its subjects, through psychic time. To paraphrase this famous quote from Gramsci (it is cited by Edward Said on the question of Palestine):

The starting point of critical elaboration is the consciousness of what one really is, and is 'knowing thyself' as a product of the historical process to date which has deposited in you an infinity of traces without leaving an inventory.[29]

—these are traces which persist and colour the present to the exact extent
that everything inside people and psyche are willing themselves not to
remember, not to know. Like Gramsci, Freud too called up the Delphic
oracle 'Know thyself' (he was writing about the slips which reveal us to
others better than we know).[30] But his starting premise was that such knowledge would have to pass through the defiles of the unconscious.

Read through the filter of the present, this last work of Freud's seems like
an advance warning, a caution against the belief that statehood could ever
be the total psychic redemption of its people. Freud was sympathetic to
Zionism and by 1935, when Nazism was established, he was in favour of a
Jewish nation state in Palestine, but earlier in the 1930s he had spoken out
against the idea.[31] Driven into exile, it is as if he were almost demonstrating
in his person how loss, historic deprivation, transmute themselves into
necessity, one which soon—he did not live to see it—would entrench itself
beyond all negotiable reach. The state, lost in reality, turns into metaphor
and takes refuge deep within (it is a truism in psychoanalysis that the lost
object is the one that never lets go). Run the line from Freud's analogy to
his own historical condition and I read him as diagnosing statehood as the
symptom of the modern world. Run the line from here back to 1897 and
the Moses narrative can be read as the last chapter in Freud's attempt to
link public, collective life to the unconscious, fantasmatic, life of the mind.

The final epigraph of this introduction is taken from Muriel Spark's 1963
novel, *The Mandelbaum Gate*, set in Jerusalem and Jordan in 1961, the year
of the Eichmann trial.[32] The novel tells the story, mainly, of an Englishwoman—Barbara Vaughan—who puts herself and all those who seek to
pursue or protect her at risk by crossing over to Jordan through the
Mandelbaum Gate. Every Christmas up until 1967, Palestinian Israelis with
relatives in Jordan, when permitted and under restriction, would do the
same. There is of course no real symmetry here. In the 1986 novel *Arabesques* by Anton Shammas, the Palestinian Israeli author writing in Hebrew,
such paltry and diminished forms of contact are represented as the point
where all real connection and memory slip away.[33]

Spark's novel appears in the pages that follow as a way of situating the
issue of modern statehood at the heart of Englishness. It shows the English
on location in refined and semi-farcical panic, confronted by a legacy which
in some deep sense, since Balfour at least, could be said to be theirs. But the
novel, and epigraph, are also there because of their hesitancy: the question,
only partly answered by the book, as to whether this Englishwoman, Jewish through her mother's side, should in fact be in this part of the world at
all. For the Israeli guide who confronts her, Barbara Vaughan's presence is

acceptable only if she is willing to shed the non-Jewish part of her identity, only on condition that—without reservation or qualification—she identifies. She must make the imaginative project of Israel her own.

During my visit to Israel in 1980, I encountered something of the same demand. It was matched by the contrary recrimination from one Palestinian woman—assuming from the fact of my being Jewish that I saw Israel as my homeland—of identifying or belonging, not too little, but too much. Out of that double reproach, and the dilemma it focused for me of how to participate in a history not exactly of my own making (I was born the year after the creation of Israel when the United Nations Armistice lines were laid down) but to which I feel an intense and continuing connection, emerged much of what follows here.

When Virginia Woolf wrote that women are fortunate to be denied the full 'stigma of nationhood', that a woman wants no country, 'as a woman my country is the whole world', she offered a vision of feminized migrancy which it is tempting to lift as a solution to the political ills of the contemporary world (tempting perhaps, too, as the solution to the personal dilemma just described).[34] The epigraph from Spark is therefore also there as a caution, for its reminder that the encounter with modern statehood cannot be indefinitely deferred: 'You have too long deferred | Your visit to the modern state'. You can't, even as a woman, just float off. Woolf was not reckoning with the post-war legacy which engendered Israel/Palestine.

There is a point of more general significance. It has often been remarked that when the white critic talks of post-colonial culture, there is always the risk that she will simply reappropriate that culture back into her own language, repeating the original (colonial or imperial) offence. Two alternatives, it is suggested, confront her: either the barrier is insurmountable, or it can—perhaps—be challenged, rendered precarious, by the migration of all identities in the post-modern world. But Israel came into being to bring the migrancy of one people to an end. Uniquely, perhaps, it saw its task as the redemption, not just of that people, but of the horrors of modernity (which is not to ignore the equally strong impulse to give the Jew her place as fully modern citizen). Displacing the Palestinians, it then produced on the spot a new people without statehood, not just by oversight or brutal self-realizing intention, but as if it had symptomatically to engender within its own boundaries the founding condition from which it had fled.

In this context, the Jewish critic who wishes to address Israel as an outsider marks herself immediately as a participant by default: even more so today when, in the words of Israel Shahak, the issue for Rabin's generation is no longer, as it was for the first generation of leaders, the benefit of the

Israeli state for the Jews, but the benefit of the Jews for the security of the state.[35] But the status of diaspora intellectual cannot be invoked as a solution when, for the nation in question, the diaspora is the source of the problem, the place where historically it begins. And if in defiance—it is impossible for this not to be partly a gesture of defiance—she invokes this status as freedom, as releasing a permission to identify with the oppressed group (as many Jews outside and inside Israel do), she immediately hits the buffers of statehood once again. For the Palestinians, statehood is the demand. It is the only condition of freedom for the group with which she has chosen so undutifully to identify (a device for talking 'peace without statehood' was how one commentator defined the 1993 Oslo accord).[36]

In recent literary discussion, the terms 'culture' and 'identity' have been the common currency. In fact they are inseparable, since it is assumed that culture, as opposed to, say, class, is the process through which lines of identity, especially in the field of sexuality, are drawn. But culture has a tendency to become its own history; as the place where identities are not just formed but contested, it seems at times to acquire a political valency which allows it to set off all on its own (politics as culture and nothing else). And identity, most famously in what has come to be known as identity politics, challenges the dominant but without changing the rhetorical or psychic rules; recognized for a moment as unstable, it then immediately reasserts itself as counter-identity, and starts to mirror the forms of unswerving conviction it was meant to have left behind (question everything but identity itself).

If we replace the terms 'culture' and 'identity' with 'states' and 'fantasy', it seems to me that we avoid both of these problems at once (since sexuality is often what is being talked about, 'identity' seems too 'hard', 'culture' too 'soft'). However far it travels , the term 'state' always holds its reference to the founding political condition of the modern world. And 'fantasy', however much it threatens subjects with the prospect of its own and their dissolution, keeps sight of the peculiarities with which identities, not only consciously but also unconsciously, make and unmake themselves. To place 'state' and 'fantasy' together is not only to propose a new theoretical turn but is also, as I have tried to suggest here, to uncover the history of their intimate relation. Long before psychoanalysis got the idea—although Freud's involvement with these matters has been mostly overlooked—fantasy has been where statehood takes hold and binds its subjects, and then, unequal to its own injunctions, lets slip just a little. We cannot bypass modern statehood; we are still living in its world. Fantasy allows us first to acknowledge that as a more than external matter. But we should not forget, either, that fantasy's supreme characteristic is that of running ahead of itself. There is something coerced and coercive, but also wild and unpredictable, about it. If fantasy can give us the inner measure of statehood, it might also help to prise open the space in the mind where the worst of modern statehood loses its conviction, falters, and starts to let go.

PART ONE

The Clarendon Lectures

ONE

In the Land of Israel

I N 1968, one year after the six-day war, Amos Oz's *My Michael* was published, the novel which established his international reputation.[1] At one point in the book, the Michael of the title explains to Hannah, the woman narrator of the story, the principles of geomorphology—a discipline, as he puts it, which lies on the border between geography and geology:

Most people are of the mistaken opinion that the earth was formed and created once and for all many millions of years ago. In fact, the earth's surface is constantly coming into being. If we may employ the popular concept of 'creation' we can say that the earth is continuously being created. Even while we are sitting here talking. Different and even opposed factors co-operate in forming and changing both the visible contours and also the underground features which we cannot perceive.[2]

Hannah is not interested in Michael's profession—the novel tells the story, in her voice, of her sexual, emotional, and political disaffection from him—but on one occasion she looks over his shoulder as he writes:

The words made me shudder: Extraction of mineral-deposits. Volcanic forces pressing outwards. Solidified lava. Basalt. Consequent and subsequent streams. A morphotectonic process which began thousands of years ago and is still continuing. Gradual disintegration, sudden disintegration. Seismic disturbances so slight that they can be detected only by the slightest instruments.[3]

What, we might ask—rephrasing these two passages—goes on under the surface of the earth? Is it beneficent or harmful, continuous or complete; how can we get in touch with it, and do we need to do so? What, exactly, in terms of time, solidity, disintegration, is happening beneath our feet? Questions for the geomorphologist, but also, it would seem, for the literary student and/or critic. Resuming her literary studies after her marriage to Michael, Hannah is greeted by her professor:

Mrs . . . ah yes, Mrs Gonen, I have just heard the good news and I must hasten to congratulate you on your, ah, nuptials [. . .] What a very symbolic conjunction of subjects. Both geology, on the one hand, and the study of literature, on the other, delve down into the depths, as it were, in quest of buried treasures.[4]

Questing for buried treasures—less politely, plundering—is one way of relating to what is present, hidden, in the bowels of the earth (to use the most common but loaded metaphor). But perhaps that quest is in itself already metaphorical, already indicates that something intangible has been turned into substance, given manageable, graspable shape. To bury into the earth can also be a way of not seeing. It can give the illusion that something is there for the taking, that a claim—like the earth itself—can be settled, and then possessed for all time.

Likewise, mere walking can be ownership, the act out of which nations are made. At the end of Oz's 1991 novel, *Fima*, the narrator quotes these lines from the poet Gilboa: '"Suddenly a man gets up one morning and feels he's a nation and starts walking."' 'The time has come,' Fima comments, 'to stop feeling like a nation. To stop starting to walk. Let's cut that crap. *A voice called to me and I went. Wherever we are sent—we'll go.* These are semi-fascist motifs. You're not a nation. I'm not a nation. Nobody is a nation.'[5] Yeshayahu Leibowitz—chemist, neurophysiologist, philosopher and, up to his death in August 1994, perhaps Israel's most renowned political commentator—makes the point in more directly political terms: '*No nation has a right to any country.* While a country is an objective datum, "right" and "nation" are constructions of the human mind . . . The historic past does not exist in the present except as an act of consciousness.'[6]

In this opening chapter, I start by putting Amos Oz and Yeshayahu Leibowitz together, not because they agree with each other—we will see the ways they do and don't—but because both, in their different ways, are asking a question central to the enquiry of this book. What acts of consciousness, what forms of belief or fantasy, constitute the seeming solidity—the *reality*—of the world and air we breathe? 'Challenge our most cherished assumptions'—we assume that is something literature does, and ought to do. But 'take the ground from beneath our feet'—that might be going too far. It might rob us of what we take for granted, what we need to be sure of, in order for that first, politer, and more restrained version of literary disorientation to proceed. Redrawing the boundaries, unsettling foundations, overturning the ground—we can start by taking these metaphors of recent literary transformation literally just for a moment. Are they all—imaginatively, psychically, or politically speaking—the same thing?

For both Amos Oz and Yeshayahu Leibowitz, to lay claim to the land is an act of constitutive blindness; for Leibowitz, it mistakes an act of consciousness for an empirical given (as in pre-given) and hence as a given right (as in bestowed); for Oz, if we run together for a moment the passages from that early and later novel, it sees process as substance, movement as event. For both of them, it is a form of distorted memory which allows mind and history to settle into congealed time. Only by stopping the movement of the earth—vertically through space, horizontally across time—can you enter the 'once-and-for-all' and take possession. Of land, of others, of yourself. Blind credence. The fantasy on which state and nationhood rely. What, I will be asking throughout the chapters that follow, are the psychic preconditions, what the price?

Literary theory of the past decade has had much to say about the fixing of language and sexuality, about the way meaning and identity deceptively and damagingly ossify into their rigid but socially acceptable place. More recently, it has turned its attention to the way that those same forms of willed, imagined self-knowing batten down and fasten the colours of nation and race. My aim in this book is to track that dynamic across what might seem at first glance somewhat unlikely places: Israel/Palestine, South Africa, England and back. The links between all these places have, of course, been historic in the most concrete sense of the term: direct from Britain to Africa since the seventeenth century, when the first ships of the East India Company sailed around the Cape, to Palestine and Israel via the British Mandate and Balfour Declaration of 1917; indirectly between Palestine and South Africa in the form of the simultaneous late-nineteenth- and early-twentieth-century emigration to both countries of Eastern European Jews; more directly and troublingly between Israel and South Africa. To take just one instance, Daniel François Malan, head of the first National Government of South Africa which founded apartheid, was the first foreign head of state to visit Israel in 1953.

But alongside those connections, it is another form of linkage and belonging that interests me—the link between historic destiny and the fantasies which support and lend to that destiny their shape. In each of the chapters that follow I will be arguing that there is the most intimate relation between what goes on underneath the surface—call it the unconscious—and territorial stake-out of people, places, and things. In each case I have chosen writers who seem to me to throw into particular relief the question of how we build in fantasy our claim to solidity in the world. I start with

Israel/Palestine because of the way in which, in everything I have read, the claim to possession seems to lay bare its unconscious undercurrents, its own peculiar vulnerability, and its dangers, with such exemplary clarity and such disturbing force.

Amos Oz will be the central concern of this first chapter not only because, as these opening quotations will have suggested, his writing seems driven by this concern: not simply, not unequivocally—Oz's preoccupation with the land can also be read as sharing the investment of which it is also the critique—but also because, in ways that are eloquent of the problem of translation and representativeness, he is seen, and not only by himself, as a spokesman. The most translated Hebrew novelist into English (he has in fact been translated into 30 languages), and until recently the most often-cited critic of the Israeli government in the West (up to the September 1993 Declaration of Principles between Israel and the PLO and the subsequent accord), Amos Oz is for many what Israel—in English literary and cultural consciousness—is allowed to be. There are others, like A. B. Yehoushua and more recently David Grossman, but it is from Oz that we have heard most. He's the voice that repeatedly gets through. Ammiel Alcalay, Smadar Lavie, and Ella Shohat have all written about the other voices—Sephardic, Levantine, Palestinian—which, partly as a consequence, don't.[7] This is one reason why Oz's writings will here be deliberately woven into others, even and including voices from the 'other' side.

So, who passes *into* English? Who decides? And at whose expense? One of the things that Oz can help to bring into focus is the way in which that 'into English' is already, again, becoming part of a myth-making process, framing and binding our access to what we like to think of today as a wider, more inclusive literary and cultural world. Seen in this light, it is not just the political content of his writing that makes Oz controversial. It is his standing. Oz, we might say, straddles two political boundaries—the boundary, tangible, visible, violently contested, between Israel and Palestine; and the boundary, far less obvious but none the less carrying its own historical baggage, between Israel/Palestine and English literary culture; or between English literary culture and the worlds it partially and irregularly acknowledges as its own.

If, then, Oz has much to say about the 'land of Israel' (it is the title of one of his books)[8], he also demonstrates something about the task of literary inclusion and expansion—what often goes under the name of the 'canon' debate—its 'interminability', as we might say: not just in the sense that there are and will always be other writers, but more in the sense of interminability that we can take from Freud. Psychoanalysis starts from the

assumption that behind every new utterance that is spoken, for every rais-
ing to the surface of our consciousness, likely as not are regathering the
voices of the unheard. Certainly it believes that conscious volition—the
best will in the world—will never be enough to redraw any one individual's
psychic terrain: because it is not consciously that we enter our history, not
willingly (in both senses) that we inherit the parameters with which our
psychic reality begins. But if the idea of the unconscious has decisively
affected how we think about the agon of writers, the vertical transmission
of cultural inheritance across time, it is striking how absent it has been as
a concept from debates about the contemporary redrawing of the literary
globe.

To argue—as Stanley Fish did in the 1993 Clarendon lectures—that literary study has tried to be too political, that it has made false political
claims for itself, is amongst other things to miss this point.[9] It is to miss the
extent to which it is not solely through will, intent, and reason (all claims
of conscious volition) that we fashion and experience our political worlds.
Precisely because the very idea of 'claim' is the problem, it can serve as the
place where this particular dialogue between literature and politics will
begin. It is the starting presupposition of everything that follows that, like
the earth's surface, we might say, such dialogue is ongoing, always coming
into being, creating and recreating itself, hardly a claim since always in
process, of necessity incomplete. Literary study could, then, never be too
political; its virtue would be to be never political *enough*. The politics of
literature is not something to be calculated or computed in terms of meas-
urable effects. The issue is not whether literature, or one way of reading
literature, directly and immediately impacts or transforms the political world,
but the ways that our literary and political being, along the same or different distress lines, are, at any given moment, transforming or blocking themselves. At the very least, we need to find a language which would allow the
dialogue to be pursued in non-territorial terms.

Or, to turn the same point round the other way, if we are talking about
boundaries (Fish's argument finally was, after all, for the preservation of
literary criticism as a distinct and separate craft), then we might start by
looking at how territory can be object and source of its own peculiar form
of passion.

* * *

If you really love the land, if you really have a deep religious feeling for the land,
then love it unconditionally, love it even if the masters of that part of the land are
going to be the Palestinian people.

Amos Oz talking on the BBC 'Assignment' Programme, 'My Homeland, Your Homeland', a journey round the state of Israel in dialogue with Palestinian writer in exile, Hisham Sharabi, returning for the first time since 1947, shown on Israel television, October 1993

To talk of the 'land of Israel' is already to start with a politically weighted term, to enter non-neutral ground. What exactly is the land? Most concrete of referents, the one whose tangible, manipulable substance it would be pointless to deny, the land immediately forces us up against the heavy symbolic quotient which gives to any referent its shape. In Oz's short story, 'The Hill of Evil Counsel', set at the time of the British Mandate, the child Hillel writes to the King in London and the British High Commissioner in Palestine: 'Our land belongs to us, both according to the Bible and according to justice. Please get out of the Land of Israel at once and go back to England before it is too late.'[10] Hillel's parents quarrel about the meaning, history, potential, of the land:

Father used to say that the beautiful lands had vomited us up here in blind hatred, and that therefore we would build ourselves a land a thousand times as beautiful here. But Mother would call the land a backyard.[11]

The semantic dispute is already a scandal, the mother's disaffection in language signalling in advance her sexual 'treachery', which is how the story ends (she goes off with the Hero of Malta, Admiral Sir Kenneth Horace Sutherland, VC, KBE, Deputy First Sea Lord).

One might in fact say that the meaning of the 'land of Israel' is to have *no meaning*, that it is pure self-referentiality, beyond contestation ('according to the Bible and according to justice, get out and go'). In 1973, at the Lydda Military Court in the West Bank which tried Palestinians suspected of political sabotage, the Jewish lawyer, Felicia Langer, contested on appeal the use by the court President, Yehoshua Ben-Zion, in all the sentences he passed, of the phrase 'the Land of Israel' ('the word Israel [on its own]' she objects, 'never appears').[12]

In his book *The Third Way*, Raja Shehadeh, a Palestinian lawyer also working in the West Bank, coined the expression 'land pornography' to describe the way exile and loss transmute themselves into the most fervent forms of nationalist possession. Over-valuation of the object, Freud would call it, when a tree—to take Shehadeh's example—becomes filled out, symbolized beyond recognition with the weight of desire, and then manipulated in fantasy to its purpose. Shehadeh comments: 'It is not *any* symbolism, but *national* symbolism that makes you into a land pornographer. It is the identification of the land with your people and through that with yourself.'[13]

What Shehadeh describes, Langer protests in court, Roland Barthes once famously described as the mythological impulse, the way belief-systems write themselves as nature, dissolve into the landscape, start to look as if they were always, and will always, be there.[14] Emptied of its history, the land is packed with appropriating, mythological, intent. Perhaps no expression more than the 'the land of Israel' shows the speed with which a signifier can race across the pages of history from empty—the presupposition was of course that this land *was* empty—to (over)full sign. 'As though', Oz writes of the landscape of the settlements in his book of essays, *In The Land of Israel*, 'everything has already been said, once and for all, and not a word can be added.'[15] If the land has meaning, its ultimate promise is to bring all meaning to an end. As you read this body of literature you can watch the movement of language, its fixing and undoing, take on the most tangible political shape.

In the same chapter of *In The Land of Israel*, Oz cites a passage he wrote to the daily newspaper, *Davar*, two months after the Six-Day War, to protest against the redemptive-cum-triumphalist rhetoric in which Israel's crushing victory (and the grounds of the subsequent occupation) were being dressed: 'Only in the twilight of myths can one speak of the liberation of a land struggling under a foreign yoke. Land is not enslaved and there is no such thing as a liberation of lands. There are enslaved people, and the word "liberation" applies only to human beings. We have not liberated Hebron and Ramallah and El-Arish, nor have we redeemed their inhabitants.'[16] In his 1988 book on *Israel*, the Israeli fiction writer, A. B. Yehoshua, also writes: 'Land cannot be liberated, only man can be.'[17] In Oz's case, the protest is intrinsic to his Zionism. Zionism, he writes in 1982, is a movement 'to liberate people' ('not a movement to liberate territory'); the occupation therefore breaks the terms—or, one could argue, makes too transparent the history—of Zionism's own self-definition.[18] In fact in 1967 Oz considered the occupation of the territories to be justified, provisionally, as 'a pressure tactic to secure peace'.[19] For Leibowitz, there could be no justification for the occupation, no more in terms of security than in terms of redemption of the land, neither as reason nor as passion of state. The idea of redeeming the land was, as he saw it, in the nature of a category mistake. Anyone who attributes religious meaning to anything 'in the natural or historical domain' is, he writes, guilty of an act of idolatry—'deification of the nation and a fetishism of the land'.[20]

Corruption, perversion, fetishism, racist chauvinism—these are the terms Leibowitz used to describe that transference of religious categories onto the historical entity of Israel through which the occupation justified—

redeemed—itself. There can be no redemption of the land, because redemption is, in his terms, a reality 'that always transcends any existing
state, which one never reaches but towards which one must always strive'.[21]
Like nationhood, redemption is only ever a form of projected consciousness, a state to be achieved. 'A Messiah who actually comes,' Leibowitz
comments, 'is a false Messiah.'[22] Echoing Leibowitz, Oz also writes: 'The
messianic idea can exist only in the grammatical (and psychological) future
tense . . . every messianic idea translated into the present tense is false.'[23]
Paradoxically, then, every step on the land which sees itself as the fulfil-
ment of a religious purpose violates not only the land but also its own
intent. 'The Messiah will come', as Kafka put it in his parable 'The Coming
of the Messiah', 'only on the day after his arrival.'[24]

It is worth pausing here to ask what type of investment, as in psychic
investment, is involved. For it might be that what we are witnessing, what
is being inflated in this historically over-determined instance, is an all-too-
familiar process, but one which we barely notice, and that is the way we
use our objects in order to legitimate our desires: rather than desire because
we value, we value in order to sanction, i.e. confer value on, desire. In a
much-cited moment in the *Three Essays on a Theory of Sexuality*, Freud suggested that the sexual object is merely 'soldered' onto the instinct: 'a fact,'
he writes, 'which we have been in danger of overlooking in consequence
of the uniformity of the normal picture. We are thus warned to loosen the
bond that exists in our thoughts between instinct and object.'[25] It looks,
Freud is saying, as if the instinct knows what it wants, but in fact the
instinct is indifferent to its object, intent only on fulfilling and (thereby)
justifying itself. In the normal picture the object—'it is you I desire'—spares
us embarrassment; it gives the rationale to a search which is blind, furious,
in its own self-propelling. Hence Freud's insistence to Adler that there was
no need to posit an aggressive drive. There is no drive without aggression.
Being driven is always a ruthless state.

One way of reading Oz's fiction would be to see him as giving a political
content of another kind to Freud's already radical insight (that the apparent
normal picture of heterosexuality is merely cobbled together, as it were).
So that to the question: 'What are those who seem most ruthlessly driven
after?', 'being driven' would be the reply. The drive to be driven (the desire
to desire) is repeatedly offered by Oz as the propelling force of historical
catastrophe, the chief unconscious input into the making and unmaking of
political identities and worlds. In the short story 'Crusade', the first of the
two stories in his 1971 collection *Unto Death*, the crusader Guillaume de
Touron wreaks havoc in the service of his ideal without ever quite knowing
what he yearns for, without ever quite being able to give a name, shape,

or substance to what stands in his way: '[he] felt a wild desire to overpower or crush some obstacle whose nature was hidden from him until the day he would be permitted to be reborn anew.'[26] In 'Late Love', the complementary story in the same collection, Shraga Unger, veteran lecturer for the Israeli Central Committee, travels from kibbutz to kibbutz warning of a Soviet plan against Israel and world Jewry. At one point he describes his states of panic:

a blind wave of fervor boils up inside you and floods your soul, and you find yourself suddenly expecting an instantaneous illumination, a break in the clouds, something must, absolutely must reveal itself, a formula, a dazzling system, a purpose . . . surely there is something, something must make itself known, there must be something.[27]

'Something must, absolutely must, reveal itself', 'surely there is something': in these moments of blind panic, 'absolutely', 'surely' offer themselves as the two great performatives of uncertainty; imperatives with no content, in search of their obstacles, as one might say. In Oz's writing this is a repeated refrain: '*Climb the mountain, crush the plain. All you see—possess it [. . .] Darkness to expel.*'[28] Redemption becomes a declaratory, italicized condition; in *Touch the Water*, Oz places all exhortations of the 'Climb the mountain, crush the plain' variety in italics. In *My Michael*, Hannah makes the link between this form of exhortation and brutal possession (it is central to her disillusionment with her husband). In addition to seeing the rhetoric of the Six-Day War as crazy, she rejects the language of the Hebrew enlightenment and prefers the dark: 'In the literature of the Hebrew enlightenment there are frequent references to the conflict between light and darkness. The writer is committed to the eventual triumph of light. I must say that I prefer the darkness. Especially in the summer.'[29]

Such triumphalism, which Oz tracks across his writing, could be described as fantasmagoria, but it is equally a perfect form of logic. The only way for this vision of redemption to actualize itself, make good in the world, is in terms of what obstructs it. How else can it move forward given that its meaning is to have no meaning in and of itself? Redemption in action is therefore necessarily belligerent, since belligerence is no more nor less than the return of its own projective state: 'Those Bolsheviks [those planning his destruction], I know them backward', Unger declares. Later, he elaborates, 'And so my contention is that we ought to get moving right away and do terrible things. . . . What conclusions do I draw? The Jewish people, I say, must at last wake up and establish a sort of world shadow government, the same kind of terrible sinister conspiracy as our worst enemies credit us with.'[30] In Oz's *The Black Box*, Alexander Gideon, world-famous author of a book on fanaticism, writes: 'The annihilation of death resembles death in every respect . . . We annihilate ourselves (and shall soon wipe out our entire species) precisely because of our "higher longings", because of the theological disease.'[31]

In the first Chadwick-Healey lecture delivered in London in April 1994, Henry Louis Gates, Jr. talked of the 'virus of messianic hatred' in the context of a discussion of Black-Jewish relations (the lecture was called 'A Killing Rage: Black-Jewish Relations'). The problem with the word 'virus', however, is that it suggests a condition afflicting only those infected—like the expression 'lone derangement', the term repeatedly applied to Baruch Goldstein after the Hebron massacre of February of the same year, partly Gates's reference point, when Goldstein shot at Muslims at prayer in the mosque, killing twenty-nine. It suggests that we are dealing with something that can be isolated or expelled (since we're talking of messianism, this would be the illness as its own cure). But one of the questions which this writing raises is how far these versions of so-called extremism are wholly detachable, separable states. Is messianism something aberrant, or one face, not so crazy, not so uncommon, of collective identities, something which merely blows up and out of all proportion one way identities have of going about making sure—*absolutely sure*—of themselves?

Seen in these terms, messianism, redemption, appear more like the last stage of psychic self-entrapment: shadow boxing against the remnants of history, armoury against whatever dribbles out of the corners of body, mind, and time. Unger complains: 'Hell, that's what always happens to me. Here I was, meaning to talk about great themes, to say something about national deliverance, and all of a sudden the sewage raises its head'; or in the words of the narrator of *Touch the Water*: 'Metaphysical wrong cannot be perceived, while perceptible wrong emits a powerful stench of pork fat' (this in the same paragraph as this italicized exhortation: '*Far away in the Promised Land, All our hopes will be fulfilled*').[32]

We should, then, expect to find on the other side of such annihilating logic all those moments of uncertainty where identity fades against the day—a familiar opposition for theory, but one which steps forth here in new guise, declares its presence in the heartbeat of political time. We should expect to find all the instabilities of language and self-knowing which turn identity inside out. The central character of Oz's novel *To Know a Woman*, Yoel, is a retired member of the Secret Service whose task is to decode what he sees. As he comes more and more to question his profession, he starts to notice all those aspects of language and meaning that, in order to function in the service of the state, he has had to ignore:

And everything you have deciphered you have only deciphered for an instant. As though you were forcing your way through thick ferns in a topical forest that closes in behind you as soon as you have passed, leaving no trace of your passage. As soon as you have managed to define something in words, it has already slipped—crawled—away ... There is no limit to the number of possibilities, and each of them may indicate a different interpretation. An alternative meaning. Not necessarily a deeper, or more fascinating, or more obscure interpretation: just a totally different one.[33]

Yoel's ultimate betrayal and disillusionment is that he has lost the conviction (without which he could not have operated) that meaning, like the world itself, could be brought triumphantly to its end. He has lost the fantasy that meaning can be arrested—not just owned as in censored, but halted as in definitively deciphered—by the state. It is not of course the first time that this link between the autocracy of language and the polity has been made. Writing on fascism in 1938, Virginia Woolf commented in *Three Guineas*: 'And if words have meaning, as perhaps worlds should have meaning, you will have to accept that meaning and do what you can to enforce it.'[34]

But what gives a new colour to these political turns in relation to Israel is the way that their glaring emptiness, lack of foundation—alongside the accompanying messianic rhetoric (or in direct proportion to it)—constantly rises to the surface and reveals itself. This is a nation built on sand (by building cities, Unger comments, Israel wrested the sand dunes from the sea).[35] Running under all of this there is a form of uncertainty which no securing of language, boundary, identity could be expected to repair. To the extent that Jewishness resists concretization (we will see in the next chapter how Freud, as others since, have tried to make a virtue of this), so it has become the recurrent trope of the (post)modern. But the issue here is rather the ramifications of that uncertainty on the being of Israel itself. In 1975, Leibowitz wrote: 'We have no mark by which to define Jewish identity today'; and in his 1988 book on *Israel*, Yehoshua talks of the 'astonishing emptiness of the definition' of the Jew.[36] In response to this problem—the problem Israel was meant to resolve—messianism appears as a symptom, a way of railing against the constant risk of failed embodiment inherent to the Israeli nation-state. This is Anton Shammas, Palestinian Israeli author who writes in Hebrew, in conversation with Smadar Lavie:

Zionism gave the Jews a territory in the form of language. Hebrew is the only real victory of Zionism. The whole business of the nation-state that came later failed along the way. It's a paradox. Israel doesn't have internationally agreed-upon official borders—it's a blob of colour floating around without defined edges.[37]

Talk of the land of Israel as if it were singular, one, redeemed for all time, would then be a way of filling or staking out not just territory but the historic, repeated uncertainty of national self-definition.

What all these moments seem to brush against is the point at which, like security, the requisite differences and defences most dramatically fail to hold their bounds. If 'security has no bounds', as David Grossman puts it in *Sleeping On A Wire*, his collection of interviews with Israeli Arabs, then one of the most cherished self-fulfilling myths (and necessities) of Israel's statehood loses its rationale.[38] 'It is a sin, a crime, a folly,' Oz writes in his second collection of essays, *The Slopes of Lebanon*, written in response to the 1982 Israeli invasion of Lebanon, 'to pin everything on the question: Where will our borders be drawn?'[39]

*   *   *

But if this body of writing shows over and over again the dangers of certainty—political, psychic, linguistic—in its redemptive mode, it no less forces us to question the celebration of identity's self-othering which has so often been proposed by recent theory as political alternative, answer (also redemptive) to that first critique. The argument goes something like this. If the ego is the site of deluded mastery, let the unconscious have its say. If possession is always willed appropriation, let us renounce all ownership, let us dispossess ourselves. The problem of this form of argument for Israel/ Palestine is that you only have to turn back one page of history to discover today's occupying, or even colonizing nation, in sway to the most brutal and traumatic form of dispossession of their own. It has almost become a commonplace to say that the Palestinians are the 'victims of the victims'; the point here, however, beyond that basic recognition, is that this history and literature overturns the grounds of a certain theoretical confidence. If certainty is belligerent and panicked, you cannot in this political context just make a virtue of its opposite, not in a world where the trauma of national indefinition—lack of a nation, yearning to be a nation—is what seems historically, and so dramatically, to engender the most ruthless of psychic and political states. In relation to Israel/Palestine, we are left with two halves of a theoretical paradigm which do not add up.

For you might say it is the sanctity of the land that underpins the violence of the state; but you might also say that it is the persecutions and deprivations of nationhood that engender the sanctity and violence of the land. You might say that the problem is the false securing of identity; or you might argue that it is only when you lose the minimal conditions for identity that the drive begins for an identity which is falsely and dangerously secure. Perhaps even more important, you might notice that these uncertainties, together with that dramatic reversal of fortune which is the constitutive history of Israel as a nation, blurs the boundaries, the psychic division of labour, between the participants on either side. Not parody—Homi Bhabha has written about the forms of mockery and mimesis which can bind oppressor and oppressed—but trauma, often barely acknowledged or spoken, is what runs the join between Israel and Palestine.[40] Raja Shehadeh, in *The Third Way*, makes the connection when he describes the affective link between Palestinian and Israeli in terms of the unconscious logic of dreams:

Sometimes I think I am the victim of the victims of the Nazis . . . fate—through nightmares, through the great subconscious—has decreed that I inherit the memory . . . I have the horrible suspicion that I am more aware of the concentration camps, think about them more and dream about them more than the average Israeli does. *He acts, and I dream the dreams that he should have.*[41]

He acts, I dream. Psychoanalytically, this would be called 'transgenerational haunting' (the term from the Hungarian émigré analysts Nicolas Abraham and Maria Torok) where one generation finds itself performing the unspoken unconscious agendas of the one that went before.[42] Except that in this case the haunting works not just down through the generations, but *across* them; and not inside one family, but, creating a monstrous family of reluctant belonging, across the Red Line.[43] What type of occupation, psychically, are we talking about here? At the beginning of his book, Shehadeh insists that you cannot *force* on someone their state of mind; but his own dream story suggests otherwise, that things are not so straightforward once the unconscious is involved. Who is dreaming whose historic dream? Who dreams, who carries the symptom—'the prop for the common infirmity'—on whose behalf?[44] 'There is,' Unger writes of Tel Aviv to a friend, 'no other city in the whole world, Hugo, where so many people dream such terrible dreams every night.'[45] According to one study cited by Grossman in *The Yellow Wind*, 17 per cent of Jewish children in the settlements of Gush Etzion and Kiryat Arba dreamt of meeting Arabs, but 30 per cent of the children in the Kalandia refugee camp dreamt of meeting with Jews.[46]

Again there is a more general theoretical point here, the limit, one might say, to that celebration of provisional forms of identity which for many have become the hallmark of the postmodern world. But as we take apart identity and selfhood in the service of more precarious, shaded forms of being, we need to ask what idealization of psychic states we might be fostering, what exactly it is that we are talking about. It can be demonic repetition, not subversion, which forces the antagonists of historic conflict under each others' skin. Far from postmodern hybridity, this is historic trauma transmitting and repeating itself across time.

On more than one occasion, Freud found it appropriate to talk of symptoms as 'alien', of the 'foreign body' of the repressed. This would make of identity a type of prosthetic body, as Allon White has put it, made up of bits and pieces imported against the will.[47] In *The Yellow Wind*, Grossman writes of the West Bank as an 'organ transplanted into my body against my wishes'.[48] 'This body does not really belong to me—I do not have a strong affinity to this fleshly tissue'.[49] 'I'm a foreign implant,' he writes in *Sleeping on a Wire*, 'I'll always be a foreign body to them.'[50] This is literal, historical—Israel *is* the occupying force (I use the present tense because, as I suggest in the introduction, I do not consider that the Oslo agreement has brought the occupation to an end). But, the moment from Shehadeh's book suggests, *not only* literal; there is something more shifting at play. If identity is uncertain—this has now acquired something in the nature of common theoretical currency—it is not clear how or where it can be halted, nor how far in theory we are willing to allow the oscillation of barriers to go (only to the point of pleasure and its return). Above all, it is not clear what lines of confluence, transmission, contact are historically in process—living, often against all our best judgement, in the realm of the unthought. For Freud the subject's ego is the precipitate of its identifications, but the subject does not choose—not consciously—who or what will take up occupation inside the mind. At the beginning of *My Michael*, Hannah recalls the words of her father: 'My late father often used to say: Strong people can do almost anything they want to do, but even the strongest cannot choose what they want to do.'[51] Or, in the words of the feminist moral philosopher, Annette Baier: 'I may change my beliefs, expectations, opinions, convictions, but I cannot change my memories.'[52] In fact analysts might define this as precisely the aim of the cure, but the point still remains that, like wants or wishes, memories have a volition all of their own.

I want to call this the reluctant side of passion. Look at this body of writing in these terms, and what is striking is the tenacity, against all political will and intention, of joins which run back and forwards across psychic and political time. As Edward Said puts it in *A Question of Palestine*, there was 'an exact (and troubling) symmetry between the concrete form of Israeli–Jewish statehood and the concrete form of Arab–Palestinian statehood in exile' (one of the Israeli Arabs interviewed by Grossman says almost verbatim the same thing).[53] The problem is not therefore how to get the two sides to the conflict to relate (lines of communication to be opened, new communal narratives of recognition to be created and shared, which is not to underestimate the importance of this agenda for what lies ahead); but rather—and as the already-existing obstacle to the first—the extent to which the two peoples have already taken up places inside each other's heads (the liberal agenda, as so often, ignores or goes straight past the more intractable unconscious determinants involved).

In this context, we can usefully compare David Grossman with Hanan Ashrawi, Palestinian spokeswoman at Madrid up to the Declaration of Principles (now ombudsman for the new Palestinian entity of Gaza, former University Professor of English, writer, and poet). For Grossman, the issue is all of distances to be traversed: 'Make room for them within us. How does one do that? It is precisely the thing that we, the majority, forbid them with such deft determination'.[54] Whereas, beyond this form of anxiety (the oppressing party berates himself for failure to connect), Ashrawi's language is all of implication, excessive closeness, the 'fatal proximity', as she puts it, between the two sides: 'the occupier cannot hide anything from the occupied . . . We are probably the one delegation to whom the Israelis are not a secret, or an enigma to be deciphered . . . with us it's not a question of lack of familiarity or overcoming psychological barriers; we don't have them. There's too much familiarity. There is this imbalance in equilibrium that has to be redressed.'[55] Taher, Arab resident in the occupied territories, says to Grossman: 'Push us, but with delicacy. Because sometimes you push so hard that we see how scared you are . . . We are dismembering you from the inside.'[56]

At the end of *The Third Way*, Shehadeh recounts another dream:

I feel empty: in the hollow centre of a wheel with rusty spokes. At the end of every spoke is a head—a haunted, hunted, greedy, cruel death-mask. The wheel begins to spin and I get dizzy trying to find my face among the masks. I look out into the other side, the backs of the masks, and instead of hollows I see twin masks—the fragmented faces of our occupiers: riveted to the backs of ours in a way that ensures that *we will never see each other*, as the wheel spins faster and faster.[57]

In his famous 1982 novel, *The Secret Life of Saeed, the Ill-Fated Pessoptimist: A Palestinian Who Became A Citizen of Israel*, Emil Habiby gives the comic version. In the city of Haifa, where Jews and Arabs live 'as brothers', only the Arabs are willing to fly the Israeli flag. Why, asks his hero: 'Imagination, brother, imagination! . . . We fly the flag so they can see them with their own eyes . . . We can see the flags of the state even when folded up inside people . . . Now that's what I call imagination.'[58]

It is as if the very term of 'occupation' were sliding between its more literal and connotative poles: you occupy my land, my mind—and then turning itself on its head: you think you have the upper hand, but your unconscious only I can see. If this has a political logic, it might also provide a better model for psychoanalytic practice (or rather, be a structure inherent to its dynamic). Do not assume as analyst, because you are in a position of seeming authority, that the patient, the one who suffers, is not reading *you*.

* * *

To return to Amos Oz. Up to this point, I have more or less presented him as a type of diagnostician of absolutist fantasy in Israel, reader of the psychic subtext of territoriality, a writer who buries beneath the possession and dispossession of the land. But there is another side to this. For while Oz may have been one of the most vocal critics of the occupation up to 1993, we need to ask in what terms. It is in fact hard not to see his features in the last Israeli figure, 'in some ways more disturbing than any other', which Shehadeh picks out from his spinning-wheel—the beautiful Israeli upset by the occupation 'because it ruins his looks'.[59]

When the issue of the occupation for the Israeli is, in Oz's words, that of 'our moral distress', he has turned the occupation into a crisis of identity for the one who occupies: 'Fima presented them with the need to choose between the territories conquered in '67 and our very identity'.[60] Your territories/my self. What kind of opposition is this? As Lacan comments on the famous 'Your money or your life', the one presented with the alternative is in fact bound to lose either way. Whose identity is missing here? As though guilt could be spared too harsh a condemnation by giving itself the privilege of the moral life—the familiar move of the colonizing consciousness in its reflective mode. 'Guilt' might seem too strong, but if we go back to that opening quotation from *My Michael*, 'volcanic forces pressing outwards', we find that the translation almost reverses the original, which reads 'weigh heavily' (the expression used for conscience) 'from *within*' (my emphasis).

In direct proportion as Oz's writing undoes the rhetoric of messianic Israel, so then it could be said to offer a less obvious, but at points no less insidious, form of apologia for the Israeli state. It is, the writing suggests, the capacity of this consciousness to examine itself so brutally and without inhibition that allows it to occupy the (moral) high ground. There is an obvious affinity with Joseph Conrad; the allusions to *Heart of Darkness* are explicit: 'a slight hint of brooding evil: distant, infinitely patient, forever observing you unobserved'; 'Why did you bring me to the heart of darkness and leave me and run away'; 'The Territories are nothing but the dark side of ourselves'.[61]

When darkness becomes a political metaphor, then we always need to ask what other political histories and potentialities are being revoked (the darkness in these quotations refers respectively to Arab sector, female sexuality, and the occupied lands). We need to ask what it is that this form of moral self-scrutiny allows Oz's fiction not to see. To put it at its most basic, Oz's representation of Arab, Sephardic Jew, and female desire often, and often grotesquely, verges on pure caricature, setting the limit to Oz's own account of the task of the writer: shattering of stereotypes, recreation of new ones (the tropes are too familiar to fall into this second category of new images to be dismantled by writers to come).[62]

But, crucially, it is not in terms of a simple opposition between true and false representation, between history and metaphor, that this problem can be framed. What is missing from the writing is not, or not only, the silenced and truer voice of the oppressed (the voices evoked by Barthes when he wrote of the distortions of modern mythology, and by Achebe when he wrote of Conrad's representation of the blacks).[63] Instead the quotes from Shehadeh, Ashrawi, and Habiby offer a form of political belonging along rather different lines: not absence, but unwilling presence. At a Peace Now rally in September 1993, Oz stated, 'Even a long and bitter conflict can sometimes create a deep and secret kind of intimacy between enemies'; but that form of implicatedness you will find nowhere in the fiction.[64]

In an interview published in the 1993 collection For Palestine, Edward Said described Oz as 'Jekyll and Hyde' because his criticism of the occupation has been repeatedly backed by reaction to the Palestinians which verges on demonizing the PLO. In Oz's own words, during a 1992 lecture to Ann Arbor: 'Nor do I admire the Palestine national movement, which I have always regarded as one of the most extremist and uncompromising national movements of our time' (Said's comment was made before the later internal critique of the leadership by sections of the PLO itself).[65] On a programme on British television the week after the 1993 Declaration of Principles, Oz described as 'the second victory of Zionism' an agreement which leaves the Palestinians—again it is Said who has been most vocal in articulating this—with a mockery of self-determination or rights (elsewhere Oz rephrased his comment as the 'end of the prologue to Zionism', meaning the first chance for Israel to live in peace: 'Let the Jewish people start living as a nation').[66] On the same programme, this passage from an article in the Guardian on the Declaration was presented to him for comment: 'if the worst comes to the worst, it will always be easier for Israel to break the backbone of a tiny, demilitarized entity than to go on and on breaking the backbones of eight-year-old stone-throwing Palestinian kids.'[67] It was, he replied, the 'moderate language of a moderate man' (Oz has himself condemned the treatment meted out to the stone-throwers and called the orders behind the brutality immoral).[68] Perhaps Oz can only display the fantasmatic face of Zionism as critique in his fiction because, according to the logic I have been pursuing here, he knows one part of it—i.e. knows it psychically, backward, internally—*so well*: 'There was not one sentiment expressed by those angry and hysterical people which I did not understand, that I have not emotionally shared at some point in my life'.[69] This Zionist who said in 1973, and stood by his remark when questioned in Oxford in 1994, that nationalism is the 'curse' of mankind[70]. This is the vision: 'upon this crowded, poverty-stricken and decomposing planet of ours there should exist hundreds of civilizations, thousands of traditions, millions of regional and local communities—but no nation-states'[71] (to be a Zionist and against nation-states is of course something of a contradiction in terms). Jekyll and Hyde may be right, then, but only if we remember that the point of the tale, as much as the clash of moral absolutes, is that the two cannot do without each other.

It is not therefore a question of *placing* Oz (simply condemning, simply condoning), but of following the psychic and political tension of the writing. This in itself might help to demonstrate the vacuity of the backlash term 'political correctness', as if it were a question of judging writers— judging whether a writer should be read—according to the consistency of their political views. To read a writer politically is to unpack the points of uncertainty, to follow internally to a single writer the clash of voices pitted, clamouring, against each other in the political world outside (which simply gives an additional political turn to what Barthes once referred to as opening out the 'tissue' of voices in a text). But since the terrain and the mind are unsettled, to read in such a way is unlikely to settle the matter.

A final point about language. Go back to Shammas's quote on Hebrew as the 'only real victory of Zionism' (it could be juxtaposed with that of Oz). In the translator's note to the English version of *My Michael*, translated in collaboration with the author, Nicholas Lange explains the difficulty of rendering in English the varieties of Hebrew—Polish, Yiddish, Yemenite— which the different characters speak. The loss of that complexity in translation, the gradual erasure of that complexity in Oz's own writing, coincides with the gradual suppression, inside the Hebrew language, of the multiple traces of its past: 'Our Hebrew in those days was a jumble: a word in Turkish, a word in Hebrew, a word in Yiddish, a word in Arabic.'[72] Oz defines one of his tasks as a writer as the preservation of the (sexual) integrity of Hebrew against the dual threat of modernization and foreignness: 'Hebrew is like a person with loose morals: it has slept around and been influenced by Aramaic, Arabic, Russian, German, Yiddish, English, Polish and what-not.'[73] To read Oz in English is therefore to read a translation of a translation. Or to put it another way, you can already be a translator in your own tongue.

TWO

Black Hamlet

IN the National Picture Gallery in Siena there is a painting by the fifteenth-century artist, Sano di Pietro, of Saint Cosmos and Saint Damian 'transporting', as the booklet puts it, the leg of a Negro into a white patient. Baffled by this extraordinary image during a recent visit to Siena, I sought guidance from the two attendants in the room. 'It is impossible for a man without a leg,' they told me, 'to enter the gates of heaven' (resurrection of the body requires that the body be whole). A 'wild' interpretation, as I later discovered, but nonetheless expressive. As they saw it, the miracle repaired the dying white man's deficiency in the eyes of God, cleared his pathway to the afterlife. But what of the now-deficient Negro whose state replicates exactly that of the man he has repaired? Clearly it could only make sense if he is already outside the category of the human as potentially divine. One man's miracle, another man's curse. Uncertain as to whether the painter was condoning or celebrating this state of affairs, my interlocutors were none the less convinced of the ageless relevance of the painting in view of the resurgence of racism and the New Right in Italy and across Europe today.[1]

Looking at their reading of the painting from where so much of recent literary theory has situated itself, it is hard not to read it as internally undoing or 'deconstructing' itself. For if the Negro is inhuman—the justification for the seeming inhumanity of the miracle—then how can the transplanting of one of his bodily organs in any sense be said to *complete* the white man? And if he *is* human, then surely the miracle is a double, human and divine, affront?

This anecdote can serve as the way in to this chapter because it raises so starkly the issue of ownership—not of land, the focus of Chapter 1—but of the body. What does it mean, we might ask, to think that your body is your own? And on what forms of exclusion, what boundaries or barriers, does belief in its inviolable and potentially divine selfhood rely? This is a psycho-analytic question. It is at the centre of the work of Melanie Klein who argued, against Freud's more circumspect vision, that the child's earliest curiosities send it tunnelling in fantasy into the mother's body which it endlessly devours and rips asunder (in the very act of possession, it takes apart or dismantles its own claim).

But it is also a political question. In his best-selling autobiographical account of contemporary South Africa, *My Traitor's Heart*, Rian Malan—descendant of Daniel François Malan, head of the first National Government which founded apartheid—tells the story of the transplanted heart. An Afrikaaner traditionalist, elder of the Dutch Reformed Church and sup-porter of Andries Treurnicht's Conservative Party is fatally wounded; his wife agrees to the life support machine being switched off so that his organs can give life to others. When Malan visits her to talk about her husband, she says she can't, hinting 'at some terrible secret, something too dark and painful to be aired'. Her husband's heart had been transplanted into a black man and while she saw no wrong in that 'because she was not one to hate', the family in the country were tormented: 'They wanted the heart back.'[2] And they were prepared to hire a lawyer to sue the hospital to retrieve it so it could be buried with the rest of their son. In South Africa, Malan com-ments, in a gibe at a recent article in *Critical Inquiry*, race is no metaphor. 'Eat your heart out' finds its gruesome actualization somewhere between apartheid South Africa and Melanie Klein.

In fact Malan's book is full of metaphors. *My Traitor's Heart*—the title of the book—is one. On the same page as the story of the transplanted heart he writes: 'I have a wise friend in Johannesburg who says he knows where the race question lies. "It lies in your heart," he says, "too deep for you ever to find" '.[3] Pik Botha regularly exhorted South African whites: 'Adapt or die', 'Tame your hearts with your minds'.[4] As Malan sees it, despite Botha's real limitations, he moved things on politically, if only through the cumu-lative effect of such formulas on the psyche of the whites. Malan's grim story notwithstanding, we use the heart as metaphor whenever we want to indicate that part of the psyche where the mind's sovereignty is insuffi-cient, where something other than the ego holds sway. Look at Botha's injunction again: 'Adapt or die', 'Tame your hearts with your minds'. It is an extraordinary rewrite of that form of Social Darwinism on which so much of racist science and ideology has relied. According to that earlier belief, the white man found himself naturally—as in naturally driven—on top of the world. It now turns out that the natural impulse, left to its own devices, will kill you. Adaptation means curtailing, moulding, deflecting— submitting to reason—the seemingly self-propelling and self-justifying urge. This may also sound familiar. After all, reason was always meant to be the prerogative of the white man; such arguments were another way in which racism justified itself. Except that reason is now being called on to question that same prerogative as unreason. In Botha's exhortation—'Adapt or die'— racism, no longer survival of the fittest, now looks like or spells its own death.

The question of ownership—of hearts and/or of minds—bears the most intimate relation to the question of ownership of the land. Unlike charity, which rarely comes automatically, propriety, one might say, really does start at home. It is almost a tautology to say of the ego that it is master of its own house. For Freud, in an emphasis to be heavily underlined by Jacques Lacan, that so-called mastery is pure delusion. The ego comes to believe in its own supremacy only by blocking the shades and layers of former identifications out of which it has in fact been made. In a paradox as psychically as it appears to be politically unassimilable, what you call your own belongs to you only in so far as it originally came from, belonged to, somewhere or somebody else. Like occupied land, where your tenancy is by definition dubious, unstable, the ego is a prosthetic object. Thus David Grossman described the occupied territories in Israel as a foreign limb trans-planted into Israel against his will.[5]

In an article on the concept of moral right in relation to Israel, A. B. Yehoshua makes the same point. Critiquing the Jewish claim to a historic right to the land, he argues that such a claim would only be justified if the prior occupation had not in itself been based on conquest: 'but if he himself was a conqueror, on what right is his argument against another conqueror based?'. 'But,' he continues, 'isn't it the case that the Jewish people explic-itly assert that they conquered the land from other peoples and therein lies their historic right?'[6] Justification by conquest demolishes its own (sure) ground. In Amos Oz's *Black Box*, Michael Sommo is busily buying up land in the occupied territories, firmly convinced of the justification and the redemptive nature of his work (one of the few representatives of Sephardic Jewry in Oz's work, and a caricature). At one point, he pauses and asks, 'Am I living in error? Heaven forbid, there is nothing in Heaven? No judge and no justice? Perhaps the world is really an ownerless property?'[7]

Heaven forbid there should be nothing in Heaven: it is of course a beau-tifully self-cancelling plea. But what, then, are the grounds of possession?

Who owns what? Can any *body* ever unequivocally, surely, durably own itself or the land? From Israel in the first chapter, it is South Africa that will be the focus here; or rather, the links that run back and forth between the two. In an article, 'God and the underdog', written in 1968, the South African writer Bessie Head, exile in Botswana, makes the connection. Though she was writing after the Six-Day War and in the year when, as a direct response to that war, twenty-two post-colonial African states severed their links with Israel, for Bessie Head the impossibility of ownership is still the lesson and truth of Jewish history (she is reporting a conversation with a British volunteer):

This volunteer and I had been having an amiable discussion about the establishment of the State of Israel and during the discussion I happened to remark: 'There is nothing that moves me more deeply than the History of the Jews. They of all people have experienced most deeply and profoundly that God is the real Owner of the Universe . . .' Being caught up in this thought, I was quite taken aback when the volunteer turned on me irritably and said: 'I don't like the way you say God is the Owner of the Universe.' . . . I was enraged. Because I wanted to say something like this: 'Do you think your bloody motor-car is the Owner of the Universe? Do you think a pip-squeak jiggling little white man like you is God?'[8]

For Bessie Head, writing as a woman, the trauma of Jewish history gives to the Jews the truth of non-possession. But there is no automatic reason why the identification should go that way. Colonel Swanepoel, one of the cast of characters of *My Traitor's Heart*, was chief interrogator of the South African Security Police (his exploits were brought before the United Nations). For Swanepoel, such non-possession is anathema and leads straight to the trash-can of history: 'The West is a spent force . . . it has lost its blood.' Malan explains: 'In fact, all white nations save the Afrikaners and Israelis had *lost their blood* and would shortly wind up on the trash heap of history.'[9] Like the heart, blood figures in the language of the body as the site of true, non-metaphoric possession; or, as in this case, as the metaphoric bearer of the destiny of nations. Remarkably, Rian Malan manages to get both—heart and blood—into the title of his book; *My Traitor's Heart* is subtitled 'Blood and Bad Dreams: A South African Explores the Madness in His Country, His Tribe and Himself.'

One of the central issues that has vexed and stimulated literary study in the last several years is the question of how the map should be drawn. What does English literature exactly *include*? Where or how do you draw the lines? Bessie Head and Colonel Swanepoel are there to remind us that the fields of force between Israel and South Africa can be run, as tragic insight or as triumph, in a number of different ways. It is one of the most difficult aspects of the topic of this book that Jewish history can embody utter loss of possession in the most radical, traumatic, and corporal sense of the term, and then reappear, in the form of the nation-state of Israel, as owner, occupier, dispossessor of rights in relation to the Palestinians in turn. But these are shifts which broach the limits of recent theory or dislodge its most familiar counters—identities not so much unstable or divided as mutating and inverting themselves through the passage of historical time.

All of this suggests something of how complex are lines of affiliation and descent, political and literary, how inadequate our commonest ideas of literary transmission might be. It might also explain why the argument about the canon will get nowhere as long as its language is restricted to exclusion and inclusion: invited and uninvited guests with all the continuing colonial implication of who—that is, 'we' the literary institution—will let inside the doors. The debate can only makes sense, a point that has often been made, if it is seen as part of the uncovering and redrawing of literary–political history. But this history cannot know its parameters in advance. We need to find a place inside these discussions for a concept of the historical unseen.

What world do you want to, do you think you, belong to? How far does it stretch? To what extent are you carrying histories, geographically as well as through time, which you may not be conscious of living, that you may not want to live, histories that set off, so to speak, long before you began? And how far is this an issue which can in any way be seized or fully grasped by the idea of conscious volition alone?

In this context, gendered accounts of the writer—the agon of the male writer in Oedipal struggle with his paternal forebears, the woman writer thinking back less combatively through her grandmothers, more physically through the female body—cannot help us: not only because they so rarely, if ever, break home ground; but also because their idea of transmission, even when coloured with the language of psychoanalysis, never asks how exactly—along what lines of conscious and unconscious inheritance—histories, individual and collective, are moulded and passed down. Raja Shehadeh felt that he was dreaming the dreams of the Israelis: 'He acts and I dream the dreams that he should have'.[10] Bessie Head's most famous book, *A Question of Power*, is a semi-fictional account of her breakdown in Botswana— a breakdown in which it is both too easy and utterly appropriate to read the violent psychic legacy of colonialism (*A Question of Power* is the topic of Chapter 6 of this book). At the end of the book she writes: 'She really knew absolutely nothing, except that she had gained an insight into what the

German concentration camps must have been like.'[11] For both Raja
Shehadeh and Bessie Head, from their very different histories, the key,
decisive points of connection are the ones you cannot see, do not want—
or cannot bear—to know.

In fact it is not difficult to trace out the historical pattern which runs
underneath these lines of literary-political belonging. In the course of the
peace conference in Versailles after the First World War, President Wilson
persuaded the Jewish delegation to substitute the term 'minority' for 'national' rights at exactly the same time as Palestine fell under the British
Mandate, held in trust—as many saw it after the 1917 Balfour Declaration—
for the eventual and inevitable establishment of a Jewish state. For Hannah
Arendt only the emergence and formalization of the category of the stateless person after Versailles can explain the modern form of anti-Semitism
which reaches its fullest expression in the years leading up to and during
the Second World War. In *The Origins of Totalitarianism*, she stresses the
irony that citizenship, as soon as it was detached from property in favour
of a general category of the human, promptly attached itself to the nation-
state:

The full implication of this identification of the rights of man with the rights of
peoples in the European nation-state system came to light only when a growing
number of people and peoples [read Jews] suddenly appeared whose elementary
rights were as little safe-guarded by the ordinary functioning of nation-states in the
middle of Europe as they would have been in the heart of Africa.[12]

This is one link, more than metaphoric one might say, between Africa and
the Jews. Hence Arendt's praise for the relatively unknown French Jewish
thinker, Bernard Lazare (she contrasts him with Theodor Herzl) who, instead of concentrating on the territorial question of Palestine, saw the
emancipation of European Jewry as only possible in conjunction with the
other oppressed peoples of the world:

He knew that anti-semitism was neither an isolated nor a universal phenomenon
and that the shameful complicity of the Powers in the East-European pogroms had
been symptomatic of something far deeper, namely, the threatened collapse of all
moral values under the pressure of imperialist politics.

And she then cites in a footnote this comment by Lazare from his book on
the Jews in Romania; referring to the same pogroms, he makes the direct
link to South Africa: 'Besides what other nation dares open its mouth?
England, who wiped out the Boers?'[13]

This is to write anti-Semitism and the subsequent founding of Israel back into the history of imperialism and into a critique of the modern nation-state. As Alisdair MacIntyre puts it, 'The modern state is indeed totally unfitted to act as moral educator of any community. But the history of how the modern state emerged is of course itself a moral history.'[14] There is therefore a line which runs straight from the heart of Europe and its stateless people to the dispossessed of Africa, Asia, and the rest of the world. When Zora Neale Hurston said as much in her autobiography, *Dust Tracks on a Road*, she was persuaded by her publishers to keep the offending passages out: 'I hear people shaking with shudders at the thought of Germany collecting taxes in Holland. I have not heard a word against Holland collecting one twelfth of poor people's wages in Asia. Hitler's crime is that he is actually doing a thing like that to his own kind.'[15] (Hurston had written and submitted the passage to her publishers before Pearl Harbour, but the book did not come out until 1942).

If these are ethico-political connections, they also carry the most concrete of histories and migrations. Fleeing those East-European progroms, large numbers of Lithuanian Jews found themselves in South Africa, first at the turn of the century and then during Hitler's rise to power. In a 1926 speech aimed at inflaming Afrikaner fear of Jewish immigration, Manie Maritz, former Boer War General, pronounced: 'Jerusalem is already here' (Maritz had been imprisoned for his role in the 1914 Rebellion which aimed to restore the Northern Republics).[16] In the 1930s, German Jews, many of whom left for the United States of America, also found themselves in South Africa because, according to Benita Parry, it was often cheaper, easier, and quicker to get out. These were also, of course, two major waves of Eastern European emigration to Palestine.

So where exactly do these peoples belong, not just in the sense of ambiguous citizenship but more fantasmagorically? Addressing the United Nations in 1974, Arafat described the Palestinians as 'ghosts'. He was of course talking of exile and historic deprivation, of the effects of one flight on those it dispossessed: 'we are ghosts without an existence, without traditions or future'.[17] But haunting can also work in the other direction, not only of loss but of uncanny persistence (the expression 'to get away with something' perfectly captures the ambiguity of fleeing with unwanted baggage in your hand). It is of course a question basic to psychoanalysis whether you can ever leave anything or anywhere behind. Arab Israeli writer Yitshak Goren asks: 'Is Vilna the Jerusalem of Lithuania or is Jerusalem actually the Vilna of Eretz Israel?'[18] Take over the holy city as new beginning, as historical redemption, and the risk is that the site of the very trauma you thought you were fleeing rises up before your eyes. The lines that run from Lithuania to Israel/Palestine, to South Africa, are there to remind us that there is no place of pure beginning, not historically, politically, or culturally, in the world.

Given this history, it should come as no surprise that once you start looking, South Africa appears as one sub-text—fleeting aside, lost relative, mourned connection—in the writings of Amos Oz. In *My Michael*, Hannah and Michael's 'hysterical' neighbour, carted off in an ambulance when she attacks her husband, has a sister in Johannesburg (she also has a brother in Antwerp but this is more or less all we are told about her).[19] In *The Hill of Evil Counsel*, the fanatical Mitya who lodges in the house of Hillel has one sole surviving relative, an aunt also in Johannesburg, who dies and leaves him her jewellery in the week he moves out of his kibbutz and Hitler occupies Warsaw; her legacy then allows him to settle in Jerusalem to study 'with the aim of proving once and for all that the natives of Palestine were descended from the ancient Hebrews'.[20] And Fima, every time his ex-wife mentions South Africa, which she does repeatedly, finds himself fighting off the urge to predict a post-apartheid blood-bath—black on black, white on white—a danger which, crucially, he also sees as menacing the Jewish state.[21]

In all these moments, South Africa appears as the unlived life of Israel: mundanely, almost contingently, as the place where the Israeli might have chosen to go; more troublingly, as the sign wherever it appears—hysteria, fanaticism, apocalypse—of the barely imaginable, barely acknowledgeable, political unconscious of the nation. In *In The Land of Israel*, Oz expresses his fear that, should the settlers succeed in their cause, Israel will turn into 'a monster like Belfast, Rhodesia or South Africa'.[22] 'Every Jewish generation born in Greater Israel,' writes Israeli sociologist and military historian Yoram Peri, 'becomes more and more South African.'[23]

This is not to speak, of course, of the lines of security, investment, and recognition which have passed—more and more as the two countries came to feel the status of international pariah—between South Africa and Israel during the past twenty years. This was not always the case. Israel sided with the African States on the 1962 UN vote to impose sanctions on South Africa, whereupon the South African treasury promptly refused to approve the routine transfer of South African Jewish donations to Israel. But from 1967, Israel's policy reversed: 'Why had Israel been supporting resolutions in the United Nations which were hurtful to South Africa, when South Africa now stood revealed as one of the few countries to stand up and be counted when Israel was in peril?'[24] In fact Israeli investment in South Africa has been proportionately small compared with the multinational involvement of the United States and Western Europe, but it has been concentrated in decisive areas such as weapons technology and the Bantustans. These are the words of Ciskei's Israeli representative during a ceremony in 1984 to twin Ariel on the West Bank with Ciskei: 'It is symbolic that no country in the world (except South Africa) recognizes Ciskei, just as there is no country in the world that recognizes Jewish settlements in Judea and Samaria.'[25]

* * *

In August 1939, Wulf Sachs, Lithuanian Jew, Socialist, Zionist, and the first training psychoanalyst in South Africa, wrote to Freud in London from Johannesburg, only weeks before Freud's death and the outbreak of the Second World War, in response to Freud's last great work, *Moses and Monotheism*. This extraordinary encounter between the psychoanalyst fleeing European anti-Semitism and the Lithuanian exile sits squarely but bizarrely at the heart of the historical narrative of this book. What dialogue could there be between the psychoanalyst struggling to understand the looming shadows of anti-Semitism, global war, and the place of Jewish history in that catastrophe, and the analyst in South Africa where a no lesser tragedy of racial proportions was moving towards what seemed, until April 1994, to be its definitive historical shape?

Originally entitled *The Man Moses: An Historical Novel*, *Moses and Monotheism* was the work in which Freud argued that Moses was an Egyptian, that there was in fact not one Moses but two, the first murdered by his followers.[26] In this account, therefore, the earliest history, if not origin, of the Jewish religion is dissonant, doubled, internally self-riven (an anti-redemptive account as one might say). The response to the book had been dramatic and largely hostile; Freud himself had hesitated to publish it at the time of Hitler's rise to power. But he always insisted that his project in writing it was to understand anti-Semitism and that it was thus wholly appropriate to the historical moment which, for others, made it so unacceptable.

Freud's version of Jewish history, it could be said, shares the virtues and vices of his account of femininity whose final version he was elaborating more or less at the same time (Freud's last paper on 'Femininity' was published in 1933).[27] The point being not whether either can be discredited—they both can and have been—but something about their feel. It was as if, for reasons which go beyond mere prejudice, Freud could only produce an account of the development of femininity in terms which made it appear impossible *to itself*. Despite his best, or worst, judgement, Freud showed that there is something about so-called femininity which really won't do.

For one strand of feminism, that failure is a strength, eloquent of the non-sense of the idea of producing a satisfactory, neatly progressing story of how girls get to be girls. Look at his account of Jewish history and you could say that he is doing the same thing. This is a history that falters, falls apart at the seams, does not make it to the end. You do not enter the promised land, for it is only when you think you have made it, that it is all in your grasp, there for the possession, that everything starts to go so terribly wrong.

For Wulf Sachs, living and working as a psychoanalyst in South Africa, the value of Freud's *Moses* lay in the light it could throw on the politics of race and nation. How can one race (the whites) live among another (the blacks) in a land where they have no founding history and where, strictly speaking, they do not belong? Moses offered a role-model to Sachs because, as he saw it, Moses had succeeded in crossing over, he had—to put it simply—made himself one of the people. For Sachs, Freud's book about leaders and followers, about history and groups in the making, building themselves on the most shifting and precarious of foundations, provided a counter-narrative to the catastrophe of colonialism, notably in the field of its 'best' moral endeavour. If missionary work among the natives of Africa fails, if the white man, however benevolent, remains the enemy, it is in Sachs's view because he never becomes one of the blacks. Like Moses, he chooses the people but—this is the crucial difference—he never crosses over, never *identifies*. It is because he never risks his own identity that the apparent empathy of the missionary is a con: 'The missionaries give us *their* God and take away from us *our* land.'[28]

What Sachs sees in Freud's account is a form of political identity which would put itself at risk. This is for him the value, even though it was also about to be the most brutal form of tragedy, of the Jews. Having defined themselves as a religious group, they were now obliged to take on the trappings of nationality as the sole path to recognition in the modern world. Nationhood is the only way to avoid persecution; Sachs defined himself as a Zionist but, he insists in his letter to Freud, his Zionism has nothing to do with sentimental or national-chauvinistic ideals about returning to Zion, nothing, one might say, with the definitive appropriation of either identity or land. We are talking about lesser evils: 'in many forms of colitis we use acidopholus milk so as to let the less pathological germs overgrow the more harmful.'[29]

Watching one tragedy of expropriation in South Africa, Sachs reluctantly accedes to the creation of another (the founding of the state of Israel, the dispossession of the Palestinians). As he sees it, what the Jewish people are about to lose is their defining identity as mystery, not only to others, but to themselves. They are about to concretize something whose value resides in the fact that it belongs in the realm of the unknowable and unknown. The native formula 'their God, our land' beautifully encapsulates, in addition to the basic violation, the prior equalization between the two entities—God and land—which makes possible the abusive, unequal exchange. Inadvertently, the missionaries have turned God into a commodity. But they have simultaneously elevated the land from terrain, work, fabric of life, into an ideal. Watch the very idea of land fracture across these different histories. Perhaps it is only when land fossilizes into identity that, like the symptom in psychoanalytic language, the real trouble begins.

In 1930, following the Arab riots in Palestine, Freud had written to Dr Chaim Koffler of the Jewish Agency in reply to his appeal for prominent Jews to criticize British policy on access to the Western Wall and on Jewish immigration to Palestine:

I do not think that Palestine could ever become a Jewish state, nor that the Christian and Islamic worlds would ever be prepared to have their holy places under Jewish care. It would have seemed more sensible to me to establish a Jewish homeland on a less historically burdened land . . .

I can raise no sympathy at all for the misdirected piety which transforms a piece of an Herodian wall into a national relic, thus offending the feelings of the natives. Now judge for yourself whether I, with such a critical point of view, am the right person to come forward as the solace of a people deluded by unjustified hope.[30]

For Sachs and Freud, the psychoanalytic *and* historical question was whether it was possible, as a Jew, to hold on to more tentative ways of being in the face of the Jewish entry—forced, unavoidable—into the politics of the nation state. In this context, the value of Freud's *Moses and Monotheism* is its radical *incompletion*. Freud's self-acknowledged speculative endeavour (it *is* a novel of sorts) mirrors the peculiarities of the story he tells: race, nation, destiny, each one without a clear, singular beginning, never arriving, always on the move. Like the case-studies of his patients, which he also compared to novellas, Freud writes Jewish history in the image of the unconscious, calling up a divided, uncertain, precarious way of being against the pseudo-certainties of the age.

For Sachs, however, the issue is even more complex. Between Lithuania and South Africa, London and Berlin, he embodies the multiple dilemmas of the dispossessed *and* colonial consciousness. A Jew fleeing Eastern Europe, he becomes a white man in the tropics. How then did he deal with the problem—white man and native—which he put at the beginning of his letter to Freud? For if you take psychoanalysis to South Africa, the risk must be that, despite the best of intentions, your own forms of vicarious conversion, of inadvertent missionary zeal, will be impossible to avoid. In fact, from the very beginning Freud had always seen psychoanalysis in some such missionary terms (*Moses* can also be read, then, as Freud's own institutional self-critique). It is a question regularly put to psychoanalysis whether it has any relevance outside Vienna or, in its more recent version, the North London consulting room. Does theory travel? Or rather should it— irrevocably contaminated by its Eurocentric beginnings—even try?

In 1937, two years before that letter to Freud, Wulf Sachs had published his most famous book, *Black Hamlet*.[31] The first book of psychoanalysis ever to be published in South Africa, it is Sachs's account of his attempt to analyze John Chavafambira, a native diviner living in a slumyard in downtown Johannesberg. *Black Hamlet* was, we could say, Sachs's attempt to cross over, to be the right kind of Moses, to identify. In his 1934 book, *Psychoanalysis: Its Meaning and Practical Application*, Sachs offered, in the course of discussion of a male patient who had been a fervent supporter of women's suffrage, a moment that it is hard not to read as his own self-analysis, the briefest recognition of the psychic-cum-historical pull of the native African for the Jew:

As a Jew he felt the effects of anti-Semitism very keenly, but, as an assimilated one, he could not join his fellow sufferers in an open fight and protest, by, for instance, joining a strong national movement. Instead he sympathised to a degree of identification with women . . . His interest in the equality of the sexes was really a manifestation of his demand for equality of races. So also we often find Jews who are fighters for someone else's national or racial rights.[32]

In writing *Black Hamlet*, Sachs saw himself as effecting a dialogue across racial boundaries. Racism, he believed, could be countered by demonstrating that the unconscious of the Western and the African 'native' was fundamentally the same. What might appear at first glance as the ultimate gesture of literary appropriation (Shakespeare goes to slumtown), the clearest case of psychoanalysis in its specious universalizing mode (your unconscious is the same as mine) turns out to be, as well as all of that, part of a claim for the radical destabilizing power of the unconscious. If fantasy moves across the racial front line, it is not only the ego's self-possession that flounders; such mobility also gives the lie to the doctrinal and symptomatic rigidity of racial difference doing its deadly work above ground.

To the question most often put to psychoanalysis—what family does psychoanalysis presuppose? (the Oedipal narrative for which it is most renowned)—we can therefore add a further query: what family does it create? If we go back to the image with which this chapter began—the transplanted leg of the black man, or the transplanted heart of the dying Treurnicht supporter—we can see Sachs's endeavour in oddly similar terms. It is a paradox most clearly articulated by Paul Gilroy, that the most rigid racial categorizations *and* a belief in a universal family of man can belong equally to the rhetoric of racism.[33] *Hamlet* transplanted into the psyche of the native would be an exemplary case of inmixing in its appropriative mode. But Sachs is also, remember, a dispossessed subject. In no sense does he, any more than Freud, unproblematically or unequivocally embody the master narrative of the West. Remember, too, that if Hamlet appears in the psychoanalytic version as Oedipal man, frozen by a confrontation, in the shape of his uncle, with his own patricidal and incestuous desires—it is Hamlet's consequent failure to act, his inability to seize his political as much as his personal destiny, that is the point of the symptom and story.

John Chavafambira's father had died when he was 3, his uncle married his mother; John stalls at the point when that same uncle is meant to pass on to him his legacy as diviner, at which point he flees the kraal (the comparison with Hamlet starts from here). But in the eyes of Sachs, as he increasingly sees it, this is a *political* problem. As one dispossessed subject tries to read another via Freud, psychoanalysis starts to shift its ground and becomes a plea for the oppressed. Gradually, in the course of the story, Hamlet shifts from Oedipal man to reappear as the syndrome, coined by Sachs, of Hamletism—not neurosis, but inhibition, apathy, failure to enter a life. For Sachs, this means Chavafimbira's failure to recognize the unjust nature of the world around him and to act on behalf of his people. There is nothing, writes Sachs, wrong with John. His 'deficiencies were not characterological'. 'John's greatest need was . . . to know the society he lived in, to recognize its ills and to learn how to fight them'.[34] Sachs writes these lines in the second edition of the book, published in 1947, which he re-named *Black Anger*. The move from psychoanalysis to politics shadows the history of the Second World War.

In between the two versions, Freud publishes his story of Moses, the leader who offered his people a destiny whose force could be said to lie in its potential, transitional mode. Sachs writes himself into some such Moses-like position as he increasingly sees his task as that of political educator and inspirer of Chavafambira. But it must, surely, be unique in the history of psychoanalysis that the objective of a 'treatment' is to induce in its subject the imagined capacity to kill (it is hardly the most familiar reproach). We should not forget, however, that what Hamlet endlessly defers in Shakespeare's play is bloody revenge. As Sachs reads *Hamlet*, Hamlet's murder of Polonius makes it clear that he was an unconscious—or closet—revolutionary waiting to come out:

In the unconscious, Polonius was identified with the tyrant aspect of Caesar, the Caesar who had to be killed by a revolutionary. Those who accept the basic mechanism of identification will understand the curious identification of Polonius with Caesar: 'I did enact Julius Caesar. I was killed in the Capitol. Brutus killed me.' . . . May I remind you of the generally negative attitude of Shakespeare to Caesar and his idealisation of Brutus.[35]

Take *Hamlet* to South Africa and it becomes a revolutionary tale untold.

This is doubtless not the only, but it must be the most transparent, instance of a counter-transference in which the analyst projects onto his patient the historical unconscious, his own unlived political half-life. I am talking about Sachs rather than about Chavafambira because we are, of course, dealing above all with Sachs's own imaginings. Identification across the front line follows the tracks of a double dispossession, black and Jew, at the very moment, as Sachs's letter to Freud makes clear, when such an identification is about to become impossible to sustain. In fact it would not be until the 1967 Six-Day War that Israel's shared identity with the post-colonial African states, as joint graduates of British colonialism, finally and definitively collapsed.

We can then follow the lines that run from here to the odd and ghostly presence of South Africa in the novels of Amos Oz, and to his fear of a very different identification in the making. This is the full version of the earlier quote about Israel and South Africa, taken from his account of a visit to Jewish settlers in Ofra in 1982:

Once, many years ago in Jerusalem, I was invited to a meeting of religious boy scouts at an Orthodox high school . . . Now in Ofra, I find I must overcome my amazement at how similar these settlers are to those boys. . . . But I must also remind myself that if my hosts—genial, articulate, fired with ideals as they are—succeed in their cause, they may drag both me and my children with them, to kill and die in a perpetual and unnecessary war, or perhaps to turn Israel into a monster like Belfast, Rhodesia and South Africa.[36]

* * *

In *The Question of Palestine*, Edward Said writes:

I do not doubt that every thinking Palestinian, or those like myself whose trials have been cushioned by good fortune and privilege, knows somehow that all the real parallels between Israel and South Africa get badly shaken up in his consciousness when he reflects seriously on the difference between white settlers in Africa and Jews fleeing European anti-semitism.[37]

'But,' he continues (a big 'but'), 'the victims in Africa and Palestine are wounded and scarred in much the same sort of ways'.[38] Note the short memory span between these two sentences, how a fleeting acknowledgement of shared suffering between Jew, Black, Palestinian is unsustainable and has immediately to drop the first of the three. As if—as I read that omission—the Jews fleeing European anti-Semitism to Israel cease, with the acquisition of national identity, to be 'wounded and scarred'. As if there was only so much suffering to go around.

Said's comment is eloquent of a basic problem. That identification relies on spots of blindness—one link recognized, another immediately put back beyond memory, pushed underground. No less than personal memory, political memory is highly selective and tendentious. How far back, through how many generations, should we go? If you try, as so much of literary studies is trying today, to move across a present, geographic or racial boundary, do you have to confine yourself to the present moment, close off the other very different forms of identification, historic and potential, which are there for the taking if you also move back in time? In fact the same point can be made about memory as I have been making about the 'interminability' of recent literary debate. The links are never-ending even when, or perhaps especially when, they seem most brutally to have shut down (it was the insight of Raja Shehadeh in particular to recognize this).

Perhaps the future perfect tense, which Lacan characterized as the tense of psychoanalysis, might be of use:

What is realised in my history is not the past definite of what was, since it is no more, or even the present perfect of what has been in what I am, but the future anterior of what I shall have been for what I am in the process of becoming.[39]

This is not a random inclusiveness; nor does it have anything to do with the idea of never letting go of the past. Lacan's formula aims at a past to be discovered only in a moment of transformative activity, only on condition that it allows that past, and its bearer, to move into the future and on to the next stage.

Of course there is an obvious trajectory which runs from the historical moment that has been the focus of this chapter to the historic events—the Palestinian/Israeli accord, the South African elections—of 1993–4. But the relevance of this particular dialogue between South African and Jewish history in the making lies just as much in the psycho-political story which it tells, the unanswered questions about identities it poses and which are still with us today. Between Freud's dispossessed Moses and his people and Sach's closet revolutionary, between Palestine and South Africa, two very different conceptions of political selfhood emerge: one which sees any fixed, rigid, tyrannical identity as the danger and the source of political violence; the other which pits identity against identity, sees emancipation—political and psychic—in the ability to know your enemy and strike. But if faltering identity is incompetent (hamletism), and competent identity dangerous (redemption), then what are the desirable psychic components for a politically emancipated life in the modern age?

Perhaps one of the reasons why Freud's *Moses and Monotheism*, written in the 1930s in the shadow of impending war, is such a difficult and confused text to read, is because this 'important Jew in exile' as Auden puts it, somewhere could not quite make up his mind.[40] Moses falters but he becomes a hero in the end. He doesn't make it himself, but he leads the people to the Promised Land where they will eventually take possession: as if Freud knew that his narrative cradled the future of nations. How can the dispossessed claim their legitimate rights without taking on the psychic trappings of the oppressor? Feminists will recognize this as Virginia Woolf's question, for women, in *Three Guineas*, which she also wrote in 1938 in response to the same crisis preoccupying Sachs and Freud. How can woman stake their claim to the institutions and forms of public being without entering the procession that leads to war?

In Stevie Smith's 1938 novel, *Over The Frontier*, Pompey Casmilus muses about the significance of Gold as she watches a meeting of City Directors:

And the significance of Gold is dirt. OK Mr Freud. That's the significance of Gold . . . But round that Board Room table sit Jew and Gentile . . . And in each separate mind the significance of gold is a separate thing, in the mind of Sir Phoebus a pursuing hunt, a release from the boy's besetting boredom, a hunt a fight a hunt hurra . . . And in the mind of Empire-Blue-Eyes, the significance of gold is fury and pride and a great beacon of light and power. Blue-eyes looks like he would lay a tail of bullets around the board room table.
[. . .]
And in the eyes of Israel what is the significance of Gold? Unity, flexibility, secrecy, control . . . OK Israel, keep it under your hat.[41]

For the Empire, bullets all round the table; for Israel, not yet a nation, secrecy, flexibility, a political identity still in the making. The question we might take from this chapter is how you can stop the second (the provisional identity of a group striking out against injustice) from turning into the first (Empire-blue-eyes with his beacon of light, fury, pride, and power).

* * *

There is a more obvious sequel to this history. In 1936, Joe Slovo—then Yossel Mashel Slovo, a 10-year-old Yiddish-speaking Lithuanian Jew—arrived in South Africa. His father, Wulfus, had left Lithuania for Latin America and had just sent word for his family to join him when the Depression intervened. Unemployed, he headed off for South Africa, where he worked as a street hawker in Johannesburg until he had saved enough money for his family to join him. Head of the South African Communist Party, and from 1994 up to his death in January 1995 Minister of Housing in Mandela's first cabinet, Joe Slovo was described as the second most popular public figure after Nelson Mandela at the time of the 1994 elections. During those elections, the allusion to Moses was certainly present. At a rally for Mandela in Durban on the first day of the vote, a black South African explained to an English journalist: 'It is as though Moses has led his people to the promised land.'[42] But, although Sachs was a Socialist, not a Communist, it is Joe Slovo who could be described as Wulf Sachs's dream come true—the dispossessed Lithuanian Jew who becomes the revolutionary leader of the black people: 'He identified himself to such an extent with the black masses that he seemed to me to be our Moses'; 'Joe Slovo . . . had the good fortune to see the promised land.'[43]

The last word, however, goes to his daughter, Gillian Slovo, a writer (like her sister, who wrote the story on which the film A World Apart was based), until recently mostly of detective fiction which, as she herself has put it, she resolutely situated in North London where she now lives, as far—you might say—from South Africa as you could get. Not until 1990, not until it was psychic and political time to remember, did she write her extraodinary semi-fictional saga of South Africa, Ties of Blood, which stretches from Lithuania in 1902 to the present.[44] It is her story of how you forge an autonomous political identity when that identity is in some sense pre-given, of how you have to forget in order to remember, let go in order to retrieve. It is a story, amongst other things, of how a black and white family, across three generations, succeed and fail in identifying with each other.

One moment crystallizes this chapter's concerns. It is the 1930s and the schoolgirl Rosa, second-generation South African—her grandmother had left Lithuania in 1906—decides to repudiate her Jewishness in order to be accepted into the dominant white South African caste, in order, as she puts it, to be sure of herself. That sureness crumbles, her political and personal identity are forged, on the day she finds herself confronted with a Jewish immigrant boy, in flight from Nazi Germany (she will eventually marry him):

her new-found confidence was, it seemed, built on a floor of sand. For just when she was feeling secure, it happened: the moment she had most been dreading. She emerged from school, her arm linked with Sarah's, and saw immediately the danger that awaited her—among the gaggle of boys stood a skinny, pale-looking child. Rosa knew his type, knew it only too well. She did not need to look for confirmation at the yarmulke on his head. He would be defiant in his identity: He would be trouble, she was sure of it.[45]

Later on the same day, she will bring down the window of her car when Nathaniel, the black whose family is most closely knitted with hers, is fleeing the police in the street. Out of these moments of betrayal, which she compares with Peter's of Jesus (her third betrayal is of Communism on the same day), her own political identity will gradually be formed.

If all this sounds a bit unlikely or dramatic, I should say that what is most striking about this book is precisely its language of seduction and betrayal (the saga as the form of grand tragedy for the modern age). Or to put it slightly more soberly, it is the power of this book to write political destinies in terms of psychic affiliations, preferences, and repudiations, to write such destinies in the conscious and unconscious colours of the mind (the language of that passage is all of identities crumbling, sure, not so sure).

But, in so far as it tells Gillian Slovo's own story, *Ties of Blood* also leads us to England today, partly as the way out (the next stage of exile for Rosa and her children), partly as a way of recreating what is already—from England to South Africa—a mostly inglorious historical tie. The extent to which England, or more specifically, Englishness is inextricably part of everything I have been describing in these first two chapters—you are there whether you like it or not—is the topic of the next.

THREE

The English at their Best

I T is generally agreed that when John Major launched his 'Back to Basics' policy following the Conservative Party Conference of 1993, no one could possibly have predicted what was to follow. Within days of a speech intended to lay down guidelines for a set of seemingly commonsense but essentially punitive policies on education and crime, one MP had hit the tabloids for fathering a 'love-child' (Yeo), another for corruption in the housing market (Duncan), another for the suicide of his wife (Caithness), another for multiple affairs (Norris), with further allegations of bed-sharing between men (Ashby) and housing profiteering (Gorman) to come. When Stephen Milligan was discovered a month later hanging in women's stockings in his home, it seemed to many merely the tragic culmination of a farce. No amount of insistence on Major's part that his policy was never aimed at personal morality could alter the sense that these events, all sex and money, were the true underside of Conservatism's impossible moral claims. Or indeed that they were Conservatism writ large (go for it, as Thatcher would say). (Nor did anyone seem able to convey to Major that Mulligan's activities, despite the outcome, might also have been his way of *enjoying* himself).

In fact, as more than one commentator pointed out, Thatcher herself steered clear of ever issuing injunctions on personal moral behaviour (it would have clashed with her ruthless individualism, but she also would not have taken the risk). Others observed that the whole concept of 'back to basics' was an attempt to consign to the sphere of moral accountability the catastrophes—in terms of housing, employment, crime, educational stand-ards—which were the direct outcome of the Thatcher years themselves.

But in all of these discussions, one point seems to have been missed: that if moralism backfires, it is not just for reasons of hypocrisy, but because the law, in order to be effective, has to draw on pleasure; the more intense the moral fervour, the greater the sexual charge that is *already there*. It was one of Freud's most valuable insights to stress that moral conscience can only work by drawing on the very energies it is trying to tame (where else could they go?). Which means that morality, not only but especially in the sexual field, has a stunning propensity to defeat itself. In a gesture worthy of the Russian formalists, whose programme was to 'lay bare' the well-worn clichés of the culture, 'back to basics' proved to be exactly what it said (how much more basic can you get?).

From the outset it was clear that Major's concept of 'back to basics' was based on a particular ethos of Englishness: 'Ever since his Carlton Club speech a year ago', wrote the *Guardian* in January 1994, 'Mr Major has repeatedly tried to define his brand of Conservatism in terms of the recreation of a lost moral universe, in which a particularly English notion of social discipline and respectability is supposed to hold sway.'[1] Less well-known, perhaps, is the extent to which the whole policy of basics took root in education. In a 1993 article in *Critical Quarterly*, Marilyn Butler describes how from the early 1990s, Kenneth Clarke (appointed Education Minister by Thatcher three weeks before she was forced to resign) started to promote the question of literacy as a national concern. The concept of 'correct' English, Butler argues, caught on among the Tory grass roots because, in the year after the Poll Tax riots, it was seen as a means of holding things together, of reasserting government control. When Butler addressed a Tory educational meeting in 1993, the anxieties she encountered were all about lawlessness. Literacy, the first of the basics, one might say, had become a metaphor for something (or rather just about everything) else: 'with language it is proficiency that matters; correctness does matter, but it is an aspect of proficiency. They cared only for correctness which they understood symbolically as law.'[2] Not for the first time, the national language was being called on to secure a vision of national consciousness: 'Without a consciousness of national language', as Herbert Read put it in the Preface to his 1939 anthology, *The English Vision*, 'there can be no consciousness of a nation.'[3]

If some of this is, therefore, an old story, there is none the less something distinctive about this new run. It is rather as if well-worn arguments about the ethical imperative of educational and linguistic cohesion were drawing closer and closer to the perilous sub-stratum of all ethics. For the drive to morality—the first stirrings of back to basics—also started with the education department, with an article which appeared in the *Spectator* of April 1992, written by John Patten, Major's post-election Secretary of State for Education ('yoked or effectively handcuffed' as Butler also puts it, to Baroness Blatch 'from Major's own constituency of Huntingdon').[4] Inadvertently, the Tory concern about education creeps beyond the more transparent forms of national anxiety and electoral self-interest ('no longer a question of what Major can do for education, but what education can do for him')[5] and starts sexually to double back on itself. 'Back to basics', one could say, gives a whole new gloss to what Max Weber referred to, with reference to nationalism, as cultivating the *'peculiarity'* of the group.'[6]

In the 1994 summer reshuffle, Patten was unceremoniously dispatched. He became an embarrassment. But what embarrasses can be revealing (that is often *why* it embarrasses). Judge a party not by its words, but by what it has to get rid of in order for its basic agenda—unmanageable only when spoken—more subtly, less visibly, to proceed. In relation to one peculiar mix of ethics and Englishness, Patten's 1992 article can be read today as a symptomatic text *par excellence*.

On the cover of the April 1992 issue of the *Spectator* there is a cartoon based on Michaelangelo's God and Adam in the Sistine Chapel. God has one arm round the figure of an angel, who looks on, appalled, his other arm outstretched pointing at 'Adam' who lolls in the guise of a layabout. Fag-end in one hand, the youth's other hand, instead of reaching out to God's as in the original, has its second index finger cocked up in the air. 'Mocking God', in red type, is the caption to this image; inside the magazine, Patten's article is entitled: 'There is a choice: Good or Evil' with the gloss: 'John Patten argues that fear of damnation and hope of redemption must return, if Britain is to become civilised again.'

In view of Patten's basic theme, the cartoon is unfortunate, or at the very least ambiguous, since how you read it will depend on how you see the sequence of gestures between God and man. Is it an image of man foolishly rejecting the judgement of the Almighty? That would already distort the meaning of the original as divine creation, recognition, *before* guilt and judgement entered the world. Or does it rather suggest that judgement invites mockery, that it is in response to ethical coercion that all hell breaks loose—if you point the finger, you're asking for it (another reason perhaps why 'back to basics' went so rapidly into self-destruct). Ironically, then, the cartoon fleetingly permits a meaning which is the opposite of the one Patten seems to intend. Hardly an answer *to* sin, the call for redemption and damnation is far more likely to set it off.

Unwittingly perhaps, *The Spectator* has managed to expose one of the central flaws of this particular brand of conservative ethics. Thinking to replace a left-leaning or liberal stress on the social determinants of crime with individual moral responsibility, it merely shifts the question of determination to *inside* the language of morality itself. To put it more simply, is morality the counter to bad behaviour or its determinant, antidote to violence or one of the strongest colours that it wears?

Read in this light, Patten's article starts to look like its own diagnosis, an exemplar of ethics in its sadistic mode. Unapologetically, what Patten is calling for is a fear regime. England today lacks 'godfearingness', the ingredient missing from mid-Victorian society, where crime was low but killing rife, but central to late-Victorian society when unemployment soared but all crime plummetted: 'that near mythical age when no-one bothered to lock his door and the world was a village'.[7] There is a famous moment in Jane Austen's gothic spoof, *Northanger Abbey*, when Tinley rebukes the heroine, Catherine Morland, for imagining horrors which simply could not occur on English soil:

Remember that we are English . . . Does our education prepare us for such atrocities? Do our laws connive at them? Could they be perpetrated without being known, in a country like this, where social and literary intercourse is on such a footing; where every man is surrounded by a neighbourhood of voluntary spies?[8]

'A neighbourhood of voluntary spies'?? Tilney's sentence seems to have run away with itself to suggest, despite his best intentions, that so-called English safety relies wholly on distrust. Purity needs danger to be sure of its ground. Innocence needs guilt. In his article, Patten proposes that 'delinquent' parents who fail to get their children to behave should feel the 'contemporary lash' (that agenda has certainly not gone away).[9] Or, in the words of the famous aphorism, you have to be cruel to be kind.

Psychoanalysis has a term—'violent innocence'—coined by the contemporary psychoanalytic writer Christopher Bollas to describe a particular syndrome of denial and defence.[10] Dreading her or his own unconscious thoughts, feeling those thoughts to be criminal—guilt by association, we might say, with the troubles of the soul—the violent innocent unconsciously passes her or his 'crime into the other, who now stands accused'.[11] Psychoanalysis calls this projection or projective identification. You pass across to the other facing you what you least like inside your own head, so that they hold it and become answerable for it at one and the same time. But the mechanism might be easier to understand as the logical extension or another version of a process we have encountered before. For if, as I have been suggesting, the contents of the mind can include the lives, consciously lived or merely dreamed, of previous generations, histories barely acknowledged, lines of affiliation repudiated and yearned; if identity—no one man's property or burden—is layered across space and time, then the idea of thoughts travelling from one psyche to another might lose something of its terror and mystique. Violent innocence might, for example, be one way of describing a canon of literature shedding, blinding itself to, the unspoken or even violent histories out of which it was made. It can certainly help us understand why the individual who makes the strongest claim to purity seems to be always on the verge of incriminating himself.

A specific form of mind in action, this is, in Bollas's words, a 'never mind' because it never recognizes its own psychic activity, its compliance with what it abhors. A mind like this never sees as part of its own psychic landscape the contents it deposits and punishes elsewhere. According to this analysis, it is precisely in so far as it so ejects its own felt 'criminality' that the real punishing—the real pleasure, one might also say—begins. In relation to Patten, and at the risk of momentarily personalizing the issue, we might therefore note the violent underside of his own purity regime. In March 1994, an article about his particular brand of political dialogue appeared in the *Independent on Sunday*. Graphically, if bemusedly, it described his habit of referring to political opponents as 'pigmies' or, in one case, as a madman 'let loose, wandering around the streets, frightening the children' (he was successfully sued), of suggesting he might 'pay [one] a visit' and 'deal with him' or that another was 'on his list'. According to the same article, there was a moment during the 1992 election when the posters of both parties in Oxford, Patten's constituency, were torn down, whereupon a Conservative poster promptly appeared with the comment: 'John Patten's posters have been torn down in this street. Your vote on Thursday will decide whether crime pays.'[12] Who exactly, in this case, we might ask, is making crime pay?

A remarkable political rhetoric by any standards if only for the way it exposes itself. We should then, according to Bollas's analysis, expect to find the glare of innocence on the other cheek. 'I am appalled,' said Patten at the time of the Leeds sex-education scandal, when a health visitor provoked an uproar by answering unsolicited children's questions about Mars-Bars parties and oral sex, 'to think that children in schools should be exposed to things they shouldn't even be beginning to think of understanding'.[13] Language, the tortuous rhetoric implies, can swallow only so much innocence without doing violence to itself. And what, we might also ask, is the relation between this type of innocence and the ethics—there is a choice: good or evil'—for which Patten calls? Are Adam and Eve full ethical subjects prior to eating from the tree of knowledge? Can you have ethics at all if you don't *know*? Patten's moral vision is internally self-defeating. Underneath his image of late Victorian England we discover Paradise before the Fall. Hence, I would suggest, the relentlessness. 'Nothing but cruelty,' writes moral philosopher Judith Shklar, 'comes from those who seek perfection.'[14]

Running through all of this there is a particular ethos of Englishness. Patten's article was, by his own account, triggered by a plane ride across England:

I flew along the liturgical ley-line that links some of our greatest cathedrals and ends with Pearson's rock-solid Truro edifice. The faith that raised Salisbury, Exeter and Wells was, broadly, sustained through all the succeeding centuries until the present one. It provided a bedrock for civil behaviour. Civility led to eternal life, badness to eternal damnation.[15]

Linking civility to virtue, Patten places himself inside a long-standing tradition which assigns to England a special moral privilege in relation to the rest of the world. This has taken a number of different forms: from civilized disinterestedness as the mark of Englishness to the counter-ethos of enterprise which identified commercialism with patriotic virtue. At issue between them was the question of whether the national character resided most tangibly in acres or commerce, unmoveable or moveable goods. In her book, *Britons: Forging the Nation*, Linda Colley writes of the radical version of the latter with reference to the Wilkite activists of the eighteenth century:

by stressing their supreme solicitude for liberty and by arguing that liberty was synonymous with Englishness, they advanced their own superior claims as patriots. Individuals like themselves, men of movable property, whether dissenting or Anglican, not only had an equal right with the landed classes to active citizenship. They had a better right, for they were better Englishmen.[16]

Between these two seemingly incompatible ideas of Englishness, there was, however, an equal preoccupation with virtue in its civilized and potentially civilizing mode: civility as detached benevolence, or endeavour, free enterprise, liberty as the sign of intrinsic moral worth (hence Colley argues the preoccupation of the second with the freeing of slaves). In a formula which might seem an oxymoron today, freedom, precisely in so far as it was *English* freedom, could be associated by an otherwise liberal tradition with national prestige and power: 'In all times . . . a marked feature of the English character, [freedom furnishes] the true measure of our power as a nation.'[17]

Both conceptions were therefore used to stake out the superiority of what it meant to be English. One way of describing the ethos of Thatcherism would be as an attempt to seize the second, as in free enterprise, for the very Toryism to which it was originally opposed, to raise profit to the dignity of virtue (the Protestant ethic in new guise). One way of describing Majorism, if there is such a thing, would be as retaining that basic agenda while pretending not to do so by trying to reconnect with the first (the more benevolent mode). For Matthew Arnold it was grounds for objection that the mercantile, as opposed to the landed, version of Englishness was the one being exported to South Africa: 'The English in South Africa "will all be commercial gentleman", says Lady Barker,' and he continues: 'Their wives will be the ladies of commercial gentlemen, they will not even tend poultry.'[18]

Either way, however, and this is a central argument of Linda Colley's book, Englishness—and then Britishness as it attempted to absorb all the nations of the Union under its sway—was inseparable from more brutal forms of self-fashioning. 'Regular *and violent* contact with peoples' defined the nation-state (emphasis original).[19] Ours is, she states on the first pages of the book, 'a culture that is used to fighting and has largely defined itself through fighting'.[20] In fact the first stirrings of popular national conscious-ness can be traced to the fourteenth century in the writings and fighting experiences of the Hundred Years War.[21] Perhaps it is in the sphere of militarism that the distinction between British (as in political and institu-tional) and English (as in cultural) breaks down: there is nothing like war for engendering a spurious and temporary psycho-cultural unity which rallies everyone to the flag.

These are the words of the song that would become the National An-them by the early 1800s as first sung publicly in 1745:

> O Lord our God arise,
> Scatter his enemies
> And make them fall:
> Confound their politicks,
> Frustrate their knavish tricks.
> On him our hopes are fix'd
> O save us all.[22]

You can track the line from God, to emnity, to moral contempt (these enemies are knaves) to the redeeming but imperilled national sense of self ('O save us all'). Indeed, as Colley points out, the fact that the song came to be known as the National *Anthem* in itself shows how closely patriotic identity came to be yoked to religion. Or in the words of a clergyman celebrating the Act of Union: 'We are fenced in with a wall which knows no master but God only.'[23]

The same yoke can explain, Colley also suggests, the sometimes radical, often complacent, Protestant identification of Great Britain and the Promised Land. In fantasy, Great Britain identifies with Israel, which means that, long before the historic moment which is at the centre of this book, she was already *there*: 'In Great Britain, second and better Israel, a violent and uncertain past was to be redeemed by the new and stoutly Protestant Hanoverian dynasty.'[24] Isaacs Watts, the dissenting minister, systematically replaced references to Israel with the words 'Great Britain' in his 1719 bestselling translation of the Psalms. How, Colley asks, could Wilkes not believe that England was an elect nation, marked out by God, 'when both his father and his brother were called Israel?'[25]

'A people exposed to struggle, redeemed through faith'[26]—or, violent innocence abroad (in fact home and away). We could do worse, I would suggest, than take some such phrase as the political, national, English version of Christopher Bollas's more personal, psychoanalytic formula (in fact, Bollas starts his paper with a discussion of the McCarthy era and other such moments of American self-innocenting).

For psychoanalysis, it would be axiomatic that such a programme will be prone to internal collapse. Stake your ground on the moral narcissism of the nation, and you render yourself prey to narcissism's inherent vulnerability, to the merest inkling of the hesitancy, recalcitrance, and uncertainty out of—or against which—any identity will have been formed. For Patten, as he made clear on a separate occasion, the opposite of moralism is not so much immorality, which you might expect, as uncertainty: 'We must avoid drifting into wishy-washy consideration of hazy moral questions or quasi-religious treatment of "social problems" or "causes" in which God barely features.'[27]

If Patten belongs to the past of this phase of Conservative government, there is at least an even chance that Michael Portillo belongs to the future (more terrifyingly, some predict that the future of the Conservative Party belongs to him).[28] In a key speech to the Conservative Way Forwards Annual Dinner in January 1994, Portillo sought to wrest 'back to basics' from Major's denials by insisting on its moral dimension (Heath suggested he be sacked as a result), basing his whole argument on what he saw as 'one of the greatest threats that has ever confronted the British Nation . . . the New British Disease':

the self-destructive sickness of national cynicism . . . spread by so-called opinion formers in the British elite . . . a readiness to denigrate our country and praise others; to devalue our achievements, and envy others; to hold our national institutions in contempt and look with approval on other people's; to deride every one of our national figures . . . A country which places no value on its national characteristics cannot be stable or prosperous for long . . . [Until the 1970s] People 'knew' that we did things best in Britain.[29]

Ironically, it would seem that nationalism, rather than socialism, is the 'politics of envy' (Colley: 'a panacea for nagging doubts and a way of coping with envy').[30] Nationalism is fast emerging as the grounds on which the Conservatives will fight Tony Blair's 'new' Labour party in 1996; out of the three big issues that matter to politics—'fear, greed and a sense of belonging'—one Cabinet Minister is reported as saying he had come to realize that the third was even more important than the other two.[31] When Portillo proclaimed to the 1994 Party Conference, 'Conservatives are not xenophobic. We are patriotic,' he was making a bid for a psychic redistribution of terms. Unlike xenophobia, patriotism as sentiment is confident, unafraid. Like Britain, it is lofty, uncowed.

Superiority, however, contains derision as its motor. If you make ethical authority the grounds of your appeal, there is no way of ensuring that the contempt which upholds it won't follow you all the way home. The viciousness (the potential violence) is certainly unmistakable: 'If defeatism has become the fashion of an élite, it must be thrown out. We must temper our traditional tolerance.'[32]

*   *   *

For the rest of this chapter I will be discussing these issues as they surface in literary writing of the modern period which takes Englishness and/or ethics as its main concern: Englishness—I will argue—at the moment when the zones of influence of the two preceding chapters, Israel/Palestine and South Africa, make their presence felt underneath or even at the surface of the text. We have, I have argued, been very selective in the ways we have redrawn the literary map of the world. That quote from Matthew Arnold, published in his 1882 collection of *Irish Essays*, already points to the presence of South Africa, not just as colonial venture, but inside the English cultural imagination, part of a debate about what Englishness at home should be allowed to be. Two texts—Kazuo Ishiguro's *The Remains of the Day*, and Muriel Spark's *The Mandelbaum Gate*—can serve to illustrate Englishness under particular strain.[33] In both of these novels, Englishness appears in harness to global ties, embarrassed by historic and often violent connections which, exactly in proportion to their reality, it struggles to transform, detach itself from, or deny. Each of them tells a story of why, historically as well as ethically, one peculiar version of Englishness is impossible to sustain.

The Remains of the Day is best known for its exploration of Englishness through the lens of Nazism and the approaching Second World War. Briefly but crucially, however, South Africa appears near the start of the book. An episode dropped from the film version reveals that Stevens, the butler whose story the novel tells, had an elder brother killed during the Boer war, the casualty, as it later emerged, of 'a most un-British attack on civilian Boer settlements . . . irresponsibly commanded with several floutings of elementary military precautions, so that the men who had died—my brother among them—had died quite needlessly.'[34]

Stevens tells the story to illustrate the peculiar quality of 'dignity'—'a butler's ability not to abandon the professional being he inhabits'—a quality exemplified by his father's willingness to serve the General responsible for this carnage when he later visited his employer and, since the General arrived without a valet, 'to suffer intimate proximity for four days with the man he detested'.[35] Since the General also turned out to be insufferable, his father was deprived of even the compensation of respecting the man responsible for the death of his son.

From the beginning, then, and long before the issue of British appeasement of the Nazis which will be at the centre of the novel, this moment already puts under the severest pressure the concept of 'dignity' as the professional ethos of the serving classes. But in doing so, this 'most un-British attack' simultaneously unsettles the associated quality of 'greatness' which Stevens defines right at the start of his story as an inherent property of the English countryside:

the English landscape at its finest—such as I saw it this morning—possesses a quality that the landscapes of other nations, however more superficially dramatic, inevitably fail to possess. It is, I believe, a quality that will mark out the English landscape to any objective observer as the most deeply satisfying in the world, and this quality is probably best summed up by the term 'greatness' . . . What is pertinent is the calmness of that beauty, its sense of restraint . . . In comparison, the sorts of sights offered in such places as Africa or America, though undoubtedly very exciting, would, I am sure, strike the objective viewer as inferior on account of their unseemly demonstrativeness.[36]

What English dignity and landscape have in common, therefore, is that they don't 'make scenes'.

Stevens starts his journey across England with Mrs Jane Symons's *The Wonder of England* as his guide. Although it dates from the 1930s, he is confident that the enduring features of the countryside—its 'greatness'— will not have been disfigured past recognition by German bombs. The 'wonder' of England is unreachable by war. In fact, as the novel reveals, that same countryside, dotted with the great houses which pride themselves on being the repository of virtue in its civic disinterested mode, will play its part in allowing the horror to come. Silence, impassivity: do not be deceived; do not believe for a moment that what appears most graciously undemonstrative is not actively transforming, disfiguring, the world before your eyes. Much gets done under cover of restraint. Or, as Freud remarked famously of so-called sexual passivity: 'to achieve a passive aim may require a large amount of activity'.[37]

If you run the links like this across Ishiguro's novel—Englishness, greatness, dignity, restraint, no protest, appeasement—then Englishness and appeasement rejoin, find themselves face to face, at either end. Not immediately, not crudely: it is the strength of the book as opposed to the film that when Lord Darlington, master of the House, justifies befriending the Germans in terms of honour and justice (why indeed go on punishing and humiliating them in the 1920s after the First World War?), these terms are not shot down at once but allowed, at least for a while, to float in the air. We do not, for example, see Lord Darlington reading *Mein Kampf* as we do in the film, presumably in case we have missed the point. But, if this is the case, it is equally the strength of the book that it is not just Darlington, but a whole class, caste, category of Englishness that is implicated by the novel in the unfolding events. This is not just the story of one individual morally faltering, of one man's ethical-political demise. The class which prides itself on civic virtue, for which virtue is pure performative—all it has to do is declare or pronounce itself—is the one most likely to have the political rug pulled over its eyes:

The truth is that Herr Ribbentrop was, throughout the thirties, a well-regarded figure, even a glamourous one, in the very best houses. Particularly around 1936 and 1937, I can recall all the talk in the servants' hall from visiting staff revolving around 'the German Ambassador', and it was clear from what was said that many of the most distinguished ladies and gentlemen in this country were quite enamoured of him . . . And then again, you will hear these same persons talking as though Lord Darlington did something unusual in receiving hospitality from the Nazis on the several trips he made to Germany during those years. I do not suppose the same persons would speak quite so readily if, say, *The Times* were to publish even one of the guest lists of the banquets given by the Germans at the time of the Nuremburg Rally.[38]

The Boer War episode is there to remind us that there are other histories under cover here (the corporate household can also be read as standing for fascist Japan). It is important that the episode was deemed unrepresentable in the film which allowed another anecdote from the novel about the British in India to do service for both: a story, which his father loved to relate, of a butler killing a tiger in the kitchen so that it did not disturb the equipoise of a colonial tea-party. The film simply gets rid of the story which is the hardest to tell—dignity as mute suffering as opposed to heroic risk. In doing so, it gets rid of the other moment in the book where what is at issue is silence, something failing to pass into speech. Unprotesting, Stevens's father serves the disgraced General from the Boer war; unprotesting, Stevens serves the subsequently disgraced Darlington, whom he defends to the end (the unreliable narrator rests on his dignity, we might say). Muteness marks the spot of what will become the mostly unspeakable link from British colonialism in Africa to Nazism. Remember this quote by the French Jewish thinker, Bernard Lazare, on the pogroms against the Jews in Romania: 'What other nation dares open its mouth? England, who wiped out the Boers?'[39]

The omission of the South African moment can also serve to raise another issue. In what has come to be known as post-colonial studies, India—or rather the British in India—has received a great deal of attention. But that South Africa, or indeed the pre- and post-war Jewish question as it is central to Ishiguro's novel, should seep back into national self-fashioning has gone relatively unremarked. Perhaps because the legacy of the British presence and its continuing investment in apartheid has simply been too raw; perhaps because of the seemingly intractable difficulty of that legacy in Israel/Palestine.

It might, however, be partly as an effect of this that the term 'national identity', as scrutinized by recent literary theory, has undergone a strange and uneven division of roles. Identity—as a psychic phenomenon in its coercive, self-contradictory, internally ambivalent contours, or more simply identity gone mad—has taken off to the post-colonial; while 'national'—as in the cultivation of virtue and character—has tended to remain at home. So Englishness, while subject to historical and political critique, has escaped psychic exposure. Or to put it another way, in discussions of Englishness, relatively little has been said about the potential insanity of the moral life.

In fact it is one of the central ironies of Ishiguro's tale that the modern butler is above all characterized as possessing a new moral sense of himself (tautologically, morality is what makes this an *English* moral tale). Unlike the earlier professional, whose standing relied on whether his employer was titled or from one of the 'old' families of England, the modern butler's worth is measured by his employer's '*moral* status'. Virtue has gained a relative autonomy. It is to be its own reward. The professional ethos sanctions the great house rather than the other way around. It is, however, precisely because of the crushing weight of this moral imperative, or so it feels, that nothing can be said. Silence reigns. Morality, in this shape, defeats itself. As soon as it acquires the status of conviction or badge; when it becomes a matter of honour that there be honour in the house; when virtue, we might say, becomes a *must*, it starts internally to disintegrate, rushing headlong into the arms of its foes.

*   *   *

Fast forward to Jerusalem in 1961. Eichmann is on trial. Hannah Arendt's famous study of that trial, *Eichmann in Jerusalem*, will release into our moral vocabulary the idea of the 'banality of evil'.[40] In a later correspondence with the Jewish philosopher, Gershom Scholem, in which she defends the book against its critics, she will argue that the term 'radical evil' is a contradiction in terms: 'evil is never radical, it is only extreme . . . [it] is thought-defying because thought tries to reach some depth.'[41] For Arendt, to call evil banal, to call Eichmann banal, was therefore not just to return to the tradition of radical good. It was also paradoxically to say something about the *extremities* to which evil will go to avoid the radical complexity of ethics.

In Muriel Spark's 1965 novel *The Mandelbaum Gate*, set in the year of Eichmann's trial, Barbara Vaughan, traveller from England, and Freddy Hamilton, employee of the British Consulate in Jerusalem, sit in the gardens of their British hosts in Jordan who have managed to create an oasis of Englishness on the Jordanian hills: 'They had coffee brought out into the garden after lunch. As swiftly as water finds its own level, they had already formed a small island of mutual Englishness.'[42] As their conversation turns to the flora and fauna of the region, it turns out that one thing they, or their relatives, have in common is an incorrigible and illegal habit of scattering English seeds in foreign soil (Jordanian, Israeli, but also Indian):

'I had a cousin used to take wildflower seeds to India and scatter them there,' Freddy said. Barbara said, 'I do that from time to time when I go abroad. To tell the truth, I smuggled a few *Anthyllis* seeds—that's Lady's Fingers—into Israel and scattered them on Mount Carmel on the sea verge . . . It's wildly against the regulations, but I couldn't resist it. I never can. It's a habit.'[43]

Place *The Mandelbaum Gate* alongside the *The Remains of the Day*. Spark's novel can be read as a return to Ishiguro's, not in terms of its writing (it was written twenty years before Ishiguro's novel), but in terms of history, memory, event. Most simply, this is a story of the British in the Middle East, making sense—there is no sense—of what it means for them to be there after the founding of the state of Israel as the immediate legacy of the Second World War, aliens on what they had almost been lulled into thinking of as their own soil. As Freddy Hamilton puts it, 'we're foreigners here now'.[44]

Before and after, or even cause and effect, the two novels sit on either side of the same historical trauma. Directly represented by neither, quietly, invisibly, it shadows them both. What does it do to our modern definition of Englishness if we place appeasement on one side and on the other the ongoing drama of Israel/Palestine (the history which will partly unfold as the consequence of the first)? Blind spots of our national self-imagining, above all in relation to the very war without which they have no meaning: especially, we might add, when that war is being yoked to patriotic purpose. Not much, if anything, was heard about either during the 1994 D-Day events. I use the fairly neutral 'events' because between 'commemoration' and 'celebration', memory and denial, the issue was never wholly clear (following protests by veterans at the inappropriate nature of the euphoric, bank-holiday tone of the original plans for the day, Major agreed to tone the whole thing down). But it is generally agreed that it is because Major wanted to use the anniversary to do service for Englishness in its self-congratulatory mode that the whole thing threatened to go so dramatically wrong.

One of the central questions of *The Mandelbaum Gate* is in fact to what extent Barbara Vaughan is strictly English. The daughter of a Jewish mother, which technically makes her Jewish, she refuses to shed the non-Jewish half of her identity, refuses identity as anything other than precarious self-division, when she is interrogated with hostility on the question by her Israeli guide. Crossing backwards and forwards from Israel to Jordan, risking arrest as an Israeli spy, disguising herself as an Arab serving-woman and then as a nun (history second time round as farce), Barbara Vaughan actualizes her racial and sexual freedom as multiple belonging. This belonging, or rather this multiplicity, is, however, historic and precise. When she chooses, Barbara Vaughan knows exactly how to identify herself; she knows exactly which forms of seemingly incompatible affiliations she combines: 'I should explain to him the Gentile-Jewish situation in the West, and next, the independence of British education, and the peculiar independence of the Gentile Jew whose very existence occurs through a nonconforming alliance.'[45]

For Barbara Vaughan, to be British in this sense is to be free. Her Israeli guide, on the other hand, brings to mind the games of her childhood 'where one's own chalked-out area, once won, contained whatever features one said it did, neither more nor less'.[46] Scattering the seeds of English flowers in Israel places Barbara Vaughan as much at risk of arrest as travelling into Jordan, because the Israelis, in the words of another observer at the tea-party, are 'extremely strict about what goes into their soil'.[47] 'Burning with its mixture of religion, hygeine and applied sociology', Israel—in this year of the trial—is already doing everything, against strong Arab objections, to monopolize the water supplies: 'It was no secret . . . in this year of the Eichmann trial, that the pipes were being laid.'[48] The way to trap a spy was to drop false sections of piping, extra-grotesque in diameter, beside the railway line and then keep watch to see where the wrong information would reappear (a key turning-point of the narrative hangs on this). It is one of those narrative details weighted with historic meaning, since water has been at the centre of the Israeli–Jordanian conflict ('the King has said many times he would never go to war with Israel again except over water'); hence the momentousness of this reply by Rabin when he was challenged by his cabinet on the peace treaty of October 1994: 'A kilometre here, a kilometre there, a drop of water more, a drop of water less—what is this compared to a peace agreement?'.[49] Control of the water supplies was no less of a negotiating block to the 1993 Israel/Palestine accord, as vital, although it received much less publicity, as the boundaries of Jericho and the return of the Palestinian refugees (Israel kept control of the water supplies).

Put down roots, sow your own seed, scatter it to the winds—Englishness abroad, territoriality, or sweet freedom? Barbara Vaughan's gesture can be read as propriety or as irreverence, last-ditch colonialism or as running wild (she beautifully inherits and encapsulates the two halves of radical freedom as English prestige). In *The Remains of the Day*, Lord Darlington's godson, investigative journalist and outspoken anti-appeaser, suggests to Stevens in the course of a conversation about nature: 'I wonder if it wouldn't have been better if the Almighty had created us all as—well—as sort of plants. You know, firmly embedded in the soil. Then none of this rot about wars and boundaries would have come up in the first place.'[50] But if the suggestion seems crazy, that is in itself because of the dramatic, historical mutation in the meaning of the words. Think how far 'planting' and 'settling' have come from their earlier meanings—'to let grow', 'to place in repose'. Think of the way they have politically contaminated themselves (plantations in the colonies, settlements in occupied Palestine). Or, to put the problem in more immediate terms, is the solution to the current dramas of resurgent, self-aggrandizing nationalism to stay put and relinquish all dreams of further possession, or to get up, keep moving, and go?

At points the links between the two novels are almost uncanny, as if the *The Mandelbaum Gate* were gathering up historically earlier moments from *The Remains of the Day*, moments still to be written, into its own past. In Ishiguro's story, two Jewish girls on the staff are suddenly expelled from Darlington Hall (in the film they are German-Jewish refugees, first welcomed and then turned away); thinking back through her mother, Barbara Vaughan remembers the German refugee girl in flight from the Nazis, who took her place as youngest member of the family, the Jewish part of her family, for Seder night. In *The Remains of the Day*, South Africa appears as British disgrace; in *The Mandelbaum Gate*, the headmistress of the school from which Barbara Vaughan is fleeing is a South African émigré to England who comes after her in hot moral pursuit, marries a Jordanian Arab, and stays (it is an orientalist cliché to have a white woman sexually awakened by an Arab; but the fact that she originates from South Africa gives it an ironic political twist). Freddy Hamilton follows Barbara Vaughan into Jordan, makes himself her guide, but subsequently suffers total amnesia—coastal memory, as it is called: 'a type of amnesia that affected white men in the tropics, especially Africa'.[51] The only way for an Englishman to discard his 'tepid correctness'[52] is through unconscious identification with a white man in Africa gone mad.

From Africa, to England, to Palestine, the lines of political affiliation, past and present, cross the surface of the writing, break, and rejoin. Freddy Hamilton's symptom is a form of historical attrition, trans-generational haunting, or amnesia *as* memory, we might say. Only in a state of dissociation can he recover the history which runs from the British in Israel/Palestine to South Africa and back. But that memory should appear thrall to pathology, retrievable only in the form of psychic pain, raises another question which is also central to *The Mandelbaum Gate*. Can you have freedom *and* memory; how much does memory cost? (In Chapter 1 I suggested that celebration of postmodern hybridity is itself a form of forgetting.) Is there a way of remembering which would not turn into repetition, the grounds or justification for new forms of ownership (stealing the waterways), but release? How can you make be sure that remembering, as the alternative to denial, will be benign? In *The Mandelbaum Gate*, all these questions are at the heart of the pilgrimage of Barbara Vaughan:

She thought, my mind is impatient to escape its constitution and reach its point somewhere else . . . In the meantime, memory circulates like the bloodstream. May mine circulate well, may it bring dead facts to life, may it bring health to whatever is to be borne.[53]

Inside the novel, another form of historical memory is in the process of being made. Reluctantly, mid-point through the story of her freedom—her great escape—Barbara Vaughan attends Eichmann's trial.

My argument is that England, not even back home—especially not back home—cannot innocent itself from these histories. They are most present, most active, when you are looking the other way. It is the final *coup de grâce* in *The Mandelbaum Gate* that as the main drama takes its course in the Middle East, back in England another scenario of violence quietly, un-remittingly unfolds. Freddy Hamilton's mother—he is partly in the Middle East to escape her—is murdered by her woman servant, Benny, in what seems to be a frenzied quasi-religious attack. From the letters he receives from each of them—it is a turning-point in the novel when he flushes these letters down the toilet together with his own composed replies—it would seem that Mrs Hamilton believes her serving woman has been stealing her jewellery, while Benny believes that Mrs Hamilton is unredeemed, lacking the certain virtue of religious life: 'I have tried,' she writes to Freddy in despair, 'to bring home the Word of Jesus to her heart.'[54] This is murder as the supreme act of ownership. Benny has got it in for Mrs Hamilton; she wants her, money and soul. It is also a violent parody of the two great icons which Colley places at the centre of English national life: property and God.

Throughout the course of the novel, Freddy had lived in 'premonition of bloodshed', but it was not from 'Christian Harrogate' that he expected it to come.[55] Such things, as we know, do not happen in England. In England, the servant–master relationship avoids—it is the whole purpose of the ap-propriate 'forms'—the ugliness of class war. Violence erupting in Harrogate feels, then, like the return of the repressed of Ishiguro's Darlington Hall. What is uncountenanced—strictly unthinkable—between Stevens and Darlington is that the servant might actually *want* what his master owns, that is, want to *own* it for himself—hence the importance of the opening gesture which sets off the story, when Darlington magnanimously lends Stevens his car for his journey through the south of England—or that he might question his moral worth. Appropriately, then, it is only in terms of this class relation, in one fleeting moment right at the end of *The Remains of the Day*, that Stevens ever doubts himself: 'All those years I served him, I trusted I was doing something worthwhile. I can't even say I made my own mistakes. Really—one has to ask oneself—what dignity is there in that?'[56] By dropping this moment, the film severs the link between the fight against Nazism and defence of the democratic ideal.

In Muriel Spark's novel, the English class system seems to be redeemable only by the violence it so gracefully denies. What link is there between this

peculiar and 'incorruptible' form of ownership and the new lines of possession and disinheritance being laid down on the other side of the world?
Look out on your English garden—wherever it may be—and all will be
well: 'The day before the news from Harrogate was brought to the
Cartwright's house that Freddy's mother had been stabbed to death by a
mad old servant, Miss Bennett, Joanna was up very early and looking at her
wild flower garden.'[57]

*   *   *

It has not, according to much recent literary theory, felt desirable or even
possible to talk about literature and ethics. First Leavis, ethical critic *par
excellence*, with his crushingly unegalitarian cultural agenda, then colonialism, and the place of English letters within it, were seen to have colonized
(quarantined) the space. It seemed as if talk about ethics in relation to
literature had to be complicit with Englishness. There could be no ethical
critique of Englishness, or so this argument runs, because ethics, in its class-
restrictive, contaminated version, and Englishness, were one and the same
thing. Oddly, then, what was missing from the discussion was a historical
analysis of their link. It is as if, accusing virtue of being ahistorical (Western,
logocentric), literary studies has itself behaved ahistorically, inadvertently
buying into, or treating as immovable, one moment in the mutable history
of ethics—the moment when civic virtue detached itself from liberty, when
ethics (as refinement) for English gentlemen, and egalitarianism (as engaged morality in practice) for just about everyone else, went their separate
ways. Have we done to ethics what Julia Kristeva suggested one moment
of feminism did to motherhood—mistaken the offensive, universalizing,
ideological hype for what it might, if we worked at and struggled for it, be
allowed to be?[58] What would a form of ethical criticism look like if it was
conducted in the name of the very agendas which the earlier version seemed
designed to exclude?

In the first series of Oxford Amnesty lectures in 1992, Terry Eagleton
made an appeal for a radical return to civic humanism via egalitarianism
and, in fact, argued that Marxism in itself could be seen as reconfiguring or
rejoining the two strands (the people laying claim to the fullness of civic
life).[59] But neither virtue, nor Englishness, nor literature were the topics of
his concern. As a way of squaring the circle, therefore, this chapter ends
with Iris Murdoch who, with blithe disregard for all such reservations, has
gone on talking and writing about the ethical life as if it were the only thing
with which the English are, or should be, concerned ('sheer Englishness', in
the words of one review).[60]

She has been criticized for not being political, because her characters do not seem to belong to a recognizably political world; but that might be the whole point. In Iris Murdoch's novels, the characters are suspended from civic possibility, and yet they talk on as if they might—just might—be living in an Aristotelian, or Platonic, world where to be virtuous was to be part of a *polis* before anything else. No city state, but virtue, in its country houses, retreats, off-stage settings, at times even in the remnants of those same eighteenth-century houses where, in relation to Englishness, the concept of civic virtue took such politically restricted flight. Iris Murdoch believes in the Socratic version of virtue which attached itself to England's great country homes, even when the façade of those same houses is, literally in some of her novels, crumbling all around. Her novels can be read as the partly diagnostic, partly symptomatic return to that key point of English ethical self-fashioning which has been running underneath this discussion. Do the English of the old civic school know *how* to be virtuous when the great house—Darlington Hall, for example—is no longer or barely standing?

Murdoch presents her fictional and philosophical project as a straining towards virtue, internal scrutiny as the path—impossible, but the only path—to the perfective life. She shows her characters failing, but on the way (this is to adopt her own terms). But there is another way of looking at it; which would be to argue that when Murdoch's characters fall, it is not through personal moral inadequacy, but because virtue in this form cannot actualize itself. Her characters are trapped, lured by a hope of ethical possibility which doesn't belong here, not in this form, any more. Refusing her characters any chance of collective, political transformation, she turns the problem of ethical being in on itself (in her non-fictional writing, her rejection of politics as axiomatic and contingent as opposed to the supreme privacy of the ethical is even more clear).[61]

What is there to say about virtue when there are no longer the social relations to support it? Can you talk about virtue—can you do anything *but* talk about virtue—when the idea of virtue has lost its historical ground? That, I think, is why her characters talk so much, and in doing so often sound so completely off their heads: 'The conversation,' as the narrator of one of the novels puts it, 'was not so much difficult as mad.'[62] Perhaps this is also why many of the novels are so long. It might also explain the unqualified moral realism of this writing; as if, by actualizing the characters, in defiance of all modernist reservations, you could bring this version of morality back to life.

Grandly Murdoch continues, but also puts the screws on, a whole ethical tradition. She leaves her characters stranded in their belief (her belief) that virtue is still something available for refinement in the pure throes of consciousness. But it is only because virtue has become *persona non grata* in so much recent discussion of literature that the political wager of this writing has been missed. To dismiss Murdoch as non-political, purely ethical, is to fall into the frame of her own self-definition. It is to accept the very opposition which drives her characters round the bend.

John Patten's article is there to remind us that morality is emphatically a political concern; it is one of the most powerful ways in which the contours of a political landscape get drawn. Uncomfortably close, for me, to Patten at moments in her own language, Murdoch has her own version of redemption, her own metaphysics of morality, to use her own terms, even of original sin.[63] At moments her writing seems to confirm the old Marxist insight that if you don't move into political being, the only way is off the edge of the world. And it is worth noting that, if Jews are present in her writing, it is often as pure fetish: the mystified representatives of a 'primitive', feminized truth (Honor Klein in *A Severed Head*), or inspired and partly crazed searchers after unattainable knowledge (Marcus Villar and Alfred Ludens in *The Message to the Planet*).[64] As Clive Sinclair put it in a review of the second, there is something bizarre about centring a modern novel on Jewish identity in relation to the Holocaust with absolutely no reference to anything of relevance to Jewish history that has happened since (Nuremberg trials, the capture and trial of Eichmann, the creation of Israel).[65] To this extent, Murdoch's writing repeats even as it offers up for inspection the severance of Englishness, as a form of ethical being, from modern Jewish history in Israel/Palestine which has been the focus here.

But virtue is for Murdoch an intangible, which means that, even if 'sovereign', it is something which no one ever owns (*contra* Patten, in Murdoch's vocabulary, 'hazy' is a good word). Nobody is as dangerous, or violent, as the one who thinks he has a monopoly on the ethical life. Nothing is more destructive than to think that you might have virtue in your power, that virtue has once and for all gone over to your side—a view which also plays havoc with the version of morality with which this chapter began.

To conclude with one example from her fiction. In perhaps her most famous novel, *The Sea, The Sea*, Charles Arrowby thinks he has found his lost innocence in the person of the childhood sweetheart, Hartley, now an old, crumpled woman, whom he rediscovers by the sea where he has gone to live in retreat: 'I had given her my innocence to keep, which could now be miraculously reclaimed . . . She held my virtue in her keeping.'[66] It is impossible to convey outside the novel the full force of the catastrophe which ensues when he tries to enact this fantasy and redeem himself by taking possession of it and her (the central paradox of lodging your innocence in someone else): 'I wonder if you know,' Arrowby says, 'what it's like when you have to *guard* somebody . . . against all damage and darkness, and to sort of renew them as if you were God.'[67] Or as Hartley herself puts it, when he takes her prisoner in his house, 'It's like a murder, a killing.'[68] Innocence can only redeem itself as crime. Judgement crushes what it tries to reclaim: 'What makes you think . . . you can judge?' she asks. 'I can judge,' he replies. 'I *know*.'[69]

We are back with the cover of *The Spectator*, with a type of judgement so unswervingly convinced of its own righteousness that it makes a mockery of its own claim. What is the authority of judgement? On what or who does it ground itself? What is the relationship between (his) judgement and (her) rights? (In *The Sea, The Sea* this is the question of an old woman.) It is central to the twisted ethics of our present-day Conservatism that the first can substitute for the second, that moral judgement can do service for justice in the modern world. Wipe out individual crime and all other social ills will magically sublate themselves. The State is pure; you are, morally, the problem for the State. In the same article, Patten asserts: 'evil exists individually in the sinews of society', not 'endemically in the corridors of power'.[70] Portillo says, 'Very few countries have produced governments of such incorruptibility.'[71]

In fact it is at the heart of the Platonic tradition on which Murdoch herself draws that you cannot consider virtue and social justice apart. Or at least that could be argued to be the case. On precisely this issue, Alisdair MacIntyre takes issue with Iris Murdoch (who becomes, as Ian Hacking puts it, 'non-historical and English' in relation to Plato).[72] 'Justice', writes MacIntyre in *Whose Justice? Which Rationality?* 'names a virtue. . . . Only justice can provide the order which enables the other virtues to do their work.'[73] In fact you could argue that justice and virtue are never so bonded as through their mutual fragility. Nothing bears witness so graphically to justice's *failure* than a rhetoric of virtue frantically mouthing itself to the heavens. 'In the Platonic view,' writes Judith Shklar, 'justice fails because its very necessity proves the collapse of pious, self-enforcing, and terrifying traditions.'[74] Justice is, of course, also the issue, in a way few would contest, in South Africa and Israel/Palestine. Justice will therefore be the topic that brings the discussion of these chapters to an end.

A final point about theory. Present-day Conservatism detaches ethics from the embarrassments of history and from justice together. For that reason the modern reader needs to be historical *and* ethical at the same time (a reputed incompatibility which has served its term). Or, in the words of a formula once used to stress the place of fantasy and identity in politics, and the risk of leaving these uncomfortable, fragile, and manipulable entities to the other side: ethics is far too important to leave to the 'right'.

FOUR

Just, Lasting, Comprehensive

THE title of this chapter is taken from the repeated formula for political settlement in the Middle East. It is taken, secondly, from the fact that in virtually every book discussed so far justice has been a central, if not *the* central, concern. It is there, finally, because justice is so difficult—one could say 'impossible', but that would be too easy—to talk about. Justice is one of those terms which excites the most passionately committed investment but which, almost in proportion to that investment, seems hardest to actualize on the ground. Nowhere does this seem more vivid or pertinent than in South African and Israel/Palestine, whose haunting presence inside and on the margins of English literature and culture has been my theme. As I finished writing these chapters in their original form as lectures in April 1994, within days of each other the first non-racial democratic elections took place in South Africa, and Israel and the PLO signed their accord. It is not to underestimate the historic significance of both of these events to say that, in both cases, justice had only—and in the case of the Middle East Agreement, I would say, barely—begun.

Justice could be called an ideal, but the word is too bland; it settles the tension between wish and actuality, desire and embodiment, in advance (an ideal is only ever an ideal). We could call it rhetoric, but that would be to ignore or override too quickly the whole tradition, starting with *The Republic*, which pits justice against rhetoric as the mere play of empty verbal form. It might be called a performative, but it is rather the opposite: talking won't do it; say it and its substance seems just as likely to vanish or drift away. Justice may not be mere rhetoric, but there is no term quite like it for forcing our attention onto the possible gap between word and deed; no word which threatens so dramatically to empty itself of content at the very moment when it is declared. Whenever the word justice is spoken, you always have to look again. Justice always makes us suspicious. Whoever speaks it, chances are someone else is being conned.

I would prefer to call justice a fantasy, but on condition that fantasy is not understood as daydream, delusion, degraded desire. If the argument of this chapter is that the best way to think about justice is as fantasy, it is not because justice is something we cannot aim for, something by definition impossible to achieve. Nor is it because fantasy is something locked into private territory: your secret, my shame. Like morality or virtue, the topic of the previous chapter, fantasy shapes the contours of our political worlds. It breaks through the boundary separating inner and outer space. To think of fantasy as private *only* is a form of possession; holding on to our fantasy, we blind ourselves to the way it circulates and empowers itself in other more public, collective domains. This chapter therefore reverses the psycho-analytic dictum at the center of the last—that the patient acts out her or his fantasy in real life as a way of disowning the private, guilty fantasy-life of the mind. For you could just as well say the opposite (the two are in a sense the obverse of each other)—that the fantasy *of* fantasy as mine and mine alone is no less denial; going back in the other direction, we flee our poten-tial and actual political selves. Frozen, on hold, in retreat. That fantasy is only a private matter is perhaps the supreme fantasy, fantasy *par excellence*.

The issue of justice hovers on the edge of literary debate. Changing the canon, voicing the silenced, becoming visible, tearing the veil (two of these are the titles of early feminist anthologies)[1]—each move, each formula, models itself at least partly on the discourse of rights. To whom have we denied a hearing? With what history of oppression have we been complicit by not noticing, not allowing the ghostly political subtext of this hitherto revered piece of writing to be read? When critics respond by arguing that politics should be kept out of literature, aren't they none the less, one way or another, sharing the same language, entering the same terrain? Studying literature, as one argument goes, is no way to redeem injustice—the wish is inappropriate, the activity unequal to the task (much of Stanley Fish's case in his 1993 Clarendon lectures could be encapsulated in the slide be-tween these two).[2] Let literature and justice go their separate ways. Above all, when you read a piece of literary writing, do not *judge*. Judgement and judicious reading are incompatible. Writing of the feel for language essential to the second, Iris Murdoch states: 'Developing a *Sprachgefühl* is developing a *judicious* respectful sensibility to something which is very like another organism' (my emphasis).[3] How do you take the just measure of a text?

Somewhere in all these questions, there hovers another, perhaps founding, distinction—the conviction that you can only give literature its due
(justice *for* literature) by detaching it from the sphere of rights. Along not
wholly dissimilar lines, Derrida describes justice as an 'experience of the
impossible': 'A will, a desire, a demand for justice whose structure wouldn't
be an experience of aporia would have no chance to be what it is, namely,
a call for justice.'[4] As a call, justice is always suspended along the path of its
anticipation, which means that it is incalculable (requiring us to 'calculate
with the incalculable') whereas law (*droit*) 'may find itself accounted for'.[5]
But if you follow this path and set the incalculable infinity of justice against
the regulated and coded prescriptions of rights, you run the risk of reinforc-
ing the link between literature and justice, by placing them together beyond
all measure, out of all legal and historical bounds.

What are the links between justice, rights, and literature? This question
could be run back across all the texts, literary and non-literary, which have
been considered here. Most simply, justice as a topic has been present in
each and every one. Amos Oz writes in judgement of his nation—by his
own acknowledgement the more it fails the more he writes;[6] but in the
name of a founding ideal of justice which, for all its violations, Israel never
ceases in his eyes, at least potentially, to represent. Oz's characters fall ill,
sink into despair, go mad on Israel's behalf. Their pathos is Israel's saving
grace. Cradling the nation's unconscious, however ugly, in his writing, Oz
redeems its soul. But justice on these terms is partial; it can never go across
fully to the other side. Solipsistic, non-exchangeable, the very agony of
justice means that it cannot fully be shared. Only the Israelis have the
privilege of justice as an object of mourning; as if for the Arabs, justice is
never desire or dilemma, only pure need or demand. In this sense, Oz's
passion, what *moves* the writing in both senses of the term, undermines his
own claim for justice by letting it do only half its work. In *The Black Box*,
Michael Sommo writes to his stepson: 'In their Koran it is written: the faith
of Mohammed by the sword. And in our Torah it is written: Zion shall be
redeemed by justice. That's the whole difference. Now you choose which
of the two suits you better.'[7] Or in Oz's own words: 'We have become
specialists in Arab mentality . . . Force is the only language the Arabs
understand.'[8]

For Wulf Sachs, writing in South Africa in the 1930s and 1940s, psychoanalysis is a discourse of justice, since it can be used against scientific racism
to show that the black and white unconscious are the same. Even more, as
his narrative progresses, psychoanalysis crosses completely over and, via
Hamlet (which you might have thought would have saved it from so crude

a political destiny), passes into the service of a revolutionary ideal. 'Curing' the native diviner, John Chavifambira, means for Sachs releasing him into political agency on behalf of his race. Sachs's difficulty is, in a sense, the mirror of that of Amos Oz. Too little identification in the first instance which in the second becomes too much; even if Sachs is on the side of black liberation, it is still his psychic agenda, still therefore an appropriative gesture, which is involved.

Who, then, speaks for justice? Or to put it another way, what happens to the language of justice, is it in fact viable, when it appears in the mouth of someone other than the one claiming their own rights? Can you ever speak for justice on somebody else's behalf? When Kazuo Ishiguro adopts the voice of the English serving class and lets the butler tell his story in *The Remains of the Day*, he makes this issue the formal wager of his writing. The servant who was silent in the face of appeasement—who appeased the appeaser, we might say—now speaks. Speaks for his own class: the very fact that he achieves self-representation is an answer of sorts to the threat to democracy posed by the Second World War (it is much clearer in the book than in the film that, while the master spoke of justice, the rights of the servant were threatening to slip away). But—and here's the catch—he also speaks for the dishonoured class which right to the end he continues so honourably to serve. This is the irony, or what could be called the 'illocutionary' paradox of democracy for the oppressor class. Give voice to the oppressed, the hitherto unrepresented, and the risk is that they will endlessly reiterate your own shame.

So can you ever speak for justice on someone else's behalf? This might give another colour to the opposition between justice and rights in relation to contemporary literary debate. Perhaps one reason why there has been so much resistance to letting rights into writing is because it opens up this zone of uncertainty. If we take on the new agendas of literary studies, it is not in 'our' name or for 'our' own cause that 'we' speak (I use 'our' and 'we' advisedly and in quotations to mean not in the name of the critics who until recently had the monopoly of the profession). It is the classic dilemma of liberalism that however crucial the gesture of solidarity, your voice might be the last one in need of being heard. The fact that most of the writers discussed in these chapters do not belong unequivocally in one place, nation, or history complicates the issue. But we have moved too fast, I would argue, if we think these forms of diversity and multiple belonging can simply do away with or cure the fundamental unease.

Another way of putting the question—who speaks for justice?—would be to ask instead how, or whether, the language of justice can be shared.

This seems to be the question, or lesson, to be drawn from the Middle East Peace Process whose reiterated formula—just, lasting, comprehensive— provides the title of this chapter. Take the three terms together as they now often appear ('just' and 'lasting' first appear in the 1967 Security Council Resolution 242, the third in a 1977 joint declaration on the Middle East by the US and USSR), and it is their combined weight and finality which is so striking.[9] Let justice be done—completely, once, for all. You can read them as equivalents ('just' *and* 'lasting' *and* 'comprehensive'), as progressive quali- fiers (an all-inclusive justice that will endure), or as tautological (if justice is not comprehensive how could it be just?) In the words of the 1977 Joint Statement, comprehensive means 'incorporating all parties concerned and all questions'. 'Incorporate' seems apt. As one psychoanalytic account has it, you incorporate something by devouring it; unlike introjection, where you take someone in as part of yourself but recognize them as separate, still let them be.[10] As if it were being inadvertently acknowledged that so total a justice, instead of leaving the world standing, would simply swallow and abolish all differences, wipe out all parties to the deal.

It is a point often made in Critical Legal Studies that the language of contract is inherently self-deceptive. Roberto Mangabeira Unger, key pro- ponent of the movement, sees the language of contract as containing a fundamental contradiction between freedom and power: 'The mechanisms of egalitarian, self-interested bargaining and adjudication cannot be made to jibe with the illiberal blend of power and allegiance.'[11] The modern law of contract 'preaches equality in distrust'.[12] Unger's point is part of a larger historical argument about rights. In pre-revolutionary aristocratic and corporatist Europe, rights were meant to 'exhibit on its surface the gross structure of society, like those Renaissance buildings whose façades tran- scribe their internal design.'[13] Modern legal thought begins when rights detach themselves from the social structure and become a universal category for describing the possible relations between citizens (the transition from special to equal rights). To these two founding moves in the history of rights, critical legal theory adds a further twist. No longer a reflection of social hierarchy nor its transcendence, the discourse of rights today serves above all to *deny* the constitutive forms of social inequality on which it rests. In critical legal parlance, the language of rights is most likely to do cover for evasion; at the very least it is unequal to the forms of inequality which it attempts to mediate, travel across, or resolve. As Judith Shklar puts it, in *The Faces of Injustice*, in an unequal society the law falls unevenly on the desperate and the powerful, hence justice serves injustice 'which has an exuberant life of its own'.[14] Or in the words of Sir Thomas Bingham, Master of the Rolls: 'We cannot forever be content to acknowledge that in England justice is open to all, like the Ritz Hotel.'[15]

Far from being an argument for abandoning the discourse of rights, Unger's manifesto is more a plea for exposure (a psychoanalytic argument, one could say). Whenever someone or something—resolution, declaration—says 'rights', look for what is not being said (ever since Pierre Macherey at least, this is something that critics and students of literature have been trained to do). Go from here back to UN Resolution 242 on the Middle East.[16] This is the resolution which calls for Israel's withdrawal from the occupied territories, hence its importance for so long. But read its silences. You will then find that 'rights' means the right of every state in the area to 'live in peace within secure and recognised boundaries free from threats or acts of force'; but the word Palestinian does not appear. The expression which does appear, 'just settlement of the refugee problem', does not specify *who* are the refugees. There is in fact no mention whatsoever of political rights in the sense most commonly understood.

If Palestinian rights are not named, then the phrase 'every state in the area' cannot include, not even potentially, a state of Palestine. Since the law against deportation under the Geneva Convention can be invoked only by states and not individuals, this has meant, amongst other things, that no stateless Palestinian can make use of it.[17] 'Every' is therefore a totalizer that veils an exclusion. In this case, the term 'just' does cover for injustice; the term 'lasting' is there as the gesture towards a possibility which, because it is ruled out by the language, cannot even begin.

Only in 1974, a week after Yasser Arafat gave his historic address to the United Nations, does the expression 'inalienable rights' of the Palestinians, including self-determination, national independence, and sovereignty, appear in General Assembly resolution 3236.[18] Not until the 1993 Declaration of Principles is the compound 'Palestinian people' used for the first time.[19] According to Israel Shahak, talking in 1975, if you used the word 'Palestinian' in Israel you were 'already half a rebel' ('Usually you say "Arab"').[20] The 1993 Declaration states that elections in Jericho and Gaza 'will constitute a significant interim preparatory step toward the realization of the legitimate rights of the Palestinian people and their just requirements'.[21] 'Interim', 'preparatory', 'toward'—how many qualifiers of 'realization' can you find? (It is now acknowledged that at this point neither Rabin nor Arafat want the elections to take place). As many commentators have pointed out—Edward Said has been foremost among them in the West—all mention of the 'occupation' has been dropped.[22] By omission, the declaration also spells the end of the right to return of the 1948 refugees (a right confirmed annually since the 1948 adoption of Resolution 194 by the UN): 'Their plight seems to be forever deleted from the lexicon of the Middle East . . . it's time now to master the art of forgetting.'[23] In fact, as Rabin announced to the Knesset in May 1994, the final terms of agreement ensured the return neither of the 1948 nor of the 1967 refugees.

Like resolution 242 which was, according to Naom Chomsky, left 'intentionally vague', the Oslo Declaration is formulated, in the words of Hanan Ashrawi, so that 'every side interprets it in his own way'.[24] Even vagueness, however, can be unequally distributed: 'In order to comprehend the real meaning of the Oslo accords . . . refer to its text, which is purposely vague on issues of Palestinian rights while precise on issues of what power Israel will retain.'[25] Or in the words of one of the Kibbutzim interviewed by Oz in 1987 on the possible outcome of the Lebanon war (Israel invaded in 1982): 'We might just come out from this deal with a comprehensive, total peace, on our own terms.'[26]

None of this is to ignore, it should be stressed, the real issue for Israel, although not only for Israel, of secure and recognizable boundaries. But look again here and another version of the same problem appears. How, as Abba Eban, Israel's Foreign Minister put it in 1968, can you base the possibility of peace on secure boundaries when dispute over the boundaries is the major obstacle to peace?[27] How can you withdraw to the *status quo ante* when 'there is nothing normal or established or legitimate to which to return'?[28] How can peace be 'juridically expressed, contractually defined, legally binding'[29] when the foundations of contract—two parties to a deal—could only be the effect, and not the presupposition, of peace?

Above all, running under all of this there is a fundamental problem which no language—not of rights nor of justice—can resolve. It is one which has a particular resonance not only in the Middle East but also in central Europe today. And that is the problem of how the grounds of national entitlement can ever be definitively secured. For if national assertion is precisely *self*-affirmation, it rhetorically and ritually blinds itself to the other on whose recognition its claim finally depends. In his 1976 essay 'Rights, Law and Reality', Yeshayahu Leibowitz writes: 'Fortunate is the people whose conception of its tie to its country is recognised by others, for should this connection be contested, no legal argument could establish it. . . . Considerations of historical "justice"', he continues, 'are irrelevant. The conflict is not one of imaginary "rights". Nor is it a clash "between Justice and Justice"—since the legal (or moral) category of justice does not apply.'[30] (Oz, who has often described the Israel/Palestine conflict as one of 'right' against 'right', qualifies this in 1992 as 'claim' against 'claim' precisely because of this problem of recognition).[31]

Leibowitz's comment does not, in fact, in his terms, spell the end of justice. His remark is specifically addressed to those who justify Israel's existence in terms of a historico-religious or immemorial right to the land: 'an eternal right that cannot be called into question', in the words of the Knesset Fundamental Policy Guidelines of 1981 (the ultimate unnegotiable right, one might say).[32] Nor does it prevent him from proposing his own solution; he ends his article by calling for the partition of the country into two nations. Rather, what I take from his comment is the way it underlines the subjective, imaginative component of national belonging. Not just in the sense of imagined communities as famously defined by Benedict Anderson, but in terms of recognition.[33] Whether I—or we—can be a nation depends on your desire. The viability of a nation does not rest with its own self-imagining, but on whether the other can (chooses, wants) to recognize *me*. We have entered the terrain of political fantasy, or rather of fantasy as it works its way underneath the political terrain. Above all, we have entered a realm where justice cannot be protected from the vagaries of conscious and unconscious desires. As Unger puts it in his discussion of legal indeterminacy, 'complexity, especially in the form of ambivalent or conflicting desires, must be kept under control.'[34]

So we might put the last question—'Can justice be shared'—differently again, What is a just subject, or rather, what does justice assume or require a subject to be? It might be only at this level that justice could be called a performative, because of the image of subjectivity which has to be mobilized or called immediately into action whenever justice is evoked. Does justice have to assume a subject who is already somewhere just? The insane man, Socrates argues in *The Republic*, is beyond the bounds of justice: if a sane friend lends you a gun, goes mad, and asks for it back, you don't comply; nor do you tell the whole truth to anyone who is out of his mind.[35]

Critics have often commented that John Rawls's famous theory of distributive justice relies on a very specific concept of the mind. In a recent article in *Critical Inquiry*, he extends the theory to the law of peoples.[36] As with his earlier theory, the participants are to operate under a veil of ignorance—they do not know in advance 'the size of the territory, or the population, or the relative strength of the people whose fundamental interests they represent'.[37] An unlikely scenario but one which precisely introduces an element of the speculative, or indeed fantasmatic, into justice. Justice, Rawls seems to be suggesting, has first of all and before anything else to take a purely disembodied place in the mind (critics who reject the whole project on the grounds that the starting premise is unimaginable have therefore missed the whole point).

Seen in these terms, the problem with Rawls is not that he starts way out

in the blue, but that he does not go far enough. Once you usher the subjective component into justice, recognize its already constitutive place, why
on earth should anyone be *reasonable* about it? Look at that starting premise
again. Rawls's actors may be suspended in space and time, but they are
absolutely self-identical, utterly *sure* of themselves. His so-called ignorance
is disingenuous, not to say knowing, at least about what is going on inside
everyone else's head. Everybody is 'reasonably situated and rational', 'de-
ciding in accordance with appropriate reasons'—hence no ugly surprises,
no mistakes.[38] The problem, however, is that, if this is true, then the people
have already submitted to the moral law and this is already a perfect world:
'more than any other doctrine', Rawls states, the doctrine of this law 'ties
together our considered political convictions and moral judgements at all
levels of generality, from the most general to the most particular, into one
coherent view'.[39] Compare Socrates: 'Hardly anyone acts sanely in public
affairs.'[40]

Could there be something crazy about justice? This may sound like a
somewhat crazy suggestion, but it is a way of drawing attention to the
almost maniacal insistence on reasonableness that justice as a concept seems
to provoke. 'The special assumption I make,' Rawls states in his original
Theory of Justice, 'is that a rational individual does not suffer from envy.' (A
big assumption if you are talking about the law of nations since, as we
saw in the last chapter, envy and nationalism are often blood-brothers: 'a
panancea for nagging doubts, a way of coping with envy').[41] Justice has to—
how could it not?—aim for reason; but the fact that it is something we
yearn for suggests that it belongs as much to our passionate as to our
enlightened selves. 'They are in the right because I love them,' Jean Genet
writes of the Palestinians, 'which is not to say', he adds, 'that justice has no
role.'[42] But once that much has been granted, then we are up against the
vagaries of desire for which contract has no place, and the partial insanity
of our own self-relation which distributive justice inside nations and between peoples has to disallow. So, to put the question another way, what
kind of object is justice inside the mind? What does justice (remember what
does a woman) want?

Ironically, it might be that justice becomes harder to actualize the more
the emotive, refractory, subjective dimensions of justice are denied (this
would be the opposite of, although not unconnected to, the injunction—
most often issued to feminism—that the best way to advance a cause is to
'keep emotions out of it'). But the point here is not that human beings are
really unjust and selfish, an assumption which Rawls in a sense starts from
and which is also the unspoken bastion of Conservative ethics. This is not

an argument about the necessity, in the service of justice, of taming human desires (which assumes those desires to be more or less consistently aimed at my own advantage or good). What is at issue here is a far less cohesive, more slippery idea of subjectivity, one which starts from the assumption that subjects can be, and nowhere more than in the sphere of morality, riven—or driven, even—against themselves. Are we always on our own side? Are we, indeed, always just to ourselves? Arguing against what she calls Aristotelian common sense, Judith Shklar writes: 'We blame ourselves for acts we did not perform and feel guilty for imaginary faults. We punish ourselves irrationally.' (She is also arguing against Aquinas, who said that no-one ever willingly hurts themselves.)[43]

By calling her book *The Faces of Injustice*, Shklar places the whole issue of justice in the framework of desire. Set justice, not in opposition to rights, but to injustice, and you are up against an 'irreducibly subjective component that the normal model of justice cannot easily absorb'.[44] To ask what injustice feels like seems obvious—in fact injustice is often unrecognizable except as a subjectively registered state. But it feels weird, to say the least, to ask the same question of justice ('how was it for you?'). If there is always a risk that revenge will get the better of justice, it might be, she suggests, because in the case of justice there is nothing like the same kind of pleasure involved.[45] Justice and injustice are not 'psychologically complementary or symmetrical';[46] they neither fully cancel each other out, nor quite add up. Justice may be sought after, but it is also eminently forgettable; unlike injustice, which nobody asks for but which never goes away. Nothing establishes the psychic component of injustice more clearly than racism because of the factor of humiliation involved—a factor supplementary even if attached to the issue of rights.[47] (By trying to make pornography a civil offence against the rights of women, Catherine McKinnon, I would argue, confuses the two: systematic degradation does not necessarily involve the deprivation of rights.) Many of Nelson Mandela's speeches both before and after the 1994 election could be read in these terms, as his bid to stop the legacy of past injustice in South Africa from playing effective and affective havoc with the attempts, however partial and tentative in the first instance, towards a more just and equal world. Forgive, but above all do not humiliate the enemy—however unjust he once was (it is this which Desmond Tutu refers to as the 'miracle' of post-apartheid South Africa and one of Slovo's obituarists as the 'astounding metanoia and reconciliation which South Africa was to undergo').[48]

By stressing the passionate, subjective dimension of justice, I am, however, trying to point to something beyond, or not fully graspable, by the

moral philosopher's vision of desire. To call subjects self-riven can imply
stubborn but endearing contrariness; or it can imply, as with psychoanalysis, a far more radical cleavage of the soul. What does justice look like if
you introduce into this discussion the idea of the unconscious? So far fantasy
has been used in this chapter to signal those moments where the language
of justice follows the path of the super-rational supra-sensible ego, magically
inflating and fulfilling itself (in the words of Stephen Greenblatt, talking of
the earliest colonial ventures: 'a self-authorizing, self-authenticating representation . . . that intensifies imaginative possession of the world').[49] But
fantasy also has an almost exactly opposite meaning; it can just as well refer
to the point where the subject 'vanishes' or 'fades' into the unconscious (to
use Lacan's terms), to all those dimensions of subjectivity which most dramatically escape the ego's thrall. What happens, in the field of justice, if you
use this second meaning of fantasy to call the bluff on the first, as a way of
countering fantasy's masterful delusion of itself?

For many involved in recent literary and cultural theory, it has become
customary to turn to psychoanalysis for a radical critique of sexual norms.
The idea of a bisexual unconscious can serve nicely to upset the stifling
language of heterosexual normality which does service for virtue in so
much of the bankrupt, moralizing discourse of the modern world. It might
be, however, that all that (welcome) attention to the throes of sexuality has
meant that those of justice have been left curiously unexamined and exposed: 'The requirement . . . that there shall be a single kind of sexual life
for everyone,' writes Freud in *Civilisation and its Discontents*, 'cuts off a fair
number from sexual enjoyment, and so becomes the source of serious
injustice' ('Ungerechtigkeit').[50] And yet, as he himself puts it only a few pages
earlier, for a law to be just ('Gerechtigkeit') it *must* be universal, that is,
broken in no-one's favour; although this tells us nothing, he adds, about the
ethical value of such a law.[51]

Sexual 'injustice' (his word) thus becomes the supreme illustration of the
gap between law and ethics; it shows universality as justice *and* injustice at
one and the same time. This is a paradox internal to the concept of justice,
but one which it seems to me that, in our keenness to use psychoanalysis to
champion an 'other' sexuality against the dominant, some of us have overlooked. Or to put it another way, in turning to psychoanalysis as a potential
discourse of justice, might we have inadvertently ignored what psychoanalysis itself has to say about the difficulties—no less complex than those
relating to sexuality—of justice itself?

A long time ago, a friend suggested that it was so much easier to be a
Marxist than a Freudian because whereas, whatever your social origins, you

could wake up one morning and more or less decide to be on the side of the working class, you couldn't quite in the same way decide one morning that from that day on you would throw off all inhibition and be sexually free (or rather you put a somewhat different set of demands on yourself if you did). There is a strange belief underlying moral injunctions that inappropriate desires, whose entire 'rationale' is that they defy best intentions, can be sweet-reasoned away. 'Be good sweet maid and let who will be clever'—as I look at that formula today (one whole strand of my life could fairly be summed up as a rebellion against it), it is not just its discouraging chauvinism which seems so offensive, but its assumption, no less fraudulent, that being good is something easy or straightforward to be.

From where does the inner sense of morality arise? This would seem to be a rather important question for women, since if you are a girl it is somehow assumed that it arises spontaneously from the inside; whereas what is involved for boys is obedience to an external social law they will themselves finally appropriate and represent (this is one reason why any feminist argument that starts by assuming women are inherently more virtuous makes me so uncomfortable). In this context it becomes a strength rather than a weakness of Freud's writing that he finds it so difficult to give an adequate account of how any of this comes about. Morality and justice, he writes in *Moses and Monetheism*, 'came about with a *renunciation of instinct*' (emphasis original).[52] But, as has often been pointed out, this begs the question, since presumably you will only renounce instinct if you have already bought into societal values and accepted a non-instinctual ideal. We can dismiss this as a flaw of psychoanalytic reason, but it might also help to explain why the moral life is so hard to achieve. It is because there are no grounds, no good, earthly reason to obey you, that you bring your weight to bear on me with such unjustified—unbearable—force.

For psychoanalysis, this is a problem structural or inherent to moral law. Failure is never therefore just individual failing; it is always at the same time a measure of the impossibility of what is being required. Failure in this context is suggestive and provocative. Rather like the impossibility of femininity, or indeed of Jewish national identity, whose connection in Freud's thinking was discussed in Chapter 2 (indeed it could be argued that both these forms of pained but strategic failing take their orders from the first). 'The cultural super-ego . . . does not trouble itself enough,' Freud states, 'about the facts of the mental constitution of human beings.'[53] It doesn't bother to ask whether its commandments are possible, psychically, to fulfil. Listen again, he suggests, to one of the 'ideal demands' of 'civilized society': Love thy neighbour as thyself. Adopt a naïve attitude as though you were listening to it for the first time, and 'we shall', he predicts, 'be unable then to suppress a feeling of surprise and bewilderment': 'Why should we do it? What good will it do us? But, above all, how should we achieve it?'[54] My love is precious to me, the result of the finest discriminations, selections, and histories, without which, in some sense, I cease to be. I diminish it, and myself with it, if I offer it to every comer on the ground. 'A love that does not discriminate [does] an injustice ['*ein Unrecht*'] to its object.'[55]

Furthermore, it is only on the basis of such fine and self-defining discriminations that collective identities are made: 'My love is valued by all my own people,' Freud continues, 'as a sign of my preferring them, and it is an *injustice* ['*ein Unrecht*'] to them if I put a stranger on a par with them.'[56] 'The commandment, "Love thy neighbour as thyself" is . . . an excellent example of the unpsychological proceedings of the cultural superego. The commandment is impossible to fulfil.'[57] Or in the words of the Umbro football poster which appeared all over London in the summer of 1994: 'God says Love Thy Neighbour. Sorry God.'

This superego is a cruel taskmaster (necessarily, given the Sysiphean nature of its task). You cannot dispense with the problem of cruelty by obeying it because of the ferocity with which it imposes its ideals. Like Kant's categorical imperative, it is something of a fanatic ('Kant's imperative reeks of cruelty', 'it is a hanging judge seated within the mind').[58] Writing on the moral sense, the feminist moral philosopher Annette Baier proposes Aristotelian cultivation of virtue in the young as an alternative to a moral law which 'has to be burned in, and which tends to provoke return aggression, or more strongly working poisons' (in fact she places Freud alongside Aristotle on the side of more benign, albeit costly, forms of correction, but this is in fact a perfect description of the superego at work).[59] A line from the notes of Alexander Gideon, a character in Amos Oz's *Black Box*, captures something of the tone: ' "Thou shalt love thy neighbour as thyself"—at once or we'll fill you full of lead' (he is writing about fanaticism, but only just).[60] As if in reply, the young Israeli poet, Sami Shalom Chetrit, cited by Ammiel Alcalay as representative of the new generation of 'Oriental' Jewish writers, ends his twenty-nine-stanza poem on the *intafadah*—'Hey Jeep'—with 'but thou shalt love thy neighbour as thyself' reiterated, dully, pointedly, vacuously, thirteen times.[61]

Furthermore, the superego dispenses its moral favours unevenly, without ratio, since the more you obey it the more you feel answerable to its judgements (conscience torments the saint far more than the sinner, virtue is not its own reward). The superego draws its energies from the same unconscious impulses it is intended to tame; it turns against the ego the very force with which the ego strains to reject its commands (this gives a whole new meaning to the idea of a punishment that fits the crime). Super-ego and unconscious are antagonists, but they also have the most intimate, passionate relationship with each other: dedicated combatants, tired and devoted cohabitees. There is, as has often been pointed out, something sadistic about this version of morality. Enter this zone of punitive pleasures, and who, we may ask, is punishing, who pleasuring, whom?

Certainly, there is nothing in this account that will submit to a language of contractual negotiation which presupposes the rationality of the rules, or of the participants, in advance. Playful, perverse, savage—to call justice a fantasy in this context is to say no more or less than that it is the supreme target and embodiment of our social aspirations, our most exacting ideal. Or, to put it another way, there is no ideal without fantasy, no shortcut through the trials of fantasy to the realization of our political dreams.

When justice attempts such a short-circuit, it threatens to destroy every-thing, including justice itself. These lines are from the Israeli poet Bialik, cited in *The Land of Israel* by Amos Oz:

> If there is justice, let it be seen at once.
> But if after I am desolated under the heavens,
> justice should appear,
> let it be destroyed for ever.[62]

He then makes the link to the slogan 'Redemption Now' of Gush Emunim. Redemption, justice, now, or redemption and justice can go to hell. Justice on these terms is apocalyptic. Like the cities of the old Mediterranean de-scribed by Alcalay: 'bracketed off in expectation of either perfect time and the final correspondence of words and things, or the aftermath of global disaster'.[63] Perfection courts disaster ('peace everlasting . . . take the world by storm').[64] As soon as justice becomes its own ultimatum, it gets vicious, hell-bent on fulfilling itself (the only frame, perhaps, in which the idea of an 'end of history' makes sense). During the 1983 Jerry-Falwell-sponsored tour of the Holy Land, Grace Halsell interrogated one of the Christian Zionists about the 'new Jerusalem' they anticipate and yearn for, the final Armageddon in the plain of Esdraelon when two-thirds of the Jews living in the region will be 'purged'; she was told that once eternity begins, 'after that there are no more sequences of events'.[65] In the words of Max Weber:

the adherent of an ethic of ultimate ends suddenly turns into a chiliastic prophet. Those, for example, who have just preached 'love against violence' now call for the use of force for the *last* violent deed, which would then lead to a state of affairs in which violence was annihilated . . . The proponent of an ethic of absolute ends cannot stand up under the ethical irrationality of the world.[66]

For similar reasons, totalitarianism cannot be placed on the other side of justice as if it had no investment in it, as if justice was not one of its main concerns: 'Totalitarian lawfulness,' writes Arendt in *The Origins of Totalitarianism*, 'pretends to have found a way to establish the rule of justice on earth.'[67]

In this context, the point of the turn to psychoanalysis is that it tears a rift in this vision of justice, opening up an aporia in our social, moral being no less radical than that affecting our sexual identities, the ones which the culture most coercively presumes to know. Against that presumption, that knowledge, we have been happy (some of us) to take on the concept of the unconscious, to tie sexuality to perversion, or rather to break down the distinction between the two. But the perverse component of justice? What good—to echo Freud's query about 'Love Thy Neighbour'—will it do? Unless we turn that question round—the classic psychoanalytic move—and ask instead: What might an account of justice look like that included that perverse component in its terms, one which allowed the most difficult psychic dimension of justice to be entertained? Can we demand justice without making a virtue of it? Could there be a theory of justice that doesn't require us all, miraculously and coercively, to be good (a recipe for disaster in my mind)? I desire justice; but not if it rules out the scrutiny of desire.

Everything in the literature examined here would seem to suggest that it is only when you try to expel desire from justice and start to believe in its absolute and total perfectibility (the second move only possible on condition of the first), that justice turns nasty and starts punishing the very world it was meant to save (it is not a belief in the possibility of reason, but over-investment in one's own sure possession of reason which is the trap).

There is a passing moment in *Whose Justice? Which Rationality?* when Alisdair MacIntyre argues that only psychoanalysis, notably that of Freud and Lacan, offers a cogent account of the 'schism' of the self which the liberal order has to repress and disguise (his words) in order to produce its 'false and psychologically disabling unity of presentation' (each individual a 'single, well-ordered will').[68] This is part of MacIntyre's overall project which started with *After Virtue*, his critique first of liberalism's assumption that there is a neutral ground from which competing claims to justice can be assessed; and then of the assumption behind that one, that justice and rationality can be understood independently, that theories of justice don't always bring a very specific, historically variant account of what makes a reasoned subject in their train (hence his move from *After Virtue* to the project and title of this second book). But, as he sees it, psychoanalysis retreats from its insight into cure, patching up the liberal self by offering therapeutic solutions to an essentially historical problem: the demise of a liberal order, in itself the effect of a breakdown in consensual being to which it vainly tries to offer a solution, blind to the fact that its history has come to an end.

But supposing it is in the field of justice, far more than in the field of individual pathology, that the rational pretensions and curative aims of psychoanalysis could be shown most definitively to break down? As Freud himself acknowledged, the problem with the analysis of so-called social pathology is that, unlike the individual symptom, there is not even the pretence of a norm. You can at least argue as to whether the aim of psychoanalytic practice is the fortification of the ego as agent, or the release of the subject, against society's best (worst) moral intentions, into the vicissitudes of desire. But in Freud's account of how subjects take up their social identities, there is nothing to support what MacIntyre sees as happy, if misguided, liberal-social communing. Nothing to buttress a conviction that conflict in the modern world can be resolved in the sphere of pure reason alone ('each individual a single well-ordered will'). 'Ethics,' Freud writes, 'is thus to be regarded as a therapeutic attempt—as an endeavour to achieve, by means of a command of the superego, something which has so far not been achieved by means of any other cultural activities.'[69] (This is to put the *placebo* delusions of therapy on the other, societal, foot.)

Psychoanalysis might then be seen as the unconscious of one specific liberal tradition, the one that by requiring—to use another of MacIntyre's own formulas—that we 'conceal the depths of our conflicts', social no less than psychic, makes it impossible for those conflicts, and above all for their *relationship*, to be acknowledged, let alone understood.

* * *

When Henry Louis Gates Jr. delivered the lecture 'A Killing Rage—Black-Jewish Relations' in London in April 1994, his topic was strikingly pertinent to the theme of these chapters, which have tried to follow some of the lines between Israel/Palestine, South Africa, and England, to trace the historic and imaginative links between English culture, black, Palestinian, and Jew.[70] Gates's lecture was a plea for an end to black anti-semitism and Jewish racism. It begun with the problem of how collective guilt gets transmitted across generations, fixing and damning our political futures in advance, and ended with a call for the politics of identity (I know who I am) to be replaced by the politics of identification (I want to know you).

The politics of identity, one could say, shares all the problems of the particular version of liberalism just discussed. It is because the self it asserts against prior injustice remains forged in the image of reason, of false self-consistency—which is what it means to assert an identity—that it finds itself powerless in the face of identity's unreason, powerless to resolve the conflicts of allegiance, the incommensurable and often antagonistic demands that such a politics provokes. It is a problem which was invisible until the politics of identity actualized it so vividly (this is the opposite, note, of reacting to these new voices as if they had all the power and were on the point of taking over the world). But if you respond to this difficulty by calling for a politics of identification, then the question of what permits and forbids identifications, of what makes recognition (love of neighbour, for example) possible and impossible has to come next. Gates's crucial demand has to go further; his call for new forms of affinity, recognition, and identification ends exactly where, psychically speaking, we need to begin.

In May 1990, in an address to three hundred corporate businessmen, Nelson Mandela cited this famous speech of Shylock from *The Merchant of Venice*:

hath not a Jew eyes? Hath not a Jew hands, organs, dimensions, senses, affections, passions? fed with the same food, hurt with the same weapons, subject to the same diseases, healed by the same means, warmed and cooled by the same winter and summer, as a Christian is? If you prick us, do we not bleed? If you tickle us, do we not laugh? If you poison us, do we not die? And if you wrong us, shall we not revenge? If we are like you in the rest, we will resemble you in that . . . The villainy you teach me, I will execute; and it shall go hard, but I will better the instructions.[71]

It was a stunning rhetorical move. Jews will undoubtedly have been present in his audience. Business and radicalism were the two main destinies of Jewish immigrants to South Africa (sometimes, as with Ruth First's family, both at the same time). But there is also a long tradition of anti-semitism in the country. When Daniel François Malan, founder of apartheid, introduced his Quota Bill in 1930, limiting immigrants from 'non-scheduled' countries (Greece, Latvia, Lithuania, Poland, Russia, Palestine), it was generally recognized as an attempt, which proved successful, to halt the immigration of Jews. Since this was 1930, eighteen years before the official inauguration of apartheid, his speeches on this topic can be read as a rehearsal for what was to come: 'Nations desire to preserve homogeneity, because every nation has got a soul, and every nation naturally desires that its soul shall not be a divided one.'[72]

That, then, is the identification to which Mandela, citing those lines of Shylock, made his appeal: the line that links black to Jew as members, equally although distinctly of a persecuted race. A plea to remember, an attempt—in the words of Ammiel Alcalay—to turn 'the texture of memory ahead'.[73]

But Mandela's use of this speech was also a warning. It has another, more deadly potential future tense. From suffering to revenge, Shylock traces a curve which puts a stop, no less dramatically, to the very redeeming identification it seems to propose: 'and if you wrong us shall we not revenge?—if we are like you in the rest, we will resemble you in that'. Mandela then took out these lines: 'If a Jew wrong a Christian, what is his humility? revenge! If a Christian wrong a Jew, what should his sufferance be by Christian example?—why revenge!' He took out the lines of the speech which show virtue—humility and then sufferance as ethos—turning violently inside-out on themselves. It would undoubtedly have complicated the argument. By leaving virtue standing, as it were, Mandela could communicate far more powerfully to this audience the extent to which their future actions would determine just how far it is at risk.

Of course, it has been the case for a long time that critics trying to defend Shakespeare's *Merchant of Venice* against the charge of anti-Semitism have turned to these lines. But they tend to ignore the dark side of the message and of the humanity to which the Jew stakes his claim: that it is through self-perpetuating violence that oppressed and oppressor most often identify. It is too soon to say whether this political scenario has been averted in South Africa, although much of the energy is going towards making sure that it is. In Israel/Palestine, as I write this today, the conditions seem so unpromising that it is not even clear if the question can begin to be put. English life and letters have, of course, tended to purify themselves of all this. It has been the main purpose of this discussion to make the connection unavoidable for us all.

PART TWO

The Limits of Culture

FIVE

On the 'Universality' of Madness: Bessie Head's *A Question of Power*

Let us burst into history, forcing it by our invasion into universality for the first time.

> Jean Paul Sartre, preface to Frantz Fanon *The Wretched of the Earth*, 1961

You know, my friend, a combination such as I of two nations finally establishes the human race.

> Bessie Head, letter to Randolph Vigne, 31 October 1968, *A Gesture of Belonging: Letters from Bessie Head 1965–1979*, 1991

I T is difficult, in recent debate about literary studies, to avoid the problem of universality. How come the critic can now hear the hitherto silenced or neglected if, as the argument has gone, belief in the possibility of universal communication, across national and cultural boundaries, masked a moment of self-aggrandizing blindness? From where can such a critic listen without reproducing the epistemological privilege of the West? What happens when the discourse of universality is claimed by a voice which, according to the first analysis, was necessarily ruled out of its frame? Might the claim that 'universality' is always Western privilege in fact generate the very exclusion it is designed to contest?

The title of this chapter is therefore deliberately provocative. It contains two words—universality and madness—which are, to say the least, problematic and contentious. I put universality in scare quotes, but madness calls in many ways for equal if not greater caution. I start by assuming that to qualify the first immediately throws a critical light on the second. This chapter tries to address the hesitancy and awkwardness of both terms for a white woman writing about a black woman writer's semi-fictional account of a period of breakdown in Africa.

My argument will be that these terms are both corrupted *and* indispensable; terms of imperial naming, they cannot, however, just be discarded, not least of all because they are part of Bessie Head's own vocabulary. Borrowing an expression from Caroline Rooney's brilliant article on Bessie Head and Ama Ata Aidoo in *Motherlands*, I would say that Bessie Head 'interrogates' them 'in passing'[1]—not, however, by going straight through them and out the other side, but by putting them into dialogue with each other. One might in fact say that it is in relation to 'madness' that 'universality' shows its most dubious euro/ethnocentric colours, as it spreads its diagnostic certainty across the globe. Yet interestingly, too, the critique of universality finds it hard to free itself of the discourse of insanity—isn't the accusation that universality is always something 'projected' by the West?

The epigraph from Sartre is there to remind us that universality can also be voiced from the other side, as a claim to participation in history which has been—still is—voiced by the oppressed. In his 1993 lecture, 'Nationalism, Human Rights and Interpretation', Edward Said—citing Partha Chatarjee—put his plea for a 'new universality', *another* universality (the test case is, of course, for him, first the Palestinians but also the South African blacks), to be put alongside—against—the new pseudo-world order, post-Gulf War, post-fall of the Berlin Wall universality of the West.[2] Another way of putting this would be to say that universality is *not yet* a dispensable term. The limits of 'universality', in its most contested version, is the subject of the final essay in this book. Here I come at the problem from, so to speak, the other side.

Bessie Head was born in South Africa in 1937 (the year of the publication of *Black Hamlet*). She is a crucial writer for this book, not just because of the problem of 'universality', to which she gives her own unique and unsettling twist, but because she covers or brings together in her own writing, as we saw briefly in Chapter 2, different fragments of its terrain. Inside her mind, sometimes tortuously in the course of her breakdown, sometimes inspirationally at the moment of recovery, she orchestrates a fantasmatic scenario of their historic and potential belonging. Because her vision is both broken and transcendent, it is impossible to characterize it, psychically or historically, as either symptom or cure.

Bessie Head left South Africa on a one-way exit permit in 1964 to settle in Botswana, where she remained until her death in 1986 (she applied for Botswanan citizenship in 1977 but was not granted it until 1979). *A Question of Power*, her most famous book which will be the focus of this discussion, was published in 1973. It was the last of her three novels; she also wrote journalism, short stories, a chronicle of Serowe, and letters—one collection published, another, as well as a further manuscript novel, published for the first time in 1994.[3] At the borderline of fiction and chronicle, A Question of Power recounts, close to the detail of one episode of Bessie Head's life, the breakdown and cure in the village of Motabeng of its central woman protagonist, Elizabeth: formally from outside her consciousness (it is written in the third person), effectively from inside her mind (it is almost consistently what she sees). Charles Larson wrote:

Bessie Head's A Question of Power is important not solely because it is an introspective novel by an African woman but because the topics of her concern are also, for the most part, foreign to African fiction . . . madness, sexuality, guilt . . . almost single-handedly [she has] brought about the inward turning of the African novel.[4]

That 'inward turning' is only part of the story; Bessie Head's writing is always rooted, locally and historically, if ambiguously, in its world: 'I could not be considered as a South African exile, but as one who has put down roots. And yet, certain strength in me, certain themes I am likely to write about, have been mainly shaped by my South African experience.'[5]

To try and read Bessie Head as a white reader is to find oneself jammed in on more than one side: by what I will call, taking my title from an article by John Lonsdale, the 'mau maus of the mind'—the risk of sliding into imperial diagnosis of the type that has rushed to read derangement where legible political protest was in fact what was being expressed;[6] by the problem of retrieval or listening—how to listen to the woman writer from a different culture when any moment of felt recognition may be mere appropriation or projection on the reader's part (especially given that the issue of projection is one of the central themes of Bessie Head's book); by the fact that if it is madness we are talking about, then communication in its most obviously understood sense—I listen, you speak—is exactly what we cannot take for granted or assume. Bessie Head writes a semi-fictional account of what she herself describes as a breakdown, in which there is in fact *too much* communication—voices inside the mind. It would be odd to respond to this extraordinary piece of writing as if channels, lines, wires— how things get transmitted—were not precisely the issue, something which the book shows as available for total, hostile sabotage.

Speak, listen, learn—A Question of Power issues this injunction to its reader, while also exploring the terrorizing potential of any verbal command. Perhaps the factor of madness in this book, the questions about communication inside and across cultures which it raises, can serve to expose or lay bare the delusional component behind any uncritical belief that text, or speaker, simply speak. To put it another way, doesn't the question of who is speaking in the text and how I should listen—the issues of race, class, gender as they have become louder and louder in contemporary critical debate (not to speak of the backlash term of 'political correctness')—carry an anxiety that the text might be speaking with a hostile voice, one which is alien, unfriendly, to *me*? As Bessie Head puts it in her 1972 short piece 'Dreamer and Storyteller' on the problem of writing in South Africa: 'how does one communicate with the horrible?'[7]

One of the reasons I do not want to discard the term 'madness' too quickly in relation to Bessie Head is because I am not sure that it is possible to read this book without feeling oneself go a little bit mad. It is, I think, part of the wager of the book. Bessie Head herself said that she knew she had written a book that goes over the top: 'It might have a lower key, something that can be explained in terms of African society in general . . . it runs on this wild style at high-key level.'[8] From the beginning, Bessie Head, or her character Elizabeth, turns the tables on her reader, issues an invitation of a very specific kind: Enter my (inner) world. It is hard for the reader who accepts not to feel that she, like the persecutors who people Elizabeth's mind, hasn't walked straight into her head: 'People's souls walked right into her'; 'Obviously she was an easily invaded world.'[9] I am sure I am not the only reader to have experienced *A Question of Power* as writing by battery assault: 'He'd been doing this for months, opening her skull and talking into it in a harsh, grating voice.'[10] Amongst other things, this is a particularly raw way of undoing the patronym (Head). Bessie Head's book is the first piece of writing that has given me any real insight into what Victor Tausk, writing in Vienna in 1919, described as the 'influencing machine'—a persecutory machine 'of mystical nature', consisting of 'boxes, cranks, levers, wheels, buttons, wires, batteries and the like'[11]:

he had to fix up his electrical wiring system (her whole body was a network, a complicated communication centre); everything depended on the efficiency of it. He couldn't get the wires in the right place if she was nervy or jumpy . . . He kept on switching off and adjusting the currents . . . Suddenly, a terrible thunderbolt struck her heart. She could feel wave after wave of its power spread over her body and pass out through her feet.[12]

Going mad as a refugee in Botswana—and then transforming that madness into writing—Bessie Head violates more than one colonial stereotype and breaks a few rules. It was widely believed by colonialists in Africa that women did not go mad. African women, writes Megan Vaughan in her book *Curing their Ills: Colonial Power and African Illness*, 'were said not to have reached the level of self-awareness required to go mad'.[13] They lacked 'interiority'—twice over, as African and as woman. According to the dominant mythology, African identity was collective not individual (read more dependent, immature), but African man had gained the rudiments of individual personhood from his contact with the European, a contact which African women lacked. The contrast with European womanhood is striking. In the West, women have if anything been reduced to mere interiority; it is their restricted and privileged domain. In Africa, interiority may be a white burden and myth foisted onto the blacks—the mark of humanity in the Western mind—but that does not prevent it from being something of which the African woman is *deprived* (*When Rain Clouds Gather*, Bessie Head's first novel, can be read as her analysis of that deprivation from the point of view of the man). Paranoia—voices in the head—is of course the perfect metaphor for colonization, take-over of body and mind; in this case, the use which Bessie Head makes of it in her writing also serves to undo one of the prevalent myths—African women don't go mad—of colonization itself.

Place the issue of madness and its universality in context, therefore, and some of the expected relations between terms immediately start to shift. On this Wulf Sachs, who was at the centre of Chapter 2, is instructive. On the first page of *Black Hamlet*, he states: 'I discovered that the manifestations of insanity, in its form, content, origin, and causation are identical in both natives and Europeans.'[14] In *Black Anger* (the revised version of 1947), Sachs foregrounds the political nature of this statement by presenting it as his answer to racism—these are the opening lines:

He had lived in South Africa all his life. 'So,' he said to me, 'you are going to settle in Johannesburg. Well—here's the best advice I can give you. Leave your ideas in Europe. You're going among blacks—gentle, happy savages—children, children who never grow beyond the age of ten or twelve. So, if you have any notion of treating them as equals, forget about it.[15]

Most simply, then, one way to come at the concept of universality might be to note, on each separate occasion, the history which provokes it: 'I saw I would get nowhere with the whites. There was only one other way. I would get to know the blacks, not as blacks, but as human beings.'[16]

So what counts as mad? One of the articles I have read on Bessie Head, by Elizabeth Evasdaughter, starts by showing how Elizabeth's symptoms correspond, almost exactly, to the criteria for paranoid schizophrenia given in the American Psychiatric Association's *Desk Reference to the Diagnostic Criteria from Diagnostic and Statistical Manual of Mental Disorders* (3rd edition,

1982).[17] This seems hardly more promising, although less tempting for me, than the comparisons I have come across between Bessie Head and Sylvia Plath.[18] Early in the book, Elizabeth says to herself 'Agh, I must be mad! That's just an intangible form', when she offers a cup of tea to the white robed monk 'sitting' on the end of her bed.[19] But it is not absolutely clear whether we are dealing with paranoia or ghosts: 'The form of a man totally filled the large horizon in front of her . . . She had never seen a ghost in her life . . . She turned her head towards where he had always sat . . . a ghostly, persistent commentator.'[20]

In Schapera's famous monograph on the Tswana, he describes the earlier dominant cult of worship of the dead, the belief that each family was under the direct guidance of its agnatic ancestors: 'The Tswana believed in the survival of the dead. They held that the souls of dead people became spirits (*badimo*), which ultimately found their way to a world vaguely located underground.'[21] By 1953, the time Schapera was writing, these beliefs were no longer operative except in cases of sickness. To be sick was to be under the influence of hostile ancestors. Illness seems, then, to be the residual place of former belief, the place to which—like a ghost—the belief in spirits had migrated.

In his recent novel, *Mating*, set in the Tsau colony in 1970s Botswana, Norman Rush has his female narrator make this point: 'If you believe that the dead hate you and that all your afflictions come from offending them, this is what *we'd* call paranoia' (note that 'we' underlined—this is colonial naming); but, she continues: 'blaming your ancestors for all the bad luck and illness bound to befall you in dire terrain like Botswana was probably pro survival, group survival, in that it directed rage and suspicion backward and mostly away from contemporaries.'[22] For this female narrator slung between the devil of her own sexual colonization by the white male founder of a female native colony in the Botswana desert (*sic*—the colony did exist) and the deep blue sea of her own colonizing of the mind (she is after all a *white* woman in Botswana), this is a good try. But the moment touches on something important. Paranoia is not quite the same thing—madness is not universal—in a culture which believes that ancestors can visit you, body and mind, that the dead live underground and are liable, at any moment, to drop in. By the end of the novel, that observation by the female narrator—or rather paranoia itself—has come home to roost: 'In my attitude toward Tsau I was stuck at a paranoid level' (the ending of the book then plays out the question of 'who's paranoid?' in unexpected and startling ways).[23]

A South African refugee in Botswana, Bessie Head is mostly critical of traditional custom and belief, and the presences in *A Question of Power* are the spirits of the living, not the dead. But it none the less remains that terms like hallucination and paranoia in themselves overlook a fundamental cultural difference. To put it another way, the boundaries between reality and hallucination are culturally specific *and* historically (as well as psychically) mobile. In a 1980 letter to Charles Sarvan, Bessie Head writes:

Then I had not asked people about African attitudes to witchcraft. I had to when doing research for my history of Serowe. People then began to tell me of things I had lived through in *A Question of Power* which are normal everyday events for black people.

They told me there are two kinds of witches in the society . . . The day witches are people in the society who are evil and can be identified. The night witches are hidden. They are the baloi. They enter the body of a sleeping victim and from then on the victim feels a pain. It is either a pain in the head or a pain in the chest accompanied by disturbed sleep. The hideous and obscene is the great joy of the night witch/wizard. The other great joy of the wizard is to open the mouth of a sleeping person and poke his finger in it. A lot of this data corresponded to my own experience.[24]

Situating herself as alien to the culture—these are 'everyday events for black people'—and unfamiliar, as yet, with its beliefs—'then I had not asked about African attitudes to witchcraft'—Bessie Head is persecuted by the figures of her still unredeemed ignorance.

In *Black Hamlet*, despite that opening appeal to universality, such differences of psychic geography play a crucial part in the story. At a turning point in the narrative, John—the subject of Sachs's investigation—finds himself in court watching the murder trial of a man who kills a friend whom he believed, following warnings by John in his capacity as witch-doctor, to be an enemy ghost. The defence bases its case entirely on the reasonableness of the action in the context of African beliefs:

To the primitive African, the belief in witchcraft is real and logical. There is no such thing as imaginary feeling. There is no such phenomenon as imaginary pain or imaginary vision. It might appear so to others but not to the sufferer. The African fears malicious spirits which he actually sees and hears. He lives in constant fear and turns to the witch-doctors, in whom he places unconditional belief and trust. Mdlawani had a reasonable belief in evildoers. His fight against them was reasonable.[25]

Mitigation, in this case, depends on arguing for the *sanity* of the defendant according to customary belief. The emphasis on reasonableness in context did not, of course, stop the beliefs in themselves from being considered at the same time primitive and quite mad. Megan Vaughan gives the example of Nyasaland, where insanity was pardonable since it was held to be a real and definable condition, while bewitchment, although seen as unreal, was taken as evidence of malice and hence a punishable offence[26] (likewise John sits watching in court at real legal risk of discovery as the inciter by witchcraft of Mdlawani). The fact remains that, according to his account, Mdlawani believed he was killing a ghost—an enemy who had taken on another shape. It was for him legitimate and necessary self-defence. Elizabeth does not believe that the presences who visit her can kill her, but the struggle is a life-and-death matter and they repeatedly exhort her to die. Instead of killing them, she enters into the conversation. Even when she is hospitalized, she is not, as Evasdaughter remarks, 'prevented by drugs from continuing her internal debate'.[27] Bessie Head's character goes through something we could call—with the crucial difference that there is no analyst present—her own 'talking cure'.

The boundaries here are precarious. At the end of *Not Either an Experimental Doll*, which can be fairly described as an account of how well-intentioned white educational benevolence played its part in driving one black girl mad, Shula Marks describes how she traced the girl, Lily Moya, to her sister's, where she was living after 25 years of institutionalization in mental homes.[28] Only briefly, before being first admitted to Sterkfontein in the 1950s, Lily's family and indeed Lily herself, Marks speculates, may 'have interpreted her illness as *inkathazo* or *ukuthwaza*, the condition afflicting people, usually women, called on by the spirits of the ancestors to become diviners'.[29] In the course of his investigation, Sachs wonders if 'it wouldn't be advisable, from a psychological point of view, to employ *ngangas* in the treatment of insane natives' because of the personal and psychic information they are able to evoke. 'In any case,' he adds, 'there is nothing to lose, for our methods fail lamentably.'[30] When John visits the mental asylum where Sachs works, he is presented with a *nganga* imprisoned for life for practising witchcraft who sits crouching as he throws 'imaginary bones for imaginary patients, to whom he gave imaginary medicines'.[31] As the narrator of *A Question of Power* puts it: 'One might propose an argument with the barriers of the normal, conventional and the sane all broken down'.[32] Depending on from where you are looking at it, the same form of behaviour can be madness or cure. In the case of Elizabeth, it seems that to get rid of the presences which persecute and haunt her, she must first *entertain* them in all senses of the term (the dictionary meanings of 'to entertain' include: keep up or maintain, keep occupied the attention of, receive as a guest).

To read *A Question of Power* as a ghost story is not to bypass the question of madness, but to enter directly into its political and historical dimension. Bessie Head, like the character Elizabeth, was born in a mental hospital to a white mother put away because she was pregnant by a native. Sent first to a nursing home and then to a Boer family, both of which returned her because she was black, Bessie Head, again like Elizabeth in the novel, was finally taken in by a Coloured foster mother whom she believed to be her real mother until the age of 13.[33] In her article 'Notes from a Quiet Back-water', published in *Drum* in 1982, Bessie Head writes:

There must be many people like me in South Africa whose birth or beginnings are filled with calamity and disaster, the sort of person who is the skeleton in the cupboard or the dark and fearful secret swept under the carpet. The circumstances of my birth seemed to make it necessary to obliterate all family history.[34]

The first secret is an intimate, sexual, family secret, a trauma of begetting which speaks a whole history of racial division (apartheid as sexual apartheid as much as, if not before, anything else—Lewis Nkosi's *Mating Birds* could be read as a recovery/re-writing of this story's hidden subtext).[35] If all primal scenes are in some sense unthinkable, this one has been made doubly unthinkable—miscegenation and its silencing—for the child. In *A Question of Power*, chronologically if not in terms of narrative sequence, the first ghost to appear—and the first invocation to madness—is the mother: 'Now you know. Do you think I can bear the stigma of insanity alone? Share it with me.'[36] The call is ambiguous—is Elizabeth to share only the 'stigma', or is she to go mad? This may be another reason why it is so difficult, if not impossible, to decide on the question of madness in the book. Elizabeth's experience carries the weight, and ambiguity, of this original (mis-)naming.

In 1979, in her article 'Social and Political Pressures that Shape Writing in South Africa', Bessie Head wrote:

A sense of history was totally absent in me and it was as if, far back in history, thieves had stolen the land and were so anxious to cover up all traces of the theft that correspondingly, all traces of the true history have been obliterated.[37]

Second obliteration—of historical origins. Bessie Head's personal trauma, and its enforced forgetting, recapitulates—and is recapitulated by—the destiny of nation and race. These, then, are the dirty secrets of sex and politics. They return as obscenity (Elizabeth in *A Question of Power* as the recipient of obscenities—'just the receiver of horror', 'a ruthless concentration on the obscene')[38] but—and this seems more unlikely—also as cosmic, universal, vision. In 'Notes from a Quiet Backwater', Bessie Head writes:

Each individual, no matter what their present origin or background may be, is really the total embodiment of human history, with a vast accumulation of knowledge and experience stored in the subconscious mind. It was against this background of an individual who could possibly have lived a million different circumstances, that I began to view my relationship to Africa.[39]

There seems to be a line here that runs from a historical deprivation (which is both personal and historical) to the accumulation of history in the 'subconscious' and from there to the potentially infinite expansion of the mind: 'I am the ocean in which all things live and move'.[40]

Something of this sequence is captured by Toni Morrison's 'rememoration'. Bessie Head's novel can be put alongside *Beloved* as a novel of transgenerational haunting where the woman becomes the repository of an unspoken and unspeakable history (*Beloved* is of course another novel about ghosts).[41] The personal drama—the mother's incarceration, insanity as stigma—passes into the daughter, where it re-emerges as the history of a race (which it always already was): 'People cried out so often in agony against racial hatred and oppressions of all kinds. All their tears seemed to be piling up on her, and the source or roots from which they had sprung were being exposed with a vehement violence'.[42] Neither hidden from history, nor invisible to history (the more familiar feminist vocabulary), the woman in Bessie Head's novel is instead the place where the hidden and invisible *of* history accumulates; she is the depot for the return of the historical repressed. From loss to infinity: it is to the precise extent that history has been robbed or diminished that it starts to expand, infinitely, in the mind: 'each individual, no matter what their present origin or background may be, is really the total embodiment of human history'; 'I view my activity as a writer as a kind of participation in the whole world'.[43] In this case, therefore, history and universality are not antagonists. The second draws its energy from, spills—runs—out of, the first.

The pertinent question, then, may not be the universality *of* madness, but the relationship *between* the two terms. If in a first move, madness in Africa can only be viably read locally, i.e. historically; the second move of Bessie Head's own writing, as part and effect of that first historical self-placing, forces us—each and every one of us—to stretch our field of vision to the point where it encompasses the history—past and potential—of the whole world: 'the total embodiment of human history', an individual who could have lived a 'million' other lives.

That movement from the personal to the historical to the universal is, I think, central to Bessie Head's writing. To present it as unidirectional would, however, be misleading. The first haunting by the mother carries a sexual burden which speaks volumes of politics and history. Correspondingly, the passage into the universal is also Bessie Head's direct line back into history, locality, and race: 'it was against this background of an individual who possibly could have lived a million different circumstances, *that I began to view my relationship to Africa*' (my emphasis).

This relationship to Africa is at the centre of *A Question of Power*. At the heart of its own self-diagnosis is the fact that Elizabeth, like Bessie Head, is of mixed descent (although Head is often referred to as a 'Coloured', this term refers to a specific language-use and cultural community, particularly at the Western Cape).[44] One way of reading the book would be to say that it is this fact which drives Elizabeth to her breakdown:

'You're not linked up to the people. You don't know any African languages' . . . Someone had turned a record on inside her head. It went on and on in the same, stuck groove: 'Dog, filth, the Africans will eat you to death. Dog, filth, the Africans will eat you to death.'[45]

This onslaught against Elizabeth as 'Coloured'—'I've never been a racialist. Of course I admit I'm a Coloured. I'm not denying it'—then returns as a mirroring hatred for the African which she discovers in herself: 'A hissing, insistent undertone accompanied her thoughts: "Yes, you think like that because you hate Africans. You don't like the African hair. You don't like the African nose."'[46]

In the second version of *Black Hamlet*, Sachs removed this remark which appears in a footnote about African unity: 'The masses persist in their chauvinistic, nationalistic ideology, with an extreme intolerance of other black men and an almost fascistic hatred of coloured people.'[47] Sachs takes it out because in the second version he rewrites the story less as analytic encounter, more as political self-discovery and emancipation on the part of John.[48] Sachs de-pathologizes his patient to free him into his political dimension—he moves his diagnosis of insanity from the individual onto colonial history. For Bessie Head this is not a viable opposition. Pathology is the place where history talks in its loudest, most grating voice. *A Question of Power* takes Sachs's footnote back and fills it out with sound. What he reads as native intolerance (reinforced rather than qualified, finally, by the reference to fascism), she reads in terms of what she will call, in her 1971 novel *Maru*, the universal language of oppression: 'How universal was the language of oppression! They had said of the Masarwa what every white man had said of every black man' (these are *Maru*'s inner thoughts).[49] In a letter to Sarvan, Bessie Head makes a direct link between the two books:

the stylised beauty of *Maru* was one struggling to retain human dignity against these shouts. The passive, still girl was my own eyes watching the hideous nightmares which were afflicting me and all the girl's personality opposes the shouts of dog, filth, dog filth, you are a coloured dog.[50]

The same shout travels or carries across texts.

In this context, universality takes on another meaning—prejudice as repetition, racist voices appearing where, according to the most obvious forms of historical analysis, they do not belong. Universality, because it could be—and has been—anyone speaking in that voice: voices migrate, mimic, impersonate, and invade as a way of testing or finding out where they might land, a purely temporary instability before they freeze and ossify into place (this gives the postmodern shibboleth of flexibility and mobility its most sinister connotation).

Which means, perhaps oddly, that universality is also contingency. Perhaps the key thing to note is the way universality as a concept starts to break up under scrutiny (that Bessie Head allows us to watch this in process is for me one of the most important things about her writing). If you could have lived a million other lives, then it follows that—in the either/or logic of racism—you might have turned up on the other side. In a letter to Randolph Vigne, Bessie Head wrote: 'I could have been born a white man. I have no control over it. I shake with terror at the thought. Say, some merciful fate put me on the receiving side of brutality and ignorance, but what if I were born to mete this out to others?'[51] Since Bessie Head is half white, this moment of terrified imagining has its concrete foundation. But it is also part of a capacity for psychic cross-over and identification which adds a further dimension of 'universality' to her writing.

In *The Wretched of the Earth*, Fanon writes: 'Weigh as heavily as you can upon the body of your torturer in order that his soul, lost in some by-way, may finally find once more its universal dimension.'[52] Fanon is exhorting the oppressed to weigh on the torturer so as to force him to recognize the humanity he shares with his victim. Similarly, Manganyi, the South African psychologist, writes in his essay 'The Violent Reverie': 'Is it not true that the natural community, as opposed to the "community of victims" is the universal community of humankind?'[53] Bessie Head rewrites and inverts Fanon's injunction. Elizabeth's path to universality takes her back, so to speak, the other way. At the central turning point of *A Question of Power*— the point which marks the transition from the first to the second part, or nightmare, of the book—Elizabeth goes under:

Too often the feelings of a victim are not taken into account. He is so disregarded by the torturer or oppressor that for centuries evils are perpetrated with no one being aghast or put to shame. The tempo of it had been speeded up, brought breath-close and condensed to a high-pitched ferocity. It rumbled beneath her consciousness like molten lava. It only needed someone to bring the hot lava to the surface for her to find that a process of degradation, scorn, and wild, blind cruelty had its equivalent of wild, savage vengeance in her.[54] ·

The shaming or degradation of the victim instead of the torturer would be one way of describing *A Question of Power*: 'conclusions about [a] saner world' asserted 'under degraded circumstances'.[55] Who, we might rephrase the query at the centre of *A Question of Power*, is (to be) degraded?—'the man at the receiving end is actually strengthened, while [the torturer] is weakened and weakened and weakened, day by day.'[56] Note that this is not the issue of the victim/aggressor boundary which has so dogged discussion of the Holocaust: the question is not 'Am I guilty?' but 'Who carries the shame?'
    For Bessie Head, degradation is the other face of power. The letter to Randolph Vigne continues: 'This shout of rage of Mr Stokey Carmichael is a shout from the depths of the deep, true, exultant power he is receiving by being the man down there. It's a kind of power that leaps up from the feet to the head in a drunken ecstasy.' This is 'deep, true, exultant power', but it contains a risk (the risk of power would be another possible paraphrase for *A Question of Power*): 'I feel Mr Stokey does not know this. He might fall down on his knees and glorify his enemy. I feel these things go on in the subconscious and we give them the wrong names.'[57] In this passage, Bessie Head sets herself up as an analyst, as the subject who knows the truth of a misrecognized subconscious. What she sees, what she believes Carmichael doesn't see, are the perils of exultation, the risk of ecstasy reversing itself into abjection. Not just a revulsion *from* power, this is also an analysis *of* power—of the potentially disabling proximity between antagonism and identification (taking the enemy's place, internally as well as externally, as the only way of ensuring his defeat). It is this analysis which prevents Bessie Head—except for her early support for Robert Subokwe—from fully supporting African nationalism, something for which she has often been criticized (she writes a scathing first-person mimicry of Joas Tsepe in the 1967 short story 'Sorrow food').[58] Elizabeth says to Tom: 'It seems an indignity to me to stick a fist in the air . . . I couldn't do it. I'd feel ashamed.' 'Why?' Tom asks. 'Because of what I see inside . . . Because of what I'm learning internally.'[59]
    In a famous comment from her essay 'Some Notes on Novel Writing', Bessie Head describes the genesis of *A Question of Power*:

I found myself in a situation where there was no guarantee against the possibility that I could be evil too. I found that one only earns a slight guarantee against the possibility of inflicting harm on others through an experience which completely destroys one's own ego or sense of self-esteem.[60]

Writing again to Vigne, she talks of her 'awareness of evil and a clear vision of direct interference in my life from an outside source' (one of two disorders in her life, the other being the refusal to grant her Botswanan citizenship, which she only received in 1979).[61] This is—in psychic terms—very precise. Like history, the ego expands and inflates itself when it has been robbed. Too much of an ego—an over-peopled ego—is the outcome of an ego which has collapsed (in another letter to Vigne, Bessie Head relates the visions in her head directly to the process of ego-shattering).[62] Elizabeth asks Tom: 'What would you do if you were both God and Satan at the same time . . . it's possible, isn't it. The dividing line between good and evil is very narrow.'[63] Thus Bessie Head allows us to track the universal or cosmic—God and Satan—as it arises out of ego-shattering history.

We can also note in passing how this reverses the Sartrean dictum that the racist's problem is predominantly metaphysical, the victim's still socio-historical (compare Manganyi: 'the victim of racism suffers from a primary deficit: that of being oversocialized').[64] This is, of course, also a gendered distinction. Tom says to Elizabeth: 'The things you draw out of a man! You know, men don't really discuss the deep metaphysical profundities with women.'[65] Amongst other things, Bessie Head presents Elizabeth to us as a woman philosopher for the whole world.

For Bessie Head, therefore, inside the head is the place where you can make the links or points of connection—both deadly and of universal potential—which are invisible to the cultural, historical, and racial differentiations above ground. It is at one level very simple—we are all equally human (the enlightenment claim to universal citizenship), to which she adds: inside the mind (not so good, but the unspoken, often unspeakable, corollary to the first claim). This is not a million miles from Kristeva's recent comment: 'only strangeness is universal . . . let us know ourselves as unconscious, altered, other in order better to approach the universal otherness of the strangers that we are'.[66] Kristeva is too close to the 'universality of the unconscious' here for my liking, but inverting the expected order of things we might say, not that madness is universal, but that madness seems, in this case at least, to be the only way for universality to get a hearing, voice itself, speak. What Bessie Head seems to offer through that process could perhaps be described as an ethics of universality, on condition of distinguishing it from a universal ethics (shared participation without ethical boundaries, as opposed to a laying down of the law).

This is why I cannot finally agree with Caroline Rooney when she argues that Elizabeth's mental invasion in *A Question of Power* is 'at the expense of her active inclusion in the process and at the expense of crediting her with a soul or subject reality of her own'.[67] Persecution is a form of interiority wherever, finally, you might decide that the presences who visit her belong (real visitants or the figments of her mind). In fact Elizabeth leaves this question open: 'It gave her a strange feeling of things being right there inside her and yet projected at the same time at a distance'.[68] It it is not clear whether we are dealing with an outside-in or inside-out situation—the writing doesn't let you decide. Projection is one way, ghosts another, of reading what is taking place (this is why I also can't agree that Elizabeth is the recipient and not the agent of 'omnipotence of thoughts', if that is the appropriate term, although I accept Rooney's critique of the ethnocentric way that Freud uses the concept). Either way, Elizabeth's nightmare is her privilege. It is both alien to her and something for which she is chosen (persecution as the sincerest form of flattery), outside and inside, invasive and utterly her own. Nor does any of this, it should be stressed, cancel the force of Bessie Head's comment in her letter to Sarvan: 'There is a sturdy sanity about everything I do.'[69]

Universality therefore is a part of interiority (I realize that to say universality is a 'part' is oxymoronic, but I want to avoid suggesting that the psyche is being *wholly* universalized here), as well as being part of and a response to the specifics of oppression and race—the two realms are inseparable without being reducible to each other. Interestingly, it seems to be the combination of universal and particular which, according to Bessie Head's own analysis, made *A Question of Power* so hard for some readers to take:

they all took a dodge behind this 'mentally sick' business . . . the language is too embarrassing to handle; it hardly sounds normal or human . . . they tried to re-set the book in South Africa because this sort of thing . . . 'there's strange under-currents and events in Botswana . . .' could not apply to Botswana. They dare not examine such language as . . . 'I thought too much of myself. I am the root cause of human suffering.'[70]

Horror is admissible only if Bessie Head is mentally sick and/or the whole thing can be placed in South Africa, politically localized, distanced, and made safe. No apartheid, no problem—there could be no such undercurrents in Botswana: the idea of 'strange undercurrents and events . . . could not apply to Botswana'. That such undercurrents might move around is, for white liberal myth, the ultimate scandal. If Bessie Head seems at moments to be promoting something which might be called universal humanism (not long ago this was, of course, the worst intellectual insult), it would seem to be—for those who have promoted its specious, self-serving version—its deranging, unacceptable side.

There is more, however, to be said about universality. It has often been pointed that Bessie Head draws her cultural references from everywhere. Her writing is, as she puts it in a letter to Randolph Vigne, 'a blending of everything . . . a huge hotch potch . . . a sprawling run across the universe taking in everything'.[71] For one critic, this further universal dimension damages the book: because of these references 'from many cultures, religions, eras and political systems', Elizabeth appears as a 'universal soul'[72] (this criticism should in itself be placed alongside Izevbaye's remark, citing Senghor, that traditional African critical attitudes are distinguished from European by their 'knowledge of the universe').[73] According to Megan Vaughan, the most disturbing forms of insanity, disturbing that is for the colonialists, were the ones which contained, internal to the delusion, a European dimension—the contents of European culture showing up as fragments in the deluded self-imaginings of the blacks: 'Owns Port Herald and is married to a white girl', 'Lives at Government House which a previous governor gave him', 'Thinks himself God and principal headman of the sky' (all these were classified as 'European-type' delusions).[74] This was insanity as parody, a participation by proxy in a cultural world to which the native was meant to be inadequate. Paradoxically, the European dimension of the delusion confirmed the extent to which the African had, in reality, failed to enter the culture he hallucinated and dreamed. Elizabeth's cultural panoply goes way beyond Europe—it includes Buddhism as well as American popular culture—but its promiscuity is, in colonial terms, both insane and an affront.

Once again, the expansiveness—'I view my activity as a writer as a kind of participation in the whole world'—is inseparable from the most precise historical self-placing—'I found myself performing a peculiar shuttling movement between two lands', 'You know, my friend, a combination such as I of two nations finally establishes the human race.'[75] One into two won't go; it has—infinitely—to multiply itself. How can universality be singular or one if it contains, precisely, every-thing (universality as in 'collective' rather than as 'generality' or 'general statement'—the two meanings between which it so often slides)? This is all-inclusiveness without totalization: 'It is not as though anyone knows who God is', 'I am sure of so little', 'Contradiction or even apparent contradiction could be called the other name of truth.'[76]

*   *   *

A few points in conclusion. One of my paths to Bessie Head was via Sylvia Plath. In Plath's case diagnosis had been so offensive, the only possible response had been to politicize her suffering but in a way which, it seemed to me, had involved taking out the mind. This struck me as expressive of a more general problem. It has become a commonplace of recent literary and cultural theory to point to the unconscious as a challenge to the dominant: the psyche knows better than the worst of the culture; the mind is also, if not only, its own place. But once you grant the unconscious—if that is what we want to call it—even such partial autonomy, how do you deal with what can appear as not just its self-creating but also its self-destroying laws? What do you do, to put it more simply, when it comes up with something you don't like? Interestingly for me, both Megan Vaughan and Shula Marks in their writings on Africa refuse to read psychic disturbance purely in terms of social and racial oppression—Vaughan because the culturalist argument has been used historically to imply that the natives are not up to the strain of Western culture, Marks because of what she calls the 'unknown quantity of personal frailty' in a tragedy, Lily Moya's, which 'raises in acute form [the question of] how to relate individual psychology and psychopathology to social structure'.[77] What place, I would rephrase her, if any is there for the concept of the unconscious, with its own laws of transformation, in an 'atrocity-producing environment'?[78] I cannot think of a writer who poses that question more acutely than Bessie Head.

Finally, on universality. At the 1968 Ife conference on African literature, Ngugi cited this passage from Orlando Patterson to indicate the particular form of alienation which distinguishes the West Indian writer from the African:

We are all Jews lost in the wilderness, Brother, and we are blackmen according to the word. And the word, which is the truth, say unto I, in this world, in this life, every man is a Jew searching for his Zion. Every man is a blackman lost in a white world of grief.[79]

In a letter to Randolph Vigne, Bessie Head writes: 'I am trying to steal the thunder and might of the old Jewish testament for Africa.'[80] At the end of A Question of Power, she writes: 'she really knew absolutely nothing, except that she had gained an insight into what the German concentration camps must have been like.'[81] Bessie Head, we might say, makes the link which Ngugi sees, six years before the publication of A Question of Power, as unavailable for African writers. From blackman to Jew—I would want to add to that Said's more troubling from Jew to Palestinian—universality becomes something which can only be posited or spoken, not as universal citizenship, but from its excluded or exiled underside (it is crucial that Bessie Head is African *and* outside her country of birth).

This is, I should stress, militantly anti-sentimental: 'Had six million Africans to die in Southern Africa before black men earned a dignity too? The philosophy of love and peace strangely overlooked those who were in possession of the guns.'[82]

What emerges for me from this discussion is that universality is always a historical, political, and non-singular term. There can be no universal statements about universality; only historical—or perhaps mad ones.

SIX

Dorothy Richardson and the Jew

WHAT happens if you substitute the language of assimilation and exclusion for the more familiar feminist vocabulary of belonging and refusal? if the vexed issue of woman's sexual and aesthetic participation in modern culture is rewritten in terms of her relation to nationhood and state? It has become commonplace to point out that the project of writing *otherwise* for women arises at the time of, and is inseparable from, the emergence of high modernist writing. Most often, the fact is used to throw doubt on, or to indicate the limits of, the political emancipation or radical potential of such writing. But to point to the marriage of feminist experiment to high modernist culture as a sign of political failure may, oddly, involve overlooking some of the other more striking points of political contact at work. It cannot be a coincidence that early modernist experimentation parallels, even as it can be seen as critiquing, the emerging nation-state in which, as we saw in Chapter 2, Hannah Arendt identifies the birth of modern anti-Semitism.[1] In this chapter, I pursue the question of statehood and Jewishness (the founding of the Jewish nation-state), which has been my recurrent focus, into the heart of British modernism, to the centre of the work—Dorothy Richardson's *Pilgrimage*—where one of the most important strands of the modernist experiment for the woman writer begins.[2]

To start with an obvious example, one of the best-known, of the link between feminism and the issue of nationhood—Virginia Woolf in *Three Guineas*: 'the law of England denies us, and let us hope will long continue to deny us, the full stigma of nationality'; or again 'in fact, as a woman, I have no country. As a woman I want no country. As a woman my country is the whole world.'[3] The link is present much earlier, however. Not this time in a text by a woman writer, but in Henry James, at the heart of *The Portrait of a Lady*, where it appears not as affirmation or freedom for women, but as curse. In a famous and much-commented-upon dialogue, Madame Merle says to Isabel Archer: 'a woman, it seems to me, has no natural place anywhere; wherever she finds herself she has to remain on the surface and, more or less, to crawl.'[4] Later in the same discussion, Madame Merle will argue that a person is nothing outside the accoutrements, attachments, and objects which tie her to the world. Fiercely, and against Madame Merle's degrading vision, Isabel insists on the independence and inviolability of selfhood—free of all trappings, Isabel will not crawl but walk tall. She fails, but when we meet her, or what I see as a version of her, again, the grounds of the opposition have shifted. In this chapter, I want to suggest that in *Pilgrimage* Dorothy Richardson rewrites that dialogue between Isabel Archer and Madame Merle as a battle—a battle which constantly threatens to turn into an identification—between the woman, her ethos of independence or non-belonging, and the plea for nationhood of the Jew (the implications of this transmutation for the wider terms of contemporary literary debate is the subject of the last essay in this book).[5]

Before going into this in more detail, the argument needs to be placed in context. A fair amount has been written about the presence of anti-Semitism in modernist writing, especially with reference to T. S. Eliot and Ezra Pound; much less about the anti-Semitism of women modernist writers.[6] This may be another version of a problem that has recently become familiar to feminism—the limits to its earlier celebration of women writers, the point where feminism has had to acknowledge the other agendas and blindspots of oppression which that celebration apparently had to ignore. If the feminist reads the woman modernist for a lift into freedom, the presence of anti-Semitism in such a writer brings her (reader *and* writer) brutally back to ground. May Sinclair's *Mary Olivier: A Life* is a psychoanalytically fuelled tale of one woman's escape from pre-oedipality into self-determination (thus avoiding the tragic destiny of the heroine of *Life and Death of Harriet Frean*).[7] At the end of the novel, in an episode where Mary Olivier is savouring the joys of literary London in the presence of her lover, this passage appears, seemingly out of the blue:

It came to her at queer times, in queer ways. After that horrible dinner at the Dining Club when the secretary woman put her as far as possible from Richard, next to the little Jew financier who smelt of wine . . . His tongue slid between one overhanging and one dropping jaw, in and out like a shuttle. She tried not to hate him.[8]

There are other instances—from Woolf's *The Years*, from Stevie Smith, from Djuna Barnes (not *Nightwood*, which I read as a critique of anti-Semitism, but from the *Ladies Almanack*: 'When but five, she lamented Mid-prayers, that the girls in the Bible were both earth-hushed and Jew-touched forever and ever').[9] None of them are quite as unequivocal as the moment from Sinclair. But they all raise the same question. What is the relation between the feminist modernist project—whether that project is defined as the affirmation of autonomy and selfhood, *or* as the dissolution of all self-hood into writing (both, to put it most crudely, forms of escape)—and this castigating-caricatured representation of that *other* outsider, the Jew?

In *Pilgrimage*, the central character, Miriam Henderson, is caught between two lovers both of whom she finally rejects—Hypo Wilson, unmistakeably now if not unmistakeably then a representation of H. G. Wells, and Michael Shatov, modelled on the Russian-Jewish émigré, Benjamin Grad. She becomes pregnant by the first and miscarries before detaching herself from him; she in any case repudiates what she sees as his ecstatic appropriation of her future through her unborn child. She refuses the marriage proposal of the second, but ensures his posterity by effectively arranging his marriage to her passionate, importunate woman friend, Amabel (it is a way of getting rid of both of them at once). The thirteen volumes of *Pilgrimage*—the last of which is not published until 1967, after Richardson's death—end with her picking up Michael Shatov and Amabel's child. In *Pilgrimage*, therefore, the issue of posterity and begetting, in so far as it is played out between Hypo (H. G. Wells) Wilson and Michael (Benjamin Grad) Shatov, gives us the woman sexually suspended, so to speak, between anti-Semite and Jew.

In this context, the presence-absence of H. G. Wells in the text can be taken as doubly symptomatic. First, as one of the subtexts of *Pilgrimage* in so far as Richardson presents Hypo Wilson with all the details of Wells's intellectual identity as writer, scientific Utopian, Fabian critic, but with no hint of his extended engagement with the question of the Jew—the question which via Shatov is simultaneously working itself out elsewhere across the pages of her novel (his relationship to Jewishness appears, therefore, to be one of the suppressed contents of the text). Secondly, as the representative of a form of 'semitic' discourse, to use Bryan Cheyette's expression, more representative of this period of English literature than has until recently been acknowledged, which in Wells's case gradually hardens after the First World War into the more recognizable tropes of unequivocal anti-Semitism.[10] The following passage from Wells represents, therefore, not just that part of him which Richardson removes from the figure of Hypo

Wilson, but also a much larger component of the political moment in which she writes:

It might have been supposed that a people so widely dispersed would have developed a cosmopolitan mentality and formed a convenient linking organisation for many world purposes, but their special culture of isolation was so intense that this they neither did nor seemed anxious to attempt.[11]

Note how this takes the form of a reproach against the Jew for too much isolated belonging (a type of oxymoron meaning the wrong kind of belonging, that is, belonging to nobody but the Jews), for not being cosmopolitan enough. What Wells objected to was the failure of the Jew to realize his historic destiny as the model for emancipated world identity. It was only one step from here to Wells's comments during the Second World War—cited by Mass Observation, by Foreign Office and Diplomatic Officials—that the Jews had provoked anti-Semitism and that any treatment of them as a special category would be to replicate the Nazi ideology of which they were now the victims.[12]

Wells's comment provides one half of a paradox which haunts accusations against the Jews—reproached for being a 'nation within a nation',[13] they were also accused of being the embodiment of cosmopolitan—that is, infinitely mobile, infinitely corruptible—capital. 'The merchant is the citizen of no country' (Benjamin Kidd citing Adam Smith in 1908); in *The Modern Jew* of 1899, Arnold White expressed the anti-Semitic version: 'cosmopolitan finance is only another word for Jewish finance'.[14] According to this vision, the Jew was only ever parasitic—chameleon-like—on the community to which he became attached: 'Although the only true cosmopolitan people in the world, with the exception of the Gitanos, they reflect, like the chameleon, the texture and the tint of the rock on which they rest.'[15] Compare Madame Merle again: 'We're mere parasites crawling over the surface.'[16]

Supra-national, or micro-national, what is crucial is that in neither case does the Jew (or woman) *belong*. The Jew therefore turns up on both sides of the divide which Kidd, whom Richardson read and admired, saw as emblematic of modernity:

It was insisted that the ideal condition of the world for the maximum production of wealth, and therefore, it was said, for international peace and progress, was one in which the exchanges of both labour and capital would be . . . absolutely untrammelled by considerations of nationalism . . . No change which has taken place in the world in our time is more striking than the assertion of what has been called the passion of nationalism against the cosmopolitan political ideals of the early Victorian period.[17]

To the question of whether or not the Jew can belong, Richardson will propose her own particular, and complex, reply. Through the figure of Michael Shatov, she will provide the backdrop, from the side of the Jews, of the issue to which Wells's writings offers one representative response. Richardson met Benjamin Grad in 1896 in the middle of the decade which followed the period of highest Eastern-European Jewish immigration into the country. This wave of immigration was characterized by its poverty— relatively and strikingly in relation to the already-established Jewish community, which viewed it with anything but pleasure and often opposed it outright (the establishment of autonomous hebrots in the East End were seen by West-End Jews as separatist—precisely a nation within a nation); and by the fact that it introduced into British Jewry socialism, trade unionism, and Zionism.[18] By the 1890s, socialism in the Jewish community had declined, social-democratic trade unionism and Zionist nationalism were ascendant. More than one commentator sees this development as a split between assimilation and separatism in itself—socialism either absorbed into mainstream English trade-unionism or carried off the map of England and Europe altogether by the nationalist vision.[19] In 1892, *Die Vekker (The Awakening)*, the new journal of the Jewish Socialist movement, exhorted its brethren:

Do not stand apart from your English comrades, do not form a separate city within a city in which to live. Discard your Asiatic customs which you have brought with you from Russia. Cast away your wild tongue and learn the language of the land in which you live. Unite in unions. But, better yet, where possible enter English unions.[20]

The rise in anti-alien sentiment accompanying these developments then culminated in the Anti-Alien Bill of 1905.

One of the difficulties, and interests, for the reader of *Pilgrimage* is the double or even treble time-scale of the work—historical, referential time (the events from Richardson's life on which the novel is closely but tranformatively based), the time of the narrator (Miriam Henderson always present inside her experience but only emerging as writer at the end of the thirteen-volume work), the time of writing (the phases in which Richardson often painfully and laboriously completed her text). Running across the different instances of her life and identity, these moments are no less striking, in terms of continuities and disjunctions, in relation to the history of the Jews—from the second wave of Jewish immigration into England at the end of the nineteenth century to the rise of Hitler to power. *Pilgrimage* clearly takes its reference from Bunyan; as Jean Radford has pointed out, the title also carries the symbolic burden of the journey involved, over more than a quarter of a century, in the writing of the work.[21] But in its less familiar meaning of 'to live among strangers', it also calls up the unfolding Jewish history shadowing her novel as she wrote (note already that Richardson has given her heroine—Miriam—a Jewish name).

If we cut, then, from the turn of the century to 1932–4, Richardson is writing—with anxiety and deferral—*Clear Horizon*, the last volume of her book to appear in her lifetime (a 'complete' edition of *Pilgrimage*, one which she will be furious with for presenting itself *as* complete since she had not finished it, was published by her pubishers, J. M. Dent, in 1938). It is the volume which includes her separation from Hypo Wilson and the first stage of her attempt to bring her relationship with Shatov to an end.[22] To the rise of Hitler, clear by this time, Richardson responds, one might say, with a crisis of writing—which is not to imply that the events in Germany are the cause of her difficulty, but that they are present running in and out across the boundaries of her text. Why else, we might ask, as she struggles to complete *Clear Horizon*, would she interrupt the progress of her novel with two translations—Josef Kastein's *Jews in Germany* and Robert Neumann's novel *Mammon (die Macht)*—both so deeply implicated in the Jewish history she both lives and transcribes?

Kastein's book is a plea for Zionism—an appeal to the Jews to retrieve their historic destiny: 'an act of consciousness: the desired, and in terms of will, realised return to the Jewish community . . . the genuine avowal of Jewhood as nationality and of Judaism as a totality in itself'.[23] Ascendant anti-Semitism is for him necessary—the argument will appear almost verbatim in the words of Shatov—in order to provoke the insight among Jews which will lead to the founding of the Jewish nation: 'It required pressure from without to produce a recognition of the stronger formative force existing in the bonds of nationality.'[24]

Neumann's *Mammon* could be seen, on the other hand, as the counter-text to Kastein. The novel centres on an assimilated Jewish lawyer—Albert Rosen—who becomes the legal facilitator behind an alliance, based on forged Russian currency, between an exiled Georgian prince and German nationalists to retrieve his lands from the Bolsheviks: 'A Prince of our race' states the President of the Society for Promoting German nationalism, 'driven from his possessions by a Communism financed by international Jewry, demands our hospitality. He shall have it. His wealth will forward our aims'[25]. Why a Jew should support such a project, identify with such aims, is not clear, except as a statement of the ultimate assimilation, the furthest self-betrayal of his Jewishness. Rosen is in fact Rosenbaum; he has a brother from whom he is alienated by the fact that this brother, unlike himself, has failed to erase the most tangible traces of his Jewish identity:

Dr B. Rosen, teacher at the University and specialist in Gynaecology, lives amidst the din of a business district at the point where it is impinged upon by the Jewish suburb. His brother notes with vexation that his name-plate is the same as last year, is scarcely smaller than that of a provision-merchant's on the next floor, and bears under the name of B. Rosen, University Professor, another name, in poorer lettering and between tastelessly scrollful brackets: Dr Benedict Rosenbaum—a name that two years ago ceased to be that of the doctor.[26]

Richardson translates these two books at the same time as she attempts to complete the part of her novel which brings Miriam's relationship to Wilson and Shatov to some kind of resolution. She writes out ('gets into writing' and 'expels') the Zionist in her novel as she translates him, the anti-Semite as she introduces into English one of his most offensive representations. In 1934, she also has a nervous breakdown which is attributed by her biographer Gloria Fromm to the combined pressures of overwork and poverty. Nothing achieved, nothing concrete; too little substance, too many words— a historically traumatic cacaphony of writing—in the head. All this forms the background, although it involves stretching the term way beyond its most straightforward meaning of backdrop, context, and support, to Miriam Henderson's engagement with the Jew in *Pilgrimage*.

The main confrontations with Michael Shatov take place in *Deadlock*, published in 1921.[27] In two conversations, Shatov and Miriam Henderson split—take up their positions—over the issue of individuality versus the race:

'I would call myself rather one who believes in the *race*.'
'*What* race? The race is nothing without individuals.'
'What is an individual without the race?'
'An individual, with a consciousness; or a soul, whatever you like to call it. The race, apart from individuals, is nothing at all.'
'. . . the race is *certainly* more sacred than the individual.'
'Very well then; I know what I think. If the sacred race plays tricks on conscious human beings, using them for its own sacred purposes and giving them an unreal sense of mattering, I don't care a button for the race, and I'd rather kill myself than serve its purposes. Besides, the instincts of self-preservation and reproduction are *not* the only human motives. They are not human at all.'[28]

In this dialogue, Shatov occupies the place of Madame Merle—the individual is meaningless without his attachments or form of belonging in the world: 'You are wrong; what you call the shape affects every individual in spite of himself'.[29] Miriam occupies that of Isabel Archer, insisting on an individualism which rests in consciousness but which also, in this case, goes beyond it, is partly sacralized, since one of its possible meanings is the 'soul'. Miriam hovers between these two meanings. Only through the second can she counter Shatov's 'sacred' vision of the race; only by retaining the domain of consciousness can she hold on to individuality as a woman's potential agency and being in the world. One could argue that, with reference to Judaism, this is at once a false antagonism and a *dialogue des sourds*. Thus Kastein will insist that it is through his commitment to national identity that the Jew will establish his 'productive *individual* existence *as* a Jew' (emphasis mine); just as he will stress that the enlightenment concept of freedom as untrammelled agency has no meaning for Jewry which sees freedom as *willing* submission to authority (it thus ceases, in the enlightenment sense, to be both freedom and coercion at the same time).[30] For Miriam who, as we will see, is much closer to Shatov than might at first appear, enlightenment can also be a dirty word: '[he was] in a state of decadence and of the enlightenment that accompanies it.'[31]

But by lining up Shatov and Miriam in this way, Richardson also runs her dialogue into another opposition being formulated at this time. She assigns to the Jew the prerogative of what Freud will refer to as species being when, in a famous moment, he describes the subordination of polymorphous bisexuality to genital reproductive sex as 'a victory of the race over the individual'; 'The sexual instinct is now subordinated to the reproductive function; it becomes, so to say, altruistic.'[32] Later, when he comes to formulate it as such, this drive of the race to its own future, over the pleasures, hearts, and minds of the individuals who bear its purpose unconsciously, will come to be designated, or receive its strongest parallel-cum-analogy, in the concept of the drive to death (*Beyond the Pleasure Principle* appears in the same year as *Deadlock*).[33] Miriam, one could say, has got the point, therefore, when she says she will kill herself rather than submit to this version of the sacred—she has understood the relation of this future to death. Hence her reproach to Hypo Wilson and Shatov both: 'In Hypo there was no sense of eternity; nor in Michael, except for the race, an endless succession of people made in God's image, all dead or dying'.[34] This future, destiny, history she reads in Michael's face: 'The heavy white lids came down over his eyes and for a moment his face, with its slumbering vitality, at once venerable and insolent, was like a death-mask, a Jewish death-mask.'[35]

It is another paradox of anti-Semitism at this time that the Jew could be seen at once to represent a fierce Darwinian individualism struggling only for itself, and a racial exclusivity which will not, which refuses to, mingle its blood. In her section on the Jewish community in Booth's *Life and Labour of the People of London*, Beatrix Potter accuses the Jew of lacking all 'social morality' and describes him as the embodiment of Ricardo's economic man.[36] In a letter to Theodor Herzl, Israel Zangwill states that it is 'a positive duty to marry out'.[37] Arnold White, anti-Semite author of *The Modern Jew*, writes: 'If the Jews will consent to be absorbed and to mingle their blood with ours, all will be well.'[38] None of this gets in the way of that other form of anti-Semitism for which the main threat is the 'leavening' of British aristocracy with Jewish blood (separation and penetration as the flipsides of the same racist paranoia).

There is therefore a crucial issue here about futurity. To whom—man or woman, Jew or Gentile—does the future belong? What does it mean when a woman refuses to play her part in the reproduction of the species? By having Miriam refuse to be a Jewish woman and mother, Richardson might seem merely to be adding a powerful intensifier to the feminist issue of women's right to control or even refuse their reproductive role. She is also demonstrating how this feminist agenda came partly in response to a eugenic theory of motherhood which stressed the importance of fertility for the future of the (best of the British) race (Claire Buck has shown just how central this was to the emancipatory project—emancipation from the woman's body into writing—of May Sinclair).[39]

But by calling this version of maternal sacrificial-cum-racial destiny Jewish, Dorothy Richardson also runs Miriam's emancipation straight into some of the most vicious anti-Jewish representations of her time. Ironically, then, Shatov appeals to an ideology of racial exclusion which anti-Semitism reflected, appropriated, came at least halfway to meet; while Miriam rejects motherhood as race destiny, rejects eugenics, but in the language of anti-Semitism. The Jew as pure racial destiny—almost one might say, jumping historically, as selfish gene. Again Kastein will insist that this is to misunderstand fundamentally the Jewish conception of continuity:

The world's conception of the being and the value of race does not correspond with the Jew's conception of these things. For the Jew, the concept of the race does not begin with the production of species, but rather with the recognition that over a long period a people has represented a certain attitude of mind.[40]

Echoing Otto Weininger, Richardson opposes Jewish to non-Jewish as nature to culture, race to individual, each time staking out—as Jean Radford has demonstrated—the second term for herself.[41] It is the moment at which, for all the historical reference she packs into her novel, she misses what might be described, for the Jew, as the whole historical point: racial destiny, not as biology or species, but as tradition, shared history, the claim for a socially realizable form of life.

Thus even Beatrix Potter will acknowledge the connection between this concept of a possible future and the 'three thousand years' of persecution which have gone into the making of the East End Jew, whose religious rituals are there to secure the future, not of another world, but as historic prospect and destiny.[42] Writing on 'Kristallnacht', Kastein comments:

since the events of last year, these things [Jewish over-hasty assimilation] belong to the past, and . . . must in all circumstances be banished into that past, where, for the Jew, they will always remain present. This dismissal must be accomplished by every Jew who to-day is determined to come level with his destiny and to shape it by taking his place once more within the stream of his own history.[43]

Note how close this idea of a past still moving in the present—a past running ahead of its time—is to Dorothy Richardson's own, very specific temporality of writing: 'For both of them [Richardson and Proust] the past was a world to which they went forward rather than back, thus making of it a future that would one day be present.'[44]

As it takes shape between Miriam and Shatov, this quarrel about the future has another political resonance. The opposition between racial and individual destiny reappears in Benjamin Kidd as the grounds of his argument for socialism: 'The history of the world is not simply a history of the struggle for life. It is to an ever-increasing degree a history for the struggle for the life of the future.'[45] Not individualism for now, but socialism for tomorrow. Miriam says to Shatov: 'Are you a socialist? Do you believe in the opinions of mediocre majorities?' 'Why this adjective?' he replies, 'Why mediocre? No, I would call myself rather someone who believes in the *race*.'[46] It is at the very least a problem for feminism that Miriam's affirmation rides the back of this repudiation of socialist and Jewish conceptions of destiny at one and the same time. The point is related to, but different from, the famous argument about *Jane Eyre*—does the emancipation of the bourgeois woman require the self-immolation of the Creole?[47]

The second key dialogue between Shatov and Miriam takes place when he returns from his first visit to English Jews:

'It is sad for me, this first meeting with English Jews.'
'Perhaps you can make Zionists of them.'
'That is absolutely impossible . . . It is useless to talk to these people whose first pride is that they are *British* . . . what they do not see is that they are not, and never can be, British; that the British do not accept them as such.'

'. . . The Jews are free in England.'

'They are free; to the honour of England in all history. But they are nevertheless Jews and not Englishmen . . . The toleration for Jews, moreover, will last only as long as the English remain in ignorance of the immense and increasing power and influence of the Jew in this country. Once that is generally recognised, even England will have its anti-Semitic movement.'

'*Never*. England can assimilate anything.'

. . .

'No nation can assimilate the Jew . . . Remember that British Jewry is perpetually and increasingly reinforced by immigration from those countries where Jews are segregated and ever more terribly persecuted . . . The time for the closing of this last door is approaching.'

'I don't believe England will ever do it. How can they? Where will the Jews go? It's impossible to think of. It will be the end of England if we begin that sort of thing.'

'It may be the beginning of Jewish nationality. Ah, at least this visit has reawakened all the Zionist in me.'[48]

This conversation is prophetic in that the episode takes place before the passage of the Anti-Alien Bill and the rise of British Zionism; it also anticipates, not only Kastein on the productive link between anti-Semitism and Zionism, but Arnold White on the power of the British Jews:

The Jewish community in England, though not numerically strong, control so large a portion of the financial and journalistic power of the country that any Ministry undertaking a joust against the consolidated strength of the Jews would be infallibly unhorsed.[49]

But it is also, of course, not prophetic, because it is being *written* in 1921 long after the developments it predicts have taken place (the Balfour Declaration is made in 1917). In the figure of Michael Shatov, Dorothy Richardson has effectively condensed a set of sometimes evolving, sometimes antagonistic moments in the history of the Jewish immigrant of the second wave (Potter says of the Polish and Russian Jew: '[he] represents to some extent the concentrated essence of Jewish virtue and Jewish vice; for he has, in his individual experience, epitomised the history of his race in the Christian world').[50] In the East End of London, Zionism will start to flourish in the early years of the century among groups of those 'who were not cosmopolitan socialists yet were alienated by the forms of immigrant religious life' (according to Lloyd Gartner, Herzl was given an almost 'Messianic' reception when he delivered his first public address on political Zionism in Whitechapel in 1896).[51] While, according to Geoffrey Alderman, the children of the early Jewish socialists also, via the Labour party, become

Zionists in turn.[52] Cosmopolitan socialist, Zionist, Russian émigré, Shatov hovers—he lives in the same Bloomsbury boarding house as Miriam—between the Jewish communities of East and West. Perhaps it is because of his borderline identity that he tries, in seeking to marry a non-Jewish woman, to take on what he himself defines as a marginal and untypical historical role: 'No nation can assimilate the Jews.' 'What about intermarriage.' 'That is the minority.'[53]

Read the dialogue about Zionism through the preceding one (they occur in the same chapter of *Deadlock*), and the opposition between assimilation and Zionism becomes overlaid with the proto-feminist opposition between the individual and the race. Feminism against nationalism sounds better, perhaps, than woman against Jew, but Richardson's text does not allow the reader to disentangle the terms. With whom does the Jewish woman reader identify at a moment like this? Shatov's historical analysis is, as it were, correct (he anticipates what will happen to British Jews). And however critically—as must be clear by now—this reader might view the subsequent history of Zionism, especially its founding precondition in relation to the Palestinians, it is impossible not to recognize the grounded particularity of his wish; while Miriam's arguments against Zionism, her too-easy belief in assimilation, even in the name of liberal tolerance, back onto (the previous dialogue is there to remind us) some of the most familiar tropes of anti-Semitism. Assigning this position to Miriam, Richardson also reverses her own support for Zionism (the radical MP Josiah Wedgewood attributed to Richardson and Alan Odle his first knowledge of Zionism as a creed).[54] This is Wells on Zionism in the continuation of the quote discussed before:

After the World War the orthodox Jews played but a poor part in the early attempts to formulate the Modern State, being far more preoccupied with a dream called Zionism . . . Only a psycho-analyst could begin to tell for what they wanted this Zionist state. It emphasized their traditional wilful separation from the main body of mankind. It irritated the world against them, subtly and incurably.[55]

The case for assimilation—'England can assimilate anything'—wears many colours and takes many forms: the liberal form of tolerance-cum-intolerance (acceptance on condition of shedding Jewish identity), the demand of the anti-Semite, the delusion and/or desire of the British Jew.

What Richardson offers us through Miriam Henderson could, then, be seen as a cameo, for feminism, of the clash between a liberal plea for individual rights and the particularities of cultures and nations, a type of vision in advance of how difficult it will become theoretically and politically to square the circle between these apparently antagonistic priorities and terms. To this problem, which stretches back and forwards across the history of Europe, Miriam's position—and claim for herself—as a woman adds a particular complexity. For, as a woman, Miriam Henderson is presented to us as distanced, alien, estranged in herself, as something, we might say, of a Jew. Like being a Jew, being a woman can also be described as a state of non- or partial participation in the available or dominant cultures. Curse and privilege, this unsettled self-positioning, as Woolf expressed it, can become alternately exclusion from, or belonging to, all possible worlds: 'As a woman I want no country. As a woman, my country is the whole world.'[56]

Even more, Richardson's involvement in Quakerism—an involvement repeated by Miriam in the last volume of *Pilgrimage*—allows her to stretch out, almost infinitely expand the boundaries of this vision of woman on the edge of time. In her 1914 book on Quakerism, Richardson cites these words from Fox: 'Be a stranger unto all . . . forsake all, both young and old, and keep out of all'[57] (she also edited a selection from his works). Her account of his developing belief is remarkably close to the description in the central volumes of *Pilgrimage* of the young Miriam Henderson at the scientific and Fabian meetings she attended in London: 'He went to hear the great preachers of the day in London and elsewhere, but found no light in them'; he refused to 'be put off any longer with "notions", mere doctrines, derivative testimonies obscuring the immediate communication of life to the man himself.'[58] 'The God of the Quakers,' writes Richardson, is 'no literary obsession coming to meet them along the pages of history, no traditional immensity.'[59] Compare this comment from Miriam (it is one of many similar comments): 'It was history, literature, the way of stating records, stories, the whole method of statement of things from the beginning that was on a false foundation.'[60]

This is the other meaning of *Deadlock* (deadlocked by false reason and tradition), against which Miriam offers—anticipating another famous theoretical moment—her own rereading of Descartes: 'Descartes should have said, "I am aware that there is something, therefore I am."'[61] If this is individualism, it is also, therefore, a woman's refusal of that *cogito* in which so much recent theory has identified the worst of patriarchal self-knowing and law. Miriam's individualism thus takes the form of the woman's willing self-subordination (compare Kastein)—against the traditional immensities—to what one influential strand of feminist literary theory has come to describe as something *other*, something else.

It would be possible, therefore, to rewrite this division between Miriam and Shatov in aesthetic terms. In the penultimate volume of *Pilgrimage*, Miriam repeats her critique of Shatov: 'the Russian in him believed it, knew, in spite of his Jewish philosophy, something of the unfathomable depths in each individual, unique and irreplaceable'; but 'the Jew in him':

so far saw Amabel only as charmingly qualified to fulfil what he still regarded as the larger aspect, the only continuing aspect of himself, his destiny as part of his 'race,' the abstraction he and his like so strangely conceived as alive, immortal, sacred, and at the same time as consisting of dead and dying particles.[62]

Then she makes the link to the forms of language: 'Are all the blind alleys and insufficiencies of masculine thought created by their way of thinking in propositions, using inapplicable metaphors . . . Are all coherent words, in varying measure, evidence of failure?'[63] Despite that reference to metaphor, it is propositional logic that is being criticized here—it is in fact the falsity of Shatov's statement, 'The whole, Miriam, is greater than the parts', his view of race and nation as transcending individualism, that is at stake ('That had sounded unanswerable. But now I see the catch in the metaphor').[64] Coherence, sequence, continuity, teleology—all these insignia of patriarchal language and culture, these aesthetic markers to which so much of modernist experimentation by women, although not only by women, comes as the response, are handed over to the Jewish conception of destiny. The fact that this is the case marks the limit, calls a halt, I would suggest, to any too easy metaphoric or troped identification between forms of outsideness, between—in this case—woman and Jew.

But if Shatov is the voice of logic, he is not yet the written text. Later in the same chapter, Miriam will comment on his impatience with writing: 'Would Amabel succeed where she had failed, make him realize how prejudicial to his British career was his impatience with the written word?'[65] His future, and that of the Jews, might be said to hang on whether he can transmute his spoken desire into writing, give to the history in which he hopes to participate the requisite forms of textual authority. And in so far as Miriam's whole journey in *Pilgrimage* is in some sense into writing, we might say that this is the point of the most powerful identification-differentiation between the woman—Miriam *and* Richardson—and the Jew.

At the very least, in the battles between them, it is not clear—not finally decided—who is right:

there was no-one alive who could decide, in this strange difference, where lay right and wrong. Why should it be right to have no sense of nationality? Why should it be wrong to feel this as something whose violation would be a base betrayal? Much more than that. Something that could not be. Not merely difficult and sacrificial and yet possible. Simply impossible.[66]

*   *   *

In *The Origins of Totalitarianism*, Hannah Arendt describes total domination as the drive to 'fabricate something that does not exist, namely, a kind of human species resembling other animal species whose only "freedom" would consist in "preserving the species."'[67] For Arendt such a vision is only possible in a society where species being has already been degraded by being relegated to the domain of private labour, has already lost its link to public, civic participation and activity in the world. In *The Human Condition*, she wrote: 'none of the higher capacities of man was any longer necessary to connect individual life with the life of the species; individual life became part of the life process, and to labour, to assure the continuity of one's own life and the life of the family was all that was needed.'[68] (It is striking just how close this description comes to Beatrix Potter's reproach—lack of social participation, pure and private commitment to their descendants—against the East End Jews.)

In the article from which the last quotation is taken, Mary Dietz observes that feminism has its own particular relationship to the developments that Arendt describes. For if, on the one hand, women could be said to have carried the burden, in the domestic sphere, of that relegation of species being to the world of private concerns, it is also the case that for one form of feminism it is exactly women's privileged connection to this human dimension which should now be revalorized or celebrated by women in turn. For this feminism, the public sphere—the world of civic participation—is irredeemably corrupt, and woman take their political bearings and identity through the distance they strike from that world (the world, amongst other things, of nationhood and state). For another feminism, however, that move is contaminated by the very identification—of woman and species being—on which it relies. Miriam's project, one might say, shares this critique, and in doing so comes down on this side of feminist history.

What *Pilgrimage* demonstrates, however—as we watch Miriam moving more and more into a form of spiritual self-containment—is the way this second path can lead to the end of any form of active political being, of participation in public life. Rewriting the title of Elizabeth Young-Bruehl's biography of Hannah Arendt, we could say—as Arendt herself says—that it requires the loss (not love) of the world.[69] Arendt can be—has been—criticized for the specific form of civic life she returns to (what would such forms of civic participation look like for women today?).[70] Yet *Pilgrimage* could be said to show the price, the historic refusals—what has to be rejected for the woman but not just for her—of relinquishing the domain of public existence *even in the name* of feminist self-determination and freedom. To exist *otherwise*, free of all worldly entrapment, is to exist free of the insignia of nations and cultures as they struggle for dialogue and differentiation, for co-operation and space. Exit is not neutral. It can be an inadvertent form of collusion with what is playing itself out on the other side. Perhaps, then, it is only in relation to other histories—Jewish history would be one example—that feminism will find a way out of the disabling opposition between civic and species being, between public and private worlds.

Freud and the Crisis of our Culture

I WANT you to start by imagining yourselves in Vienna in 1897. Mark Twain is sitting in the Viennese Parliament whose sessions he regularly attended when he was living in the city. On this particular day he watched appalled as the Parliament invited in the military police to remove certain unruly members. This is how he described the make-up of the House:

the deputies come from all the walks of life and from all the grades of society. There are princes, counts, barons, priests, mechanics, laborers, lawyers, physicians, professors, merchants, bankers, shopkeepers. They are religious men, they are earnest, sincere, devoted, and they hate the Jews.

In his 1955 lecture, 'Freud and the Crisis of Our Culture', from which I take my title today, the critic Lionel Trilling tells this story and comments:

this was the only point of unity in a Parliament which was the battleground of the fiercest nationalistic and cultural jealousies . . . the weakness of Parliament meant the strength of the monarchical government, which ruled by police methods; censorship was in force, and only inefficiency kept it from being something graver than a nuisance.

Trilling cites this Viennese episode in the life of Mark Twain to give a sense of the society—'anything but free and democratic'—in which Freud developed his adversarial view of culture, his vision of culture as something in which individual subjects are irretrievably caught but to which they in no way simply or just *belong*. For Trilling, it is to the extent that the individual lives out this adversarial relation, grinds up against and thrashes at the norm, that she or he is a human subject at all. Trilling uses his story to make the general point, but I think it is hard not to be struck today by its most concrete details, the way they resonate with our contemporary political life: democratic pluralism ('all the grades of society' sit in this House) sliding into and threatened by nationalistic and cultural antagonisms; anti-Semitism as a false unifier; that unity as weakness, not strength ('the unity was the weakness' as one observer put it on the way the European Community sacrificed intervention in Bosnia to its own economic pseudo-unity during the early stages of the war); and finally a repressive government only prevented by inefficiency from being a nuisance (except that we seem to have a government in this country which remarkably manages to be inefficient and a nuisance at the same time).

Earlier in his lecture, Trilling tells another story—this time from Tolstoi—of the countess who wept buckets at the theatre while her coachman waited outside in her carriage perishing from the cold. This, he suggests, shows how the self represented by literature, or rather the self as it responds to literature, can be way ahead of the self which the wider social relations dramatize and conceive. Unlike the Mark Twain anecdote, this is a tale about empathy, or rather the lack of it, about the 'willing suspension of disbelief' which Trilling, borrowing from Coleridge's famous statement about literature, goes on to define as characteristic of ethical life: 'The essence of the moral life', he writes, 'would seem to consist in doing that most difficult thing in the world, making a willing suspension of disbelief in the selfhood of someone else.'

Writing on the unconscious in his 1914 paper of that title, Freud likewise talks of suspending disbelief when he suggests that all we need to do in order to believe in the unconscious is do to ourselves what we have to do whenever we meet another person, that is, make the leap into believing that there is someone else really there. 'Consciousness,' he writes, 'makes each of us aware only of his own states of mind; that other people, too, possess a consciousness is an inference . . . psychoanalysis demands nothing more than that we should apply this process of inference to ourselves.' Later Freud corrects himself: 'It would no doubt be psychologically more correct to put it this way: that without any special reflection we attribute to everyone else our own constitution and therefore our consciousness as well and this identification is a *sine qua non* [or condition] of our understanding.'

So which is it? Do we find it virtually impossible to believe in the mental existence of others; or do we automatically and without reflection assume that they are a version of ourselves? And is this second option—which Freud calls identification—an indispensable condition of understanding, as he puts it, or its opposite, a way of assuming that everyone is and has to be the same? Under what conditions—the tale of the countess—does one person really identify, or empathize, with another? In his famous book on justice, John Rawls argues that it is only under a veil of ignorance, only—again—by suspending disbelief and this time picturing myself without any of the conditions which make for my recognizable, personal interests and life, that I will be brought to agree to a fair and just form of social distribution (only if I don't know where I belong in the final arrangement will I agree to a system which will always be to the benefit of the disadvantaged). He has been criticized, of course, for the somewhat hypothetical, not to say unlikely nature of such a scenario, but I think this is to miss the point. What Trilling, Freud, and Rawls all seem to be saying is that empathy, like social justice, relies on the hypothetical imagination; it is nothing if not part of our fantasy life.

I want to start, therefore, by drawing Trilling's tale of the countess and his tale of the Viennese Parliament together in order to ask a set of questions which I see as amongst the most difficult confronting the teaching and study of literature today. What are the available or desirable forms of identification between different individuals and groups in the culture and what are the limits? How, in a racially and ethnically mixed culture, can you get pluralism without potentially violent antagonism? What are the affective or psychic conditions of a genuine democracy? All questions which sit on the cusp of politics, culture, literature, psychoanalysis, and ethics. Lionel Trilling was probably the most influential literary critic of his generation. If I start with him, even though, as will become clear, I do not agree finally with his form of liberal response to these issues, it is because he always insisted that, for the profession of literature, all these domains were indissolubly linked.

It is, as I have said, to Freud that Trilling ascribes our modern sense of being-in-culture: 'It was Freud who made it apparent to us how utterly implicated in culture we all are . . . [for a great many of us] it was he who made the idea of culture real.' At another moment in the essay, however, he says something rather different:

At some point in the history of the West men began to think of their fates as being lived out . . . in relation to the ideas and assumptions and manners of a large social totality. The evidence of this is to be found in our literature, in its preoccupation with newly discovered alien cultures which, in one regard or another, serve to criticize our own.

Running through Trilling's writing, alongside his vision of the adversary and authentic self for which he is best known, there is a constant preoccupation with the question of culture in this other sense—culture as something which only becomes thinkable with the discovery of new and alien worlds. In the last essay which he wrote—'Why We Read Jane Austen'—unfinished at the time of his death in 1975, Trilling took issue with the anthropologist Clifford Geertz for suggesting that there are insuperable barriers to cross-cultural understanding, and, more important, that the idea of personhood or individuality was of limited viability outside the cultural framework of the West. Geertz had written:

The Western conception of the person as a bounded, unique, more or less integrated motivational and cognitive universe, a dynamic center of awareness, emotion and judgement organised into a distinctive whole and set contrastively both against other such wholes and against its social and natural background, is, however incorrigible it may seem to us, a rather peculiar idea within the world's cultures.

Geertz's essay was called ' "From the Native's Point of View": On the Nature of Anthropological Understanding'; its main point was to criticize the belief, prevalent in anthropological circles at the time, that for the Western observer of an alien culture empathy is enough. However nice and open you might be, once you leave home—Freud of course would say long before you leave home—you can never be sure that you are seeing straight: 'In the country of the blind, who are not as unobservant as they look, the one-eyed is not king; he is spectator.'

Trilling responds:

No student of literature can read Mr. Geertz's lecture without having it borne in upon him that anthropologists conceive unfamiliar cultures to be much more difficult to comprehend than do humanist scholars or the ordinary readers they instruct . . . Humanism takes for granted that any culture of the past out of which has come a work of art which commands our interest must be the product, and also, of course, the shaping condition, of minds which are essentially the same as our own.

That, of course, is the question. That Trilling should take up Geertz in this context—he is, remember, discussing Jane Austen, not Zora Neale Hurston—brings home the extent to which the study of literature, as soon as you raise the issue of what makes for an identifiable or legible cultural moment, is something of an anthropological undertaking. There is no single automatically available culture, not even when you're reading Jane Austen.

In his essay, Geertz takes Bali, Java, and Mexico as emblematic of his point about personhood. The self in these different cultures is 'a composite, a persona, a point in a pattern'. In none of these cultures does the individual have priority over or stand outside the social and symbolic systems in which she or he takes shape. There is, we could say, using Trilling's terms, no adversarial self, no self struggling—through its unhappy, alienated, disintegrated consciousness—into authentic being in the world. In 'Freud and the Crisis of Our Culture', Trilling argues that Freud's concept of the death-drive, the subject's will to extinction, is the best place to look for that aspect of the self which can never be fully assimilated into the cultural identities on offer. Oddly, the being-in-death of the subject is the measure of her or his freedom. Something, even if it means a recourse to biology, has to escape the clutches of culture. To put it more simply, there has to be a way—even if it is the ultimate way—out.

I want now to put this in context. Trilling in the 1950s was appealing to this idea of the self, bound by history but always somehow free of the worst that history can do, as a way of saving liberalism from its contamination by Stalinism—as someone who had been a Marxist, he wanted to retrieve the vision of a political subject in search of social justice but free of the totalitarian Communist state (it's easy to see here the outlines of the figure of the dissident). But Trilling was also setting this same vision against the complacencies of American culture, the middle-class ideology of, to use his own terms,'integration', 'co-operation', 'communication', and 'whole development', which he saw as diluting what was radical and disruptive about Freudian psychoanalysis into a recipe for the good life. If you take the rejection of Stalinism without the Freud, you might think that what is involved is a familiar rejection of Communisim as an apology for the American way of life (a bit like Reagan saying that he wanted to take Gorbachov up in an aeroplane and show him middle America—I was never quite sure what was meant to happen next). 'Non-conformists together' was how Trilling summed up his sense of a once-progressive political moment gone chic (this is, I should stress, before his opposition to the counter-culture of the 1960s). When Trilling turns to Freud to buttress what he calls the 'high authority of the self in its quarrel with its society and its culture', it is, quite explicitly, a political conception that he has in mind. Subversion—his word—is what links modern literature and Freud: 'Of the writers of the last hundred and fifty years who command our continuing attention, the very large majority have in one way or another turned their passions, their adverse, critical, and very intense passions, upon the conditions of the polity.'

For the rest of this lecture I am going to take three moments from the literature of that last hundred and fifty years to which Trilling refers and look a little more closely at this concept of the self. I want to use them not as illustration, but as one way of putting to the test—it is what I think each of the passages themselves are doing—that image of selfhood, together with the liberalism which, centrally throughout Trilling's work, accompanied it.

I start with Henry James. At the end of his book on Trilling, Mark Krupnick writes: 'Like a character in [Henry] James, or like James himself, Trilling was divided between a dream of freedom and the experience of limitation . . . But the conflict within a mid-century cultural critic inevitably took a different form than in the careers of fictional characters like Isabel Archer.' So let's take Isabel Archer, in one of the best-known moments in modern literature, the moment in *The Portrait of a Lady* when James's heroine is arguing with Madame Merle, whom at this stage she believes to be her friend, about the nature and limitations of the self. They are talking about Isabel's dream of the ideal young man. Madame Merle refuses to believe that Isabel's fantasy does not include a castle in the Appenines or, at the very least, a house. She refuses, that is to say, to believe in Isabel's ideal precisely *as* ideal. I think it is crucial that this famous quarrel starts with Isabel's rejection of the trappings, both extravagant and mundane, of what is meant to be a late-nineteenth-century woman's romantic imagination. This is what Madame Merle says to Isabel when she says that she does not care about a house:

That's very crude of you. When you've lived as long as I you'll see that every human being has his shell and you must take the shell into account. By the shell I mean the whole envelope of circumstances. There's no such thing as an isolated man or woman; we're each of us made up of some cluster of appertunances. What shall we call our 'self'? Where does it begin? where does it end? It overflows into everything that belongs to us—and then it flows back again. I know a large part of myself is in the clothes I wear. I've a great respect for *things*! One's self—for other people is one's expression of one's self; and one's house, one's furniture, one's garments, the books one reads, the company one keeps—these things are all expressive.

Isabel replies:

I don't agree with you. I think just the other way. I don't know whether I succeed in expressing myself, but I know that nothing else expresses me. Nothing that belongs to me is any measure of me; everything's on the contrary a limit, a barrier, and a perfectly arbitrary one. Certainly the clothes which, as you say, I choose to wear, don't express me; and heaven forbid they should.

When Madame Merle 'interposes lightly', 'You dress very well', Isabel retorts: 'My clothes may express my dressmaker but they don't express me. To begin with, it's not my choice that I wear them; they're imposed on me by society.'

There is an obvious proto-feminist agenda here—Isabel is objecting to the way that the woman is restricted in her body by social code. The fact that she is a woman adds an extra note to her repudiation of Madame Merle's attachment to material objects and her commitment to the 'appearances' of things (woman's famous 'to-be-looked-at-ness', to use John Berger's expression). But Isabel is going further than this—she is setting the self up in opposition to all its attachments as if this was, for her, the defining property of what a self is. In *The Portrait of a Lady*, Henry James puts in the mouth of his central female character a defence of the adversarial, recalcitrant self to which Trilling will later make his appeal. We might say that it is because Isabel is a woman that in order to define herself as an autonomous agent in the world she has, so dramatically, to throw off everything, including the world itself if necessary, which society conceives her to be. There is precisely no place in the world for a woman on these terms, no place, perhaps—the text allows this implication—for a woman at all. Madame Merle, who defines the individual by her trappings, herself seems to recognize that the obverse of her own argument for such a corrupt form of belonging is that the woman has no place in the world: 'A woman,' she says, 'it seems to me, has no natural place anywhere; wherever she finds herself she has to remain on the surface and, more or less, to crawl.' By placing the defence of social belonging in the mouth of a procuress—which is what Madame Merle turns out to be—James leaves his heroine, we might say, with nowhere to go.

It is, of course, finally in direct proportion to her claim to freedom that Isabel Archer is crushed. I don't think she is crushed because she betrays her vision, although she undoubtedly does; that could only be the case if she were already the moral agent, the autonomous self, which she fails to become. Of course James is more equivocal than that—if he wasn't he wouldn't be James—Isabel is and is not the moral agent of her story; but that ambivalence tells a tale of gender and power which wraps itself around the woman's bid for freedom. This sets the first limit to Trilling's conception of the self struggling off the edge of culture, by giving back to it for women—this would be one definition of feminism—a sex, a place, and a name. The adverse self, one might say, is never sexually neutral.

I want to go back now for a moment to Mark Twain in the Viennese parliament. Remember this point: 'They are religious men, they are earnest, sincere, devoted and they hate the Jews.' In 1936, Trilling—the first Jewish professor of literature at Columbia University—was asked to leave the department. Diana Trilling suggests that if his name had been that of his maternal grandfather, Israel Cohen, he would not have been appointed in the first place (Trilling apparently thought that this grandfather looked like Freud). The grounds they offered for 'letting him go'—that wonderful expression for sacking someone which, appropriately enough for Trilling, seems to give the impetus back to the self being sacked—were that 'as a Freudian, a Marxist, and a Jew', he could not be happy in the department; but he argued against them and they allowed him to stay. Behind this story of intellectual success and self-assertion there is another one. Trilling's father had been shipped off to America from Biaƚstok because he had broken down during his Bar Mitzvah; he had failed, we might say, to be a Jew. Trilling's mother was born in the East End of London (I am gradually bringing us closer to home): 'It was to his mother's confident expectations for him,' writes Diana Trilling, 'that Lionel, following Freud, ascribed his own ambitions and such faith as he had in his intellectual capacities.' According to her account, Trilling felt he had been born with a protective caul—he would tell the story from his youth of the day he was pelted with snowballs possibly containing rocks, but walked on, convinced that, like Baldur, he would not be hurt (he was not).

In the 1920s Trilling wrote for the *Menorah* journal, but after that he progressively distanced himself from any Jewish identity. In 1944, he wrote: 'I know of no writer in English who has added a micromillimeter to his stature by "realising his Jewishness", although I know of some who have curtailed their promise by trying to heighten their Jewish consciouness.' In one of his early short stories, 'Impediments', the narrator flees his Jewish classmate, Hettner: 'I felt always defensive against some attempt Hettner might make to break down the convenient barrier I was erecting against men who were too much of my own race and against men who were not of my own race and hated it'. This, then, is the cultural provenance, or at least backdrop, of Trilling's adversarial self suspended between participation and revolt. It starts to look very different—the dream of, or belief in, a transcendent selfhood again less sure—when it is seen to carry the question of Jewish cultural belonging. One reason Trilling told the Mark Twain story in 'Freud and the Crisis of Our Culture' was to convey the extent to which Freud, as a Jew, was necessarily at odds with his culture.

I would suggest that Jewishness shadows Trilling's conception of selfhood; that it provides the living, concrete history from which he himself increasingly detached it. In the reply to Clifford Geertz, it returns to set the limit to Trilling's universalist, humanist vision: 'Of course,' he writes in 'How To Read Jane Austen', 'neither the Jews nor the Greeks thought like humanists— they believed that nothing could be, or should be, more incomprehensible than alien cultures, the ways that *goyim* or *barbaroi* chose to go about being

persons or selves.' Traditional humanism crashes up against the barrier of
unassimilable difference. What do you do when illegibility appears not as
obstacle (the anthropological dilemma), but as something a group positively
intends or desires? In 1892 the new journal of the Jewish Socialist movement
in London, *Die Vekker* or *The Awakening*, exhorted its brethren:

Do not stand apart from your English comrades, do not form a separate city within
a city in which to live. Discard your Asiatic customs which you have brought with
you from Russia. Cast away your wild tongue and learn the language of the land
in which you live.

I take my second literary moment from the pioneer woman modernist
writer Dorothy Richardson (students are always amazed when they are told
that it is in relation to her, not Virginia Woolf, that the phrase 'stream of
consciousness' was coined). 'What shall we call our self? Where does it
begin? where does it end?' In Richardson's 1921 *Deadlock*, volume six of her
monumental thirteen-volume novel, *Pilgrimage*, Madame Merle's question
is asked again. This time it appears in the course of an argument between
Miriam Henderson, central character and consciousness of the whole work,
and the Russian-Jewish émigré, Michael Shatov. She will refuse to marry
him, but she passes him across to her closest woman friend, and the thirteen volumes of *Pilgrimage* end with her holding their child. In the dialogue
between them, the earlier conversation between Isabel Archer and Madame Merle is rewritten as a battle between the woman's ethos of independence or non-belonging, and the plea for race and nationhood of the Jew.
Shatov begins:

'I would call myself rather one who believes in the *race*.'
'*What* race? The race is nothing without individuals.'
'What is an individual without the race?'
'An individual, with a consciousness; or a soul, whatever you like to call it. The
race, apart from individuals, is nothing at all.'
'. . . the race is *certainly* more sacred than the individual.'
'Very well then; I know what I think. If the sacred race plays tricks on conscious
human beings, using them for its own sacred purposes and giving them an unreal
sense of mattering, I don't care a button for the race, and I'd rather kill myself than
serve its purposes. Besides, the instincts of self-preservation and reproduction are
not the only human motives. They are not human at all.'

I want to suggest to you that this complicates matters no end. Note how
close Shatov is to Madame Merle in *Portrait of a Lady*: 'You are wrong', he
says to Miriam; 'what you call the shape affects every individual most profoundly in spite of himself.' Against such shaping, Miriam Henderson—like

Isabel Archer—makes her bid for freedom (one thing she is doing here is
rejecting the biological destiny of women). Unlike Isabel Archer, she will
succeed. But by putting the case for that destiny in the month of a Russian-
Jewish émigré, Dorothy Richardson runs this feminist agenda into and
up against another history of oppression. In the following scene, Shatov
returns from his first meeting with West End Jews, horrified at their
'Britishness'; with uncanny foresight he predicts the anti-semitism which
will follow the second wave of Jewish immigration into London's East End;
as he sees it, this will be the only chance for Zionism to take hold in Britain.
Whatever one's views on Zionism and its subsequent development, it is
impossible not to recognize the grounded, historical particularity of this
wish. Against such particularity, Miriam gradually retreats from her earlier
socialist and feminist involvement; she moves into a form of quietism which
bears an uncanny resemblance to Trilling's vision of freedom as the suspension of all being into death. On one side the loss of the world; on the other
a traumatic history of cultures and nations clashing, which may at this
moment, although I am not convinced, be in the process of being resolved—
I am referring to the recent Palestinian-Israeli agreement.

It is as if that moment from Richardson were giving us in cameo, drama-
tizing the impasse of Trilling's version of selfhood, or rather of any version
of selfhood when it tries to take off from the world. At the very least
Dorothy Richardson muddies the waters: it is because of his place *in* culture, as a way of being-in-culture, that the Jew appeals to the biological
destiny of his race; it is as a woman that Miriam aims for universal spirit,
transcending her history and time (only some forms of feminism would
claim this agenda as their own). Most important, this is not only a clash
between the self and her or his culture; it is also a clash between two
conceptions, individual and collective, of the self. Shatov is there as a re-
minder of the possibility that the self's existence *and* its redemption might
reside collectively, politically, with the group.

In her account of the London East End Jewish Community published in
Charles Booth's *Life and Labour of the London Poor* in 1902, Beatrix Potter
describes a visit to a *chevra*, one of the autonomous religious associations of
the community each named after the town or district in Russia or Poland
from which the majority of its members had emigrated:

It is a curious and touching site to enter one of the poorer and more wretched of
these places on a Sabbath morning . . . To reach the entrance you stumble over
broken pavement and household debris; possibly you pick your way over the rick-
ety bridge connecting it with the cottage property fronting the street . . . You enter;
the heat and odour convince you that the skylight is not used for ventilation . . .

Scarves of white cashmere or silk, softly bordered and fringed, are thrown across the shoulders of the men, and relieve the dusty hue and disguise the Western cut of the clothes they wear. A low, monotonous but musical-toned recital of Hebrew prayers, each man praying for himself to the God of his fathers, rises from the congregation, whilst the reader intones, in a somewhat louder voice, the recognised portion of the Pentateuch. Add to this the rhythmical cadence of numerous voices, the swaying to and fro of the body of the worshippers . . . and you may imagine yourself in a far-off Eastern land . . . At last you step out, stifled by the heat and dazed by the strange contrast of the old-world memories of a majestic religion and the squalid vulgarity of an East End slum.

Though it takes place up the road from here (it is the world that Shatov anticipates and describes), this is—I would say—a piece of anthropology. Beatrix Potter writes up her experience as if she were a traveller to the East (she is, of course, but I don't mean of London). She offers her encounter with the Jewish community as exotica—strangeness hovering on the edge of revulsion (the odour of the place), redeemed by reverie. When Clifford Geertz replies to Trilling's last essay, he starts with a long description of *sati* or widow immolation in Bali. He takes this description from the account of a late-nineteenth-century Danish traveller, Helms, who had apprenticed himself to a white rajah-type merchant adventurer 'straight out', as Geertz puts it, of *Heart of Darkness*. Reading Helm's account, I was struck by the similarities with Beatrix Potter's picture of the Jewish East End (I am not of course suggesting that anything like *sati* was going on in the *chevra*— although anti-Semitism has imputed equivalently hideous rituals to the Jews). Helms is enraged and enchanted by what he sees. Like Potter, he turns a trauma of recognition into a garden of delights. In 'Why We Read Jane Austen', Trilling had read Bali spectacle—the way it seemed to perform the self—not as unbreachable cultural difference, but as an example of the universal aesthetic response to life. By answering him with Helms, Geertz suggests that in this context the aesthetic response might be a form of imperial naming. 'It is', he writes, 'out of such foul plagues—foul and splendid—as this that the West earns its credentials to conquer and transform the East.' There is nothing more suspect than responding to difference by declaring that it is out of this world.

Helms's ethical outrage against *sati and* his appreciative wonder are both part of his imperial history; far from transcending that history, they condone and repeat it. The answer to the anthropological dilemma cannot therefore lie in such transcendence, in lifting yourself and the other off the ground. If empathy is, or can be, empire, perhaps we should give up the myth of perfect understanding and turn the interpreting strategy back onto ourselves. The only way to read another culture, Geertz suggests, is *through*, not *behind* the interfering glosses that connect us to it: 'It is not only the Balinese and Helms who seem morally elusive when we finish this remarkable account. So, unless we are willing to settle for a few embroidery mottoes of the eating-people-is-wrong variety, do we.' The account of Bali destabilizes perspective, meaning, judgement—equivocality emerges in every line; it decentres perception (these are all Geertz's terms—I am not quoting Terry Eagleton's *Literary Theory*) 'through first, second, third and nth order inter-pretation'; 'Professor Trilling's nervousness about the epistemological complacency of traditional humanism,' Geertz concludes, 'is not misplaced. The exactest reply to it is James Merrill's wrenching observation that life is translation, and we are all lost in it.' You can only start seeing—this was Freud's most basic insight—when you know that your vision is troubled, fallible, off-key. The only viable way of reading is not to find, but to dis-orient, oneself.

I take this as my way into the final text that I wish to refer to today. I should say first that the passage from Beatrix Potter is there to suggest that the imperial dilemma can play itself out on home ground. It is not, has never been, safely away. Jews can be natives: 'strange exotics in a land of prose', to use the Jewish novelist Israel Zangwill's own words from his famous novel *Children of the Ghetto* (Trilling's mother boasted Zangwill as an intimate; she also claimed a family resemblance to Queen Victoria [I think that's called ambivalence]). The East End of London is now filled with a whole new generation of immigrants—from Jamaica and the Indian sub-continent from the 1950s; from Somalia in the last few years. In fact, Asians have been in the East End of London since the seventeenth century; and although slavery was illegal, the first black settlers in the East End were freed slaves. This college is situated in the part of London which bears the strongest legacy of empire. Imperialism rolled into reverse gear, to use David Widgery's expression from his book *Some Lives! A GP's East End*. Or in the words of one of the migrant associations' neatest slogans: 'We are here because you were there.'

One of the places the British Empire was, of course, is South Africa, another history which might be—again one cannot yet know—in the pro-cess of being at least partially resolved. The tropes that have worked their way into the literary imagination from Africa are amongst the most powerful of the modern English tradition—hence that reference by Geertz to Conrad's *Heart of Darkness* slap bang in the middle of his discussion of Bali. My final text also comes from South Africa, but it is more recent—Rian Malan's 1990 *My Traitor's Heart*—the best-selling account of contemporary South Africa, written by a white Boer South African, descendant of Daniel François Malan, head of the first Afrikaner National Government which founded apartheid and came to power in 1948. Malan subtitles his book: 'Blood and Bad Dreams: A South African Explores the Madness in His Country, His Tribe and Himself.' The title in itself feels wilfully confusing—madness explored by madness; who, then, is calling the shots? In *My Traitor's Heart* the anthropological dilemma plays itself out across the blood and bad dreams of the nation. The epigraph of the final book starts:

And you must know this law of culture. Two civilisations cannot know and understand one another well. You will start going deaf and blind.

Of the texts I have chosen to discuss today, *My Traitor's Heart* undoubtedly presents the strongest and most difficult challenge to the vision of the empathetic, ethical imagination to which Trilling held throughout his life. In South Africa, Malan's book starkly and brutally demonstrates, there is no place for the white liberalism which venerates other cultures as the mark of its own imaginative capacities, no place for cultural empathy without bounds:

Elsewhere in the world, veneration and respect for non-Western cultures is the hall-mark of the humane and open-minded white man . . . in South Africa it is quite the opposite . . . any acknowledgement of different cultural values threatens to sound like an oblique argument in apartheid's favour and an insult to Africans besides . . . In my circle of hell, the circle of white left liberals, discussions of such matters are fraught with curious peril.

For Dr Motlana in Soweto—redoubtable physician, community leader, outspoken foe of apartheid—culture is an irretrievably contaminated term: 'Culture, is a word that became disreputable because of Hitler, who made culture synonymous with race. I worry about the misuse of that word. We use it to divide mankind.' But what is Motlana to do when the people whom he speaks for claim back the word 'culture' in terms in which he cannot recognize himself? Crusading against superstition in the name of reason, Motlana risks adding insult to the injury of his people under the aegis of Enlightenment Man. In South Africa the very term 'culture' belongs to a war of attrition and attribution. Point of blindness and attraction, it can no longer—because the language has been corrupted—speak its name.

I am not, however, going to leave the issue of liberalism there, not least of all because the book doesn't leave it there. Liberalism, even white liberalism, does not, of course, only take the shape of imperial goodwill; it is in itself a historical and mutating term. Writing in 1949, Trilling could say, with an assurance that made me gasp, that 'liberalism is not only the dominant but even the sole intellectual tradition. For it is the plain fact that nowadays there are no conservative or reactionary ideas in general circulation.' By 1975, Diana Trilling will be arguing that the term had been commandeered by those unwilling to speak out against Communism *and* by the emerging new Right. The second should be familiar—it was, after all, a central platform of Thatcherism to seize for the Conservatives the liberal agenda of individual rights.

At the same time we can hardly dismiss that agenda, given that in Palestine and South Africa it has hardly begun. Patricia Williams, in her remarkable *The Alchemy of Race and Rights*, insists—against those who reject the concept of rights as pure bourgeois individualism—that it be retrieved for a contemporary politics of race. We should perhaps remember that in the US, as recently as the Dukakis-Bush election campaign, liberalism could still be too radical; it could still be a dirty word. Making a pre-emptive bid for the next Republican nomination and the Presidency, Pat Buchanan said in a speech last month:

Never will we raise a white flag in the cultural war. Our culture is superior because our religion is Christianity, and that is the truth that makes men free.

The meaning of liberalism is something still in process, constantly fought over and reclaimed; read into the spirit of Vaclav Havel, and then almost as immediately appropriated by those rushing to see in the fall of Communism the triumph—yet again—of the West.

In *The Liberal Imagination*, Trilling wrote:

The word liberal is a word primarily of political import, but its political meaning defines itself by the quality of life it envisages, by the sentiments it desires to affirm.

It is for me, finally, the weakness of Trilling's position that the sentiment increasingly substituted for the politics; but I don't think this has to be the case. Re-read that statement and it takes us back to the question with which I started—of the psychic conditions of freedom, the affective colours of political life: 'Unless we insist', says Trilling again, 'that politics are imagination and mind, we will learn that imagination and mind are politics, and of a kind we will not like.'

At the end of *My Traitor's Heart*—this is the last literary moment to be put alongside the passages from Henry James and Dorothy Richardson—the most extraordinary woman, and I think it is crucial again that it is a woman, rises up out of the violence Malan has so graphically and despairingly described, to put Trilling's vision of liberalism once more to the test. It is

Creina Alcock, widow of Neil Alcock: together as a couple they had defied all sound political warnings and judgement by making their home in the Zulu reservation of Msinga. Let me remind you of first lines of the epigraph which opens this final section of the book: 'And you must know this law of culture: two civilisations cannot know and understand each other well. You will go deaf and blind'. It continues:

signals from the other country will be as incomprehensible to you as if they had been sent by the inhabitants of Venus. If you like you can become an explorer in your own country . . . But I doubt that you will have such a desire. Such expeditions are very dangerous and you are no madman, are you?

By the time Malan meets Creina Alcock, Neil Alcock has been murdered while intervening, at local request, to try and resolve a Msinga dispute. It had been his belief that it was the task of the white man to put himself and his skills at the disposal of the black peasantry (advise, don't dictate) and on that basis the couple had been part of the most cost-effective development project in Africa. When Malan meets Creina and asks her how to live in South Africa, she answers him with questions: whether he believed in truth and sought to serve it honourably, what sins he had committed in his life, what he understood by the word 'love', throwing out quotes from D. H. Lawrence and T. S. Eliot on the way. Malan thinks he is hallucinating. It is the most bizarre of moments. Rather like a cross between a mystic encounter and a seminar on modern literature, this meeting is weighted with such expectation that you feel as a reader that the destiny of the nation, and perhaps not only of this nation, rests with Creina Alcock's words.

After the death of Neil Alcock, Creina Alcock is almost driven off the edge: she is robbed by the Zulu boys she most trusted; her land is invaded and destroyed by black-owned goats. At one point, like the Boers she has spent her life fighting, she stalks her own land armed with a gun: 'There is an old Afrikaaner philosophy—*kragdadigheid*—the act of power: you took what you wanted and held it with your gun and fists.' This woman who had, as Malan puts it, entered Africa 'an enlightened creature', 'head full of reason and rationality', of Lawrence and Eliot, so sickened by violence that she could not sit through a Hollywood action movie (note all the tropes of enduring femininity), decides now that, having tried to love, it was time to kill.

She pulls back. Later Rian Malan puts to her again the question he asked the night they met: 'How do you live in this strange place'—note the personal and generic reference of that you (you personally or you as in anyone), and she replies:

love is worth nothing until it has been tested by its own defeat . . . You said one can be deformed by this country, and yet it seems to me one can only be deformed by the things one does to oneself. It's not the outside things that deform you, it's the choices you make. To live anywhere in the world, you must know how to live in Africa.

Liberalism as insane love—you have to be a little bit crazy to believe in this. You might also have to be a woman; this is one of those moments when a stereotype brushes against its radical potential (which is to say nothing about Creina Alcock in reality as distinct from Malan's picture of her). You also have to work out how to get from here to the political next stage. This is liberalism *in extremis*, brought to its limits by the racial politics of the modern world.

*   *   *

In his famous book on ethics, *After Virtue*, Alisdair Macintyre argues that we have lost the framework which would allow us to live a grounded or consistent ethical life. For him, the problems of cultural dialogue which I have focused on here would merely be an instance of the radical incommensurability of moral priorities and judgements in the world today. You cannot have virtue in a context where the community which would sustain it—he takes Aristotle's as his model—is no longer present; in South Africa such a community is not only missing, it is literally, brutally, tearing itself apart. Seen in these terms, Creina Alcock would be calling up virtue, or love, as the solution to the impossibility of virtue itself. But that, of course, would be the pessimistic conclusion.

I have tried in this lecture to take you round the world—or round the houses, at moments literally, as one might say. The point is that much of that world is here—as legacy, personal history, hope for the future, acknowledgement of the past. Imperialism in reverse gear, in David Widgery's formula, or—in terms that would be closer to the spirit of Trilling—colonialism turned back on, taken up into, the self. It is for this reason—the fields of force and history which run from this country to all the cultural instances I have described and back again—that the debate about the canon of English literature—whether we should read and study literatures of the old or new worlds—seems to me to be so misconceived. The links are there, those 'other' voices present. What needs explaining is why that fact could have been ignored for so long. That is why, starting with Henry James and the highest modern tradition, I have moved, via the woman writer and then South Africa, progressively off the edge of what still gets called, despite all the vital shifts of content and register, the canon.

As I see it, the task for literary studies is to find the forms of language, and they will have to be more than one, which allow for the connections between cultures—of affiliation, recognition, antagonism—without dissipating the voices in which they clash. In this context, pluralism—the ideal of happy co-existence—seems as useless finally as that form of liberalism which believes all cultures can be brought harmoniously into a single view. The rhetoric of pluralism can also be a way of concealing the depths of our conflicts. It can also be a way of promoting them. In the words of Norman Tebbit—never shy about exposing the dirty secrets of the Conservative unconscious—at Blackpool last week, 'Many traditional labour voters realized that they shared our values—that man is not just a social but also a territorial animal; it must be part of our agenda to satisfy those basic instincts of tribalism and territoriality.' The shocking election of the BNP member to Tower Hamlets council in September has, I think for many of us, brought all of this dramatically home.

'The great Australian philosopher, John Anderson,' writes Macintyre, 'urged us "not to ask of a social institution: 'What end or purpose does it serve?' but rather, 'Of what conflicts is it the scene?' " ' Shift the point slightly and we might say that we should look to university departments of literature, not just—with relish—for the conflicts inside the discipline, but to those conflicts as an index of what the wider culture is often unwilling to acknowledge or speak (in this sense conflict would be a virtue, not a vice). This could not, however, expect to take the traditional form of comfortable dialogue, but would have to be something which wrenches open our utterances into their histories. It is in this sense that I return finally to Freud, for whom language was always redolent of what is both hardest to articulate and most pressingly in need of speech. Psychoanalysis has in any case, I would argue, much more to say about the problem of recognition—hence its continuing importance for these issues—than about the eternal sameness of the self.

This, then, is the task as I see it facing the teaching and study of literature today. I wanted to use this lecture to give you a sense of the difficulty, but also the challenge. It is more than a formality to say that I am honoured to inaugurate this Chair in this department in this college of the University of London.

Delivered at Queen Mary and Westfield College, October 20 1993

Notes

Notes to Introduction

1. Sigmund Freud, *Extracts from the Fliess Papers* (1892–9), The Standard Edition of the Complete Psychological Works (London: Hogarth, 1966), i. 250.
2. Freud, *Fliess Papers*, 253. Note that these quotations are all taken from letters written in 1897 only months before the famous letter of 21 Sept. 1897, when Freud confesses to Fliess that he no longer believes in his own earlier theory of the origins of hysteria in infantile seduction.
3. Ammiel Alcalay, 'Understanding Revolution', *For Palestine*, ed. by Jan Murphy (London: Writers and Readers, 1993), 80.
4. *Jerusalem Post*, 30 Zionist Congress Supplement, Nov. 1982; cited by Michael Jansen in *Dissonance in Zion* (London: Zed, 1987), 53.
5. Amos Oz, 'The Israeli-Palestinian Conflict: Tragedy, Comedy and Cognitive Block, A Storyteller's Point of View', *Israel, Palestine and Peace* (London: Vintage, 1994), 112.
6. George Eliot, *Daniel Deronda* (1876; Harmondsworth: Penguin, 1967), 190.
7. Freud, *Fliess Papers*, 247–8.
8. I take this concept from the work of Hungarian émigré analysts, Nicolas Abraham and Maria Torok; see esp. Abraham, 'Notes on the Phantom: A Complement to Freud's Metapsychology', in Abraham and Torok, *The Shell and the Kernel*, ed. and trans. with an Introduction by Nicholas T. Rand (Chicago: Univ. of Chicago Press, 1994); originally publ. as 'Notules sur le fantôme', *Etudes freudiennes*, 9–10 (1975), and in *L'écorce et le noyau* (Paris: Aubier-Montaigne, 1978).
9. Freud, *Fliess Papers*, 249, 253.
10. Josef Breuer and Sigmund Freud, *Studies on Hysteria* (1893–5), Standard Edition, ii. 165.
11. Cited in *Dissonance in Zion*, 42.
12. 'State', *Oxford English Dictionary* (Oxford: Oxford Univ. Press, 2 edn., 1991), 551.

13. Maria Torok, 'Fantasy: An Attempt to Define its Structure and Operation' (1959), in *The Shell and the Kernel*, 35.

14. Freud, *Moses and Monotheism*, 1934–8 (1939), Standard Edition, xxiii. 76.

15. Olive Schreiner, *Woman and Labour* (1911; London: Virago, 1978), 139; Sheila Rowbotham, Lynne Segal, and Hilary Wainwright, *Beyond the Fragments: Feminism and the Making of Socialism* (London: Merlin, 1979).

16. Machiavelli, *The Prince*, extract included in *States and Societies*, ed. by David Held *et al.* (Oxford: Blackwell, 1983), 67.

17. Max Weber, 'Politics as a Vocation', in *From Max Weber: Essays in Sociology*, ed. by H. H. Gerth and C. Wright Mills (London: Routledge, 1991), 79.

18. Weber, 'Politics as a Vocation', 78.

19. Weber, *Economy and Society*, ed. by Guenther Roth and Claus Wittrich (New York, 1968), i. 9–10, 14.

20. Quentin Skinner, *The Foundations of Modern Political Thought* (Cambridge: Cambridge Univ. Press, 1978), ii, 358.

21. Karl Marx, 'On the Jewish Question' (1843), *Writings of the Young Marx on Philosophy and Society*, ed. and trans. by Loyd D. Easton and Kurt H. Guddat (New York: Doubleday, 1967), 240.

22. Cited in Elie Kedourie, *Nationalism* (1960; Oxford: Blackwell, 1993), 30.

23. For a particularly informative account, see Conor Gearty, 'The Party in Government', *London Review of Books*, 9 Mar. 1995.

24. Weber, *Economy and Society*, 56.

25. Weber, 'The Sociology of Charismatic Authority', *From Max Weber*, 245.

26. Antonio Gramsci, 'The Conception of Law', *Selections from the Prison Notebooks* (1929–35), ed. and trans. by Quintin Hoare and Geoffrey Nowell-Smith (London: Lawrence and Wishart, 1971), 246–7.

27. Friedrich Engels, 'The Origins of the Family, Private Property and the State', 1884, *Marx and Engels: Selected Works* (London: Lawrence and Wishart, 1968), 577.

28. Emil Habiby, *The Secret Life of Saeed, the Ill-Fated Pessoptimist: A Palestinian Who Became A Citizen of Israel*, trans. from the Arabic by Salma Khadra Jayyusi and Trevor le Gassick (New York: Vantage Press, 1982), 70.

29. Gramsci, *Prison Notebooks*, 324; cited by Edward Said, *The Question of Palestine* (New York: Times Books, 1979; Vintage edn., 1992), 73; also cited in Said, *Orientalism* (New York: Pantheon, 1978), 25.

30. Freud, *The Psychopathology of Everyday Life* (1901), Standard Edition, vi. 211 n.

31. Letter to L. Jaffe of the Keren Ha-Yesod, financial arm of the World Zionist organization, 1935; 1930 letter to Dr Chaim Koffler in response to an appeal by the Jewish Agency to prominent European Jews for criticism of British policy on access to the Wailing Wall in Jerusalem and on Jewish immigration to Palestine, cited by Yosef Hayim Yerushalmi, *Freud's Moses: Judaism Terminable and Interminable* (New Haven: Yale Univ. Press, 1991), 13 and p. 48 below; as Yerushalmi points out, many committed Zionists, including Martin Buber and Gershom Scholem, shared Freud's 1930 view.

32. Muriel Spark, *The Mandelbaum Gate* (London: Macmillan, 1965; Harmondsworth: Penguin, 1967).

33. Anton Shammas, *Arabesques*, trans. from the Hebrew by Vivian Eden (New York: Harper and Row, 1988), 23, 235, 243.

34. Virginia Woolf, *Three Guineas* (1938), ed. with introduction by Morag Shiach (Oxford: Oxford Univ. Press, 1992), 273, 313.
35. 'An Interview with Israel Shahak', *Journal of Palestine Studies* (Spring 1975), 5: 'For Ben-Gurion, the state of Israel was an instrument for doing a presumed benefit for the Jews. But for Rabin's generation, Jews are instruments for the security of the state of Israel. It is very much worse.' Shahak has been one of the most consistent and outspoken internal critics of Israel and Chairman of the Israeli League for Civil and Human Rights.
36. Martin Woollacott, 'After the slaughter Israel must search its soul', *Guardian*, 16 March 1994.

Notes to Chapter One

1. Amos Oz, *My Michael* (1968), trans. from the Hebrew by Nicholas de Lange with the collaboration of the author (London: Chatto and Windus, 1972; Vintage, 1991).
2. Ibid. 102.
3. Ibid. 34.
4. Ibid. 41.
5. Oz, *Fima*, trans. from the Hebrew by Nicholas de Lange (London: Chatto and Windus, 1993), 162–3.
6. Yeshayahu Leibowitz, 'Right, Law and Reality' (1976), in *Judaism, Human Values and the Jewish State*, ed. by Eliezer Goldman, trans. by Eliezer Goldman and Yoram Navon and by Zvi Jacobson, Gershon Levi, and Raphael Levy (Cambridge, Mass.: Harvard Univ. Press, 1992), 231.
7. Ammiel Alcalay, *After Jews and Arabs: Remaking Levantine Culture* (Minneapolis: Univ. of Minnesota Press, 1993); Smadar Lavie, 'Blow-Ups in the Borderzones: Third World Israeli Authors' Gropings for Home', *New Formations*, 18 (Winter 1992); Ella Shohat, *Israeli Cinema: East/West and the Politics of Representation* (Austin: Univ. of Texas Press, 1989). I am grateful to Smadar Lavie for letting me see typescripts of her article, co-authored with Helene Knox, 'Translating by Dialogue: Tracing the Problems of Metonymy', forthcoming in *Women Writing Culture*, ed. by Ruth Behar and Deborah Gordon, as well as her translations of Sephardim Hebrew poetry.
8. Oz, *In The Land of Israel*, trans. from the Hebrew by Maurie Goldberg-Bartura (New York: Harcourt Brace Jovanovich, 1983).
9. Stanley Fish, 'Why Literary Criticism is like Virtue', in *London Review of Books*, 10 June 1993.
10. Oz, 'The Hill of Evil Counsel', in *The Hill of Evil Counsel* (1976), trans. from the Hebrew by Nicholas de Lange in collaboration with the author (London: Chatto and Windus, New York: Harcourt Brace Jovanovich, 1978; Vintage, 1993), 13.
11. Ibid., 15.
12. Felicia Langer, *With My Own Eyes: Israel and the Occupied Territories 1967–1973* (London: Ithaca Press, 1975), 126.
13. Raja Shehadeh, *The Third Way: A Journal of Life in the West Bank* (London: Quartet, 1982), 87–8.
14. Roland Barthes, *Mythologies*, 1968 (New York: Hill and Wang, 1971).

15. Oz, 'An Argument on Life and Death (A)', in *In The Land of Israel*, 120.
16. Ibid.
17. Frederic Brenner and A. B. Yehoshua, *Israel* trans. from the Hebrew by Philip Simpson (London: Collins Harvill, 1988), 74.
18. Oz, 'From Jerusalem to Cairo: Escaping from the Shadow of the Past', in *Israel, Palestine and Peace* (London: Vintage, 1994), 37.
19. Oz, 'An Argument on Life and Death (A)', 120.
20. Leibowitz, 'The Uniqueness of the Jewish People' (1976), 'The Religious and Moral Significance of the Redemption of Israel' (1977), in *Judaism, Human Values and the Jewish State*, 86, 113.
21. Leibowitz, 'Redemption and the Dawn of Redemption', in *Judaism, Human Values and the Jewish State*, 126.
22. Ibid.
23. Oz, 'An Argument on Life and Death (B)', in *In the Land of Israel*, 150.
24. Franz Kafka, *Parables and Paradoxes* (New York: Schocken, 1961), 81.
25. Sigmund Freud, *Three Essays on the Theory of Sexuality* (1905), Standard Edition, vii. 148.
26. Oz, 'Crusade', in *Unto Death* (1971), trans. from the Hebrew by Nicholas de Lange in collaboration with the author (London: Chatto and Windus, 1971; Vintage, 1992), 37.
27. Oz, 'Late Love', in *Unto Death*, 99–100.
28. Oz, *Touch the Water, Touch the Wind* (1973), trans. from the Hebrew by Nicholas de Lange in collaboration with the author (London: Chatto and Windus, 1975; Vintage, 1992), 71.
29. Oz, *My Michael*, 16.
30. Oz, 'Late Love', 132, 108, 139.
31. Oz, *Black Box* (1987), trans. from the Hebrew by Nicholas de Lange in collaboration with the author (London: Chatto and Windus, 1988; Vintage, 1993), 127, 231.
32. Oz, 'Late Love', 96; *Touch the Water, Touch the Wind*, 16.
33. Oz, *To Know a Woman* (1989), trans. from the Hebrew by Nicholas de Lange in collaboration with the author (London: Chatto and Windus, 1991; Vintage, 1992), 91–2.
34. Woolf, *Three Guineas*, 255.
35. Oz, 'Late Love', 127.
36. Leibowitz, 'The Uniqueness of the Jewish People', in *Judaism, Human Values and the Jewish State*, 82: 'In our times, we lack an objective criterion, independent of the subjective beliefs, views, and opinions of those who apply it, to determine whether someone is a Jew.' Yehoshua, *Israel*, 55.
37. Lavie, 'Blow-Ups in the Borderzones', 103.
38. David Grossman, *Sleeping on a Wire: Conversations with Palestinians in Israel*, trans. from the Hebrew by Haim Watzman (New York: Farrar, Straus and Giroux, London: Jonathan Cape, 1993), 141.
39. Oz, *The Slopes of Lebanon* (1987), trans. from the Hebrew by Maurie Goldberg-Bartura (New York: Harcourt Brace Jovanovich, 1989; London: Chatto and Windus, 1990; Vintage, 1991), 51.
40. Homi Bhabha, *The Location of Culture* (London: Routledge, 1993).

41. Shehadeh, *The Third Way*, 64.
42. Abraham, 'Notes on the Phantom', in Abraham and Torok, *The Shell and the Kernel*.
43. 'The Israeli occupation is boundaried by the "Green Line," the armistice line drawn in 1949 to separate Israel from Jordan, and now used popularly to demarcate the borders of the occupied West Bank and Gaza Strip from Israel before the 1967 War. Some Israelis, out of respect for national boundaries and opposition to the occupation, refuse to cross the Green Line uninvited [. . .] This refusal to collaborate with the apparatus of occupation is sometimes referred to as drawing a "red line." In other words, a red line marks the personal, moral or psychological limit beyond which one is willing to transgress; or conversely, by which one is compelled to action, perhaps consciously, to incur risk.' Deena Hurwitz, Introduction, *Walking the Red Line: Israelis in Search of Justice for Palestine*, ed. Deena Hurwitz, Preface by Rabbi Marshal T. Meyer (Philadelphia: New Society Publishers, 1992), 3. See also Grossman, *Sleeping on a Wire*, 43.
44. Expression used by psychoanalyst Jacques Lacan to describe the role of Freud's patient 'Dora' in bearing the weight, through her bodily symptoms, of the unconscious agendas and anxieties of her family; Lacan, 'Intervention on Transference', *Feminine Sexuality: Jacques Lacan and the école freudienne*, trans. by Jacqueline Rose, ed. Rose and Juliet Mitchell (London: Macmillan, 1982; New York: Norton-Pantheon, 1983), 70; first delivered as 'Intervention sur le transfert' and published in *Ecrits* (Paris: Seuil, 1966).
45. Oz, 'Late Love', 168.
46. Grossman, *The Yellow Wind*, trans. from the Hebrew by Haim Watzman (New York: Farrar, Straus and Giroux, London: Jonathan Cape, 1988), 30.
47. Allon White, 'Prosthetic Gods in Atrocious Places: Gilles Deleuze/Francis Bacon', in *Carnival, Hysteria and Writing* (Oxford: Oxford Univ. Press, 1993).
48. Grossman, *Yellow Wind*, 213.
49. Grossman interviewed on *Bookmark*, BBC, 15 Dec. 1993.
50. Grossman, *Sleeping on a Wire*, 116.
51. Oz, *My Michael*, 5.
52. Annette Baier, 'Mixing Memory and Desire', in *Postures of the Mind* (Minneapolis: Univ. of Minnesota Press, London: Methuen, 1985), 8.
53. Said, *The Question of Palestine* (New York: Times Books, 1979; Vintage edn., 1992), 148; Grossman, *Sleeping on a Wire*, 129: 'up until now, the Jewish Israeli and Palestinian Arab are the two most similar nations in this region, and the most different from the others'.
54. Grossman, *Sleeping on a Wire*, 20.
55. Jay Murphy, 'Interview: Hanan Mikhail-Ashrawi', in *For Palestine*, 167–8. Compare Haydar 'Abd al-Shafi in his opening statement to the 1991 Madrid Middle East Peace Talks, 'The occupier can hide no secrets from the occupied'; *The Palestinian-Israeli Peace Agreement: A Documentary Record* (Washington: Institute for Palestine Studies, 1993), 18.
56. Grossman, *The Yellow Wind*, 92, 96.
57. Shehadeh, *The Third Way*, 137–8.

58. Habiby, *The Secret Life of Saeed, the Ill-Fated Pessoptimist: A Palestinian Who Became a Citizen of Israel*, 101.

59. Shehadeh, *The Third Way*, 138. Oz is a member of 'Peace Now'. Cf. however the words of the Mapam (United Worker's Party) Platform of 1981: 'Annexation distorts our image.' *Documents on the Israeli-Palestinian Conflict 1967–83*, ed. Yehuda Lukacs (Cambridge: Cambridge Univ. Press, 1984), 123.

60. Oz, *In the Land of Israel*, 132; *Fima*, 27.

61. Oz, *The Hill of Evil Counsel*, 18; *Black Box*, 84; *Fima*, 43.

62. Oz, 'Telling Stories Under Seige', in *Israel, Palestine and Peace*, 98.

63. Barthes, *Mythologies*; Chinua Achebe, 'An Image of Africa: Racism in Conrad's *Heart of Darkness*', in *Hopes and Impediments: Selected Essays 1965–1987* (London: Heinemann, 1988).

64. Oz, 'Clearing the Minefields of the Heart', in *Israel, Palestine and Peace*, 128.

65. David Barsamian, 'Edward Said: Interview', in *For Palestine*, 177; Oz, 'The Israeli-Palestinian Conflict', in *Israel, Palestine and Peace*, 110.

66. Oz, *Fima*, 206.

67. Oz, 'At the Bridge', in *Guardian*, 1 Sept. 1993, repr. in *Israel, Palestine and Peace*.

68. 'Whose Holy Land?', in *Israel, Palestine and Peace*, 88.

69. Remark made by Oz during a visit to the settlers filmed on the programme 'My Homeland, Your Homeland', BBC broadcast in Israel, Oct. 1993.

70. Oz, 'An Argument on Life and Death (B)', in *In the Land of Israel*, 131.

71. Oz, 'Peace and Love and Compromise', in *Israel, Palestine and Peace*, 70.

72. Zvi Bachur, cited in Oz, *In the Land of Israel*, 198; Anton Shammas's comment on Hebrew as the sole victory of Zionism continues: 'The Hebrew that was resurrected was not the Mizrahi Hebrew. And that was the tragedy. For the non-Jewish Arab writer, Ashkenazi Hebrew is not only the homeland of the Jews—it's the language of threat.' Lavie, 'Blow-Ups in the Borderzones', 103.

73. Oz, 'Between Europe and the Negev Desert', in *Israel, Palestine and Peace* 54.

Notes to Chapter Two

1. According to *The Golden Legend* (the collection of saints' lives put together about 1260), the miracle involved transposing the leg of a dead Ethiop into the body of a man, devoted to the service of the holy martyrs, whose leg was consumed by a cancer, whereupon he made a total recovery. The severed cancerous limb is anointed and attached to the body of the dead Moor in his tomb. I am grateful to Andrew Martindale for elucidating this for me.

2. Rian Malan, *My Traitor's Heart—Blood and Bad Dreams: A South African Explores the Madness in His Country, His Tribe and Himself* (London: Bodley Head, 1990; Vintage, 1991), 273 (original emphasis).

3. Ibid.

4. Ibid., 268.

5. Grossman, *Sleeping on a Wire*, 213.

6. A. B. Yehoshua, 'D'un droit à l'autre', in *Repenser Israel: Morale et politique dans l'état juif*, ed. Ilan Greilshammer (Paris: autrement, 1993), 108.

7. Oz, *Black Box*, 209.

8. Bessie Head, 'God and the Underdog', in *A Woman Alone: Autobiographical Writings*, selected and ed. by Craig MacKenzie (London: Heinemann, 1990), 45.

9. Malan, *My Traitor's Heart*, 81 (my emphasis).

10. Shehadeh, *The Third Way*, 64.

11. Head, *A Question of Power* (London: Heinemann, 1974), 200.

12. Hannah Arendt, *The Origins of Totalitarianism* (New York: Harcourt Brace Jovanovich, 1951; new edn., 1979), 291.

13. Arendt, 'Herzl and Lazare' (Oct. 1944), in *The Jew As Pariah: Jewish Identity and Politics in the Modern Age*, ed. with an introduction by Ron H. Feldman (New York: Grove Press, 1978), 128.

14. Alisdair MacIntyre, *After Virtue: A Study in Moral Theory*, 1981 (London: Duckworth, 2nd edn., 1991), 195.

15. Zora Neale Hurston, *Dust Tracks on a Road: An Autobiography* (1942; 2nd edn. ed. and with an introduction by Robert Hemenway, Chicago: Univ. of Chicago Press, 1984), 342.

16. Cited in Milton Shain, *The Roots of Anti-Semitism in South Africa* (Charlottesville, Va.: Univ. of Virginia Press, 1994), 129.

17. 'Speech of Yasser Arafat at the UN, 13 November, 1974', *Documents on the Israeli-Palestinian Conflict*, 169.

18. Cited in Alcalay, *After Jews and Arabs*, 220.

19. Oz, *My Michael*, 129.

20. Oz, *The Hill of Evil Counsel*, 34.

21. Oz, *Fima*, 235.

22. Oz, 'An Argument on Life and Death (B)', *In the Land of Israel*, 127.

23. *Davar*, 3 Aug. 1984, cited by Jansen, *Dissonance in Zion*, 13.

24. Breyton Breytenbach, 'Isolation and Cooperation' in *Africa Report*, Nov.–Dec. 1980, cited by Jane Hunter, *Israeli Foreign Policy: South Africa and Central America* (Boston: South End Press, 1987), 27.

25. Cited by Hunter, 74.

26. Freud, *Moses and Monotheism*, 23.

27. Freud, 'Femininity', 1933, Standard Edition, xxii.

28. Wulf Sachs to Freud, 1 Aug. 1939, Freud Museum.

29. Ibid.

30. Cited in Yerushalmi, *Freud's Moses*, 13.

31. Wulf Sachs, *Black Hamlet: The Mind of an African Negro Revealed by Psychoanalysis* (London: Geoffrey Bles, 1937), reprint ed. with introductory essays by Saul Dubow and Jacqueline Rose (Baltimore: Johns Hopkins Univ. Press, 1996).

32. Sachs, *Psycho-Analysis: Its Meaning and Practical Application*, foreword by Sigmund Freud (London: Cassell, 1934), 140–1.

33. Paul Gilroy, *There Ain't No Black in the Union Jack: The Cultural Politics of Race and Nation* (London: Hutchinson, 1987).

34. Sachs, *Black Anger* (New York: Grove Press, 1947), 275. For a fuller discussion of the two versions, see Saul Dubow, '*Black Hamlet*: A Case of "Psychic Vivisection"?' in *The Psychoanalytic Study of Society*, 18, ed. L. Bryce Boyer *et al.* (Hillside, New Jersey: Analytic Press, 1993), 171–210, and *African Affairs*, 90/ 369 (Oct. 1993).

35. Sachs, *Psycho-Analysis*, 205.

36. Oz, *In the Land of Israel*, 127.
37. Said, *The Question of Palestine*, 119.
38. Ibid.
39. Jacques Lacan, 'The Function and Field of Speech and Language in Psycho-analysis', in *Ecrits: A Selection*, trans. by Alan Sheridan (London: Tavistock, 1977), 86; first delivered Rome 1953 as 'Fonction et champ de la parole et du language en psychanalyse', and published in *Ecrits*, 300.
40. W. H. Auden, 'In Memory of Sigmund Freud (d. September 1939)', *Collected Shorter Poems* (London: Faber, 1966), 166–70.
41. Stevie Smith, *Over the Frontier* (London: Jonathan Cape, 1938; Virago, 1980), 85–6.
42. Stephen Glover, ' "We are all so happy. It is as though Moses has led his people to the promised land." ' *Evening Standard*, 28 Apr. 1994.
43. Mandla Sibeko, Anglican priest at Slovo's funeral, cited Hugh Pope, 'Joe left the world a "better place" ', *Independent*, 16 Jan. 1995; Jonathan Steele, 'The prize of a lifetime', Obituary, *Guardian*, 7 Jan. 1995.
44. Gillian Slovo, *Ties of Blood* (London: Virago, 1990).
45. Ibid., 192.

Notes to Chapter Three

1. 'Living up to Back to Basics', *Guardian* leader, 7 Jan. 1994.
2. Marilyn Butler, 'Ambush: The Politics of National Curriculum English, 1990–3', *Critical Quarterly*, 35/4 (Winter 1993), 11.
3. Herbert Read, Preface, *The English Vision: An Anthology* (London: Routledge 1939), p. ix. In his 1983 book on nationalism, Ernest Gellner argues that in a secular, individualistic world, where allegiance to the nation is above all cultural, 'one's prime loyalty is to the medium of our literacy and its protector'. Language—as in the language of high culture—policed by the state substitutes its authority for that of God. *Nations and Nationalism* (Oxford: Blackwell, 1983), 142.
4. John Patten, 'There is a Choice: Good or Evil', *The Spectator*, 18 Apr. 1992; Butler, 'Ambush', 10.
5. Ibid.
6. Weber, cited in *States and Societies*, ed. Held, 116.
7. Patten, 'There is a Choice', 10.
8. Jane Austen, *Northanger Abbey* (1798–9; Oxford: Oxford Univ. Press, 1975), 175–6.
9. Patten, 'There is a Choice', 10.
10. Christopher Bollas, 'Violent Innocence', *Being a Character: Psychoanalysis and Self-Experience* (London: Routledge, 1992).
11. Ibid., 168.
12. Fran Abrams, 'Tongue and Cheek: The Real Measure of Patten', *Independent on Sunday*, 20 Mar. 1994.
13. Reported on Channel Four News, 23 Mar. 1994.
14. Judith Shklar, *Ordinary Vices* (Cambridge, Mass.: Harvard Univ. Press, 1984), 39.
15. Patten, 'There is a Choice', 9.

16. Linda Colley, *Britons: Forging the Nation 1707–1837* (New Haven: Yale Univ. Press, 1992), 112.

17. Samuel Smiles, *Self-Help*, cited by Robert Colls, 'Englishness and the Political Culture', in *Englishness: Politics and Culture 1880–1920*, ed. Robert Colls and Philip Dodd (Beckenham: Croom Helm, 1986), 35.

18. Matthew Arnold, 'The Incompatibles', *Irish Essays* (1882), The Complete Prose Works, ed. by R. H. Super (Ann Arbor, Univ. of Michigan Press, 1973), ix. 281.

19. Colley, *Britons*, 18.

20. Ibid., 9.

21. Colls, 'Englishness and the Political Culture', in Colls and Dodds, *Englishness, Politics and Culture 1880–1920*, 29.

22. Cited by Colley, *Britons*, 44.

23. Ibid., 17.

24. Ibid., 32.

25. Ibid., 111.

26. Ibid., 44.

27. Patten, speech to the 'Christianity in Today's World' Prize-Giving Ceremony, Sept. 1993; cited by Stephen Bates and Donald Macleod, 'Moralising Patten Fails to Learn his Lesson', *Guardian*, 2 May 1994.

28. Stephen Castle and Paul Routledge, 'Right Hails Portillo as Next Prime Minister', headline, *Independent on Sunday*, 16 Jan. 1994; Andrew Marr, 'Portillo, An Idea on the Move', *Independent*, 13 Oct. 1994; Marr refers to Portillo as the 'Prince Regent of Thatcherism'.

29. Michael Portillo, 'Poison of a New British Disease' (The Speech), *Independent on Sunday*, 6 Jan. 1994.

30. Colley, *Britons*, 35.

31. Andrew Marr, *Independent*, 15 Oct. 1994.

32. Portillo, 'Poison of a New British Disease'.

33. Kazuo Ishiguro, *The Remains of the Day* (London: Faber and Faber, 1989); Muriel Spark, *The Mandelbaum Gate*.

34. Ishiguro, *The Remains of the Day*, 40.

35. Ibid., 42.

36. Ibid., 28–9.

37. Freud, 'Femininity', 22, p. 115.

38. Ishiguro, *The Remains of the Day*, 136–7.

39. Cited by Hannah Arendt, 'Herzl and Lazare', in *The Jew as Pariah*, 128.

40. Arendt, *Eichmann in Jerusalem: A Report on the Banality of Evil* (New York: Viking, 1963; revised and enlarged edn., 1965; Harmondsworth: Penguin, 1977).

41. Arendt, 'Eichmann in Jerusalem', an exchange of letters between Gershom Scholem and Hannah Arendt, Jan. 1964, in *The Jew as Pariah*.

42. Spark, *The Mandelbaum Gate*, 75.

43. Ibid., 77.

44. Ibid., 31.

45. Ibid., 29.

46. Ibid.

47. Ibid., 77.

48. Ibid., 91, 116.

49. Sarah Helm, 'Deals on Land, Water and Economic Ties', *Independent*, 26 Oct. 1994.
50. Ishiguro, *The Remains of the Day*, 108.
51. Spark, *The Mandelbaum Gate*, 121.
52. Ibid., 165.
53. Ibid., 31.
54. Ibid., 131.
55. Ibid., 129, 132.
56. Ishiguro, *The Remains of the Day*, 243.
57. Ibid., 289.
58. Julia Kristeva, 'Stabat Mater', in *The Kristeva Reader*, ed. by Toril Moi (Oxford: Blackwell, 1986); first publ. as 'Héréthique de l'amour', *Tel Quel* (Winter 1977).
59. Terry Eagleton, 'Deconstruction and Human Rights', *Freedom and Interpretation: The Oxford Amnesty Lectures 1992*, ed. by Barbara Johnson (New York: Basic Books, 1993).
60. Ian Hacking, 'Plato's Friend', *London Review of Books*, 17 Dec. 1992.
61. Iris Murdoch, *Metaphysics as a Guide to Morals*, ch. 12, 'Morals and Politics' (London: Chatto and Windus, 1992).
62. Murdoch, *The Bell* (London: Chatto and Windus, 1958; Harmondsworth: Penguin, 1962), 115.
63. Murdoch, *The Sovereignty of Good* (London: Chatto and Windus, 1970; Routledge, 1991), 47; *Metaphysics as A Guide to Morals*, 8.
64. Murdoch, *A Severed Head* (London: Chatto and Windus, 1971); *The Message to the Planet* (London: Chatto and Windus, 1989).
65. Clive Sinclair, 'Is there anybody out there?', *Times Literary Supplement*, 20–6 Oct. 1989.
66. Murdoch, *The Sea, the Sea* (London: Chatto and Windus, 1978; Harmondsworth: Penguin, 1980), 186.
67. Ibid., 361.
68. Ibid., 305.
69. Ibid., 304.
70. Patten, 'There is a Choice', 10.
71. Portillo, 'Poison of a New British Disease'.
72. Hacking, 'Plato's Friend'.
73. Alisdair MacIntyre, *Whose Justice? Which Rationality?* (London: Duckworth, 1988), 23, 74. Likewise, Mary Wollstonecraft, although with reference to the social aspiration of equality for women, said: 'Liberty is the mother of virtue.' *Vindication of the Rights of Woman* (1792; Harmondsworth: Pelican, 1975), 121.
74. Shklar, *The Faces of Injustice* (New Haven: Yale Univ. Press, 1990), 24.

Notes to Chapter Four

1. Claudia Koonz (ed.), *Becoming Visible: Women in European History* (Boston: Houghton Mifflin, 1977), and Sue Lipschitz, *Tearing the Veil* (London: Routledge, 1977).
2. Fish, 'Why Literary Criticism is like Virtue'.
3. Murdoch, *The Sovereignty of Good*, 90.

4. Jacques Derrida, 'Force of Law: The "Mystical Foundation of Authority"', in *Deconstruction and the Possibility of Justice*, ed. by Drucilla Cornell, Michel Rosenfeld, and David Gray Carlson (London: Routledge, 1992), 16.

5. Ibid.

6. Jonathan Freedland, 'A Firebrand in the Laundry', interview with Amos Oz, *Independent*, 4 Sept. 1993.

7. Oz, *Black Box*, 110–11.

8. Cited by Fouad Moughrabi, 'Arab Images in Israel', in 'Views from Abroad', *Journal of Palestine Studies* (Spring 1977), 167. It might be worth giving this quote in full: 'We have become specialists in Arab mentality. For twenty-seven years, every Jew, here in Hulda and in other places, has been a great expert on Arab mentality . . . Force is the only language the Arabs understand. That's what they are like. Listen to me, I know them all the way back from Silberstein's orange grove in Nes Ziona in the 1920s.' Elsewhere Oz makes it clear that there is no symmetry between between Israeli and Palestinian grievance: 'They say that the Arabs (Egypt excepted) have a "Saladin complex" and the Israelis have a "Masada complex" [. . .] I reject this comparison. There is no symmetry between a destruction complex and an insecurity complex. [. . .] Moreover, the Israeli insecurity complex is, to a large extent, a product of the "Saladin complex" of part of the Arab world.' 'From Jerusalem to Cairo: Escaping the Shadow of the Past' (1982), *Israel, Palestine and Peace*, 41.

9. *Documents on the Israeli-Palestinian Conflict 1967–83*, 1, 10.

10. Abraham and Torok, 'Mourning or Melancolia: Introjection versus Incorporation', in *The Shell and the Kernel*; first publ. as 'Deuil ou melancolie, introjecter-incorporer', *Nouvelle revue de psychanalyse*, 6 (1972).

11. Roberto Mangabeira Unger, *The Critical Legal Studies Movement* (Cambridge, Mass.: Harvard Univ. Press, 1983), 65.

12. Ibid.

13. Ibid., 24.

14. Shklar, *Faces of Injustice*, 87.

15. 'Sayings of the Week', *Independent*, 7 May 1994.

16. *Documents*, 1.

17. Shehadeh, *The Third Way*, 129.

18. *Documents*, 9.

19. *The Palestinian-Israeli Peace Agreement*, 117.

20. 'An Interview with Israel Shahak', David Hirst and Charles Glass, *Journal of Palestinian Studies* (Spring 1975), 15.

21. *The Palestinian-Israeli Peace Agreement*, 118.

22. Edward Said, 'The Morning After', *London Review of Books*, 21 Oct. 1993; 'Who is Worse?', *London Review of Books*, 20 Oct. 1994; see also Robert Fisk, 'Remaining Issues', *London Review of Books*, 23 Feb. 1995, and Anton Shammas, 'Palestinians Must Now Master the Art of Forgetting', *New York Times Magazine*, 26 Dec. 1993.

23. Ibid.

24. Jay Murphy, 'Interview: Noam Chomsky', in *For Palestine*, 229; 'I know that they are tapping my phone: interview with Hanan Ashrawi', *Yediot Ahoronot*, 17 Dec. 1993.

25. Israel Shahak, 'The Oslo Accords: Interpreting Israel's Intentions', *Middle East International*, 22 Oct. 1993. The Oslo agreement can be interestingly compared with the 1979 Camp David agreement with which Palestinian leaders almost uniformly refused to co-operate. This comment, made at the time by émigré Palestinian scholar, Fayez Sayegh, makes the similarities all too clear: 'A fraction of the Palestinian people . . . is promised a fraction of its rights (not including the national right to self-determination and statehood) in a fraction of its homeland (less than one-fifth of the area as a whole); and this promise is to be fulfilled several years from now, through a step-by-step process in which Israel is to exercise a decisive veto power over any agreement.' Cited by Howard M. Sachar, *A History of Israel*, ii. *From the Aftermath of the Yom Kippur War* (Oxford: Oxford Univ. Press, 1987), 8.
26. Oz, *Slopes of Lebanon*, 6.
27. 'The Nine-Point Peace Plan, Israel's Foreign Minister Abba Eban, 8 October, 1968', *Documents*, 81.
28. Ibid., 86.
29. 'The Jarring Questionnaire and Replies, January 1971', *Documents*, 7.
30. Leibowitz, 'Right, Law and Reality', in *Judaism, Human Values and the Jewish State*, 230–1.
31. 'The term "right", at least in its secular sense, stands for something which is recognised by others, not for something which someone feels very strongly about', 'The Israeli-Palestinian Conflict', in *Israel, Palestine and Peace*, 102.
32. 'Fundamental Policy Guidelines of the Government of Israel as Approved by the Knesset, 5 Aug. 1981', *Documents*, 107.
33. Benedict Anderson, *Imagined Communities: Reflections on the Origin and Spread of Nationalism* (London: Verso, 1983).
34. Unger, *Critical Legal Studies*, 100.
35. Plato, *Republic*, trans. by G. M. A. Grube, revised by C. D. C. Reeve (Indianopolis: Hackett, 1992), 6.
36. John Rawls, 'The Law of Peoples', *Critical Inquiry*, 20/1 (Autumn 1993).
37. Ibid., 45.
38. Ibid., 48.
39. Ibid., 50.
40. Plato, *Republic*, 170.
41. Rawls, *A Theory of Justice*, (Oxford: Oxford Univ. Press, 1972), 143; Colley, *Britons*, 35.
42. Jean Genet, 'Four Hours in Shatila', in *For Palestine*, 29; extract from *Un Captif Amoureux* (Paris: Gallimard, 1986).
43. Shklar, *Faces of Injustice*, 29.
44. Ibid., 37.
45. Ibid., 101.
46. Ibid.
47. Ibid., 49.
48. Richard Dowden, 'Obituary', *Independent*, 7 Jan. 1995.
49. Stephen Greenblatt, *Marvelous Possessions: The Wonder of the New World*, (Oxford: Oxford Univ. Press, 1988), 37–8.
50. Freud, *Civilisation and its Discontents*, 1930 (1929), Standard Edition, 21, p. 104;

Das Unbehagen in der Kultur, Gesammelte Werke (Frankfurt: Fischer Verlag),
xiv. 464.

51. Freud, *Civilisation and its Discontents*, 95; *Das Unbehagen in der Kultur*, 455.
52. Freud, *Moses and Monotheism*, 82.
53. Freud, *Civilisation and its Discontents*, 143.
54. Ibid., 109.
55. Ibid., 102; *Das Unbehagen in der Kultur*, 461.
56. Freud, *Civilisation and its Discontents*, 109–10; *Das Unbehagen in der Kultur*, 468–9.
57. Freud, *Civilisation and its Discontents*, 143.
58. Shklar, *Ordinary Vices*, 41.
59. Annette Baier, 'Theory and Reflective Practices', in *Postures of the Mind*, 223.
60. Oz, *Black Box*, 176.
61. Alcalay, *After Jews and Arabs*, 272–4.
62. Oz, *In the Land of Israel*, 140.
63. Alcalay, *After Jews and Arabs*, 118.
64. Oz, *Touch the Water*, 137.
65. Grace Halsell, *Prophecy and Politics: The Secret Alliance Between Israel and the Christian New Right* (Chicago: Lawrence Hill Books, 1986), 37.
66. Weber, 'Politics as a Vocation', in *From Max Weber*, 122.
67. Arendt, *The Origins of Totalitarianism*, 462.
68. MacIntyre, *Whose Justice? Which Rationality?*, 347.
69. Freud, *Civilisation and its Discontents*, 142.
70. For one account of these connections and parts of this history, see Paul Gilroy, *The Black Atlantic: Modernity and Double Consciousness* (London: Verso, 1993), ch. 6.
71. Nelson Mandela, 'We must end the old social order and bring in a new one', *Intensify the Struggle to Abolish Apartheid: Nelson Mandela Speeches 1990* (New York: Pathfinder, 1990), 59.
72. Cited in Shain, *The Roots of Anti-Semitism in South Africa*, 138.
73. Alcalay, *After Jews and Arabs*, 284.

Notes to Chapter Five

1. Caroline Rooney, ' "Dangerous Knowledge" and the Poetics of Survival: A Reading of *Our Sister Killjoy* and *A Question of Power*', in *Motherlands: Black Women's Writing from Africa, The Caribbean and South Asia*, ed. Susheila Nasta (London: The Women's Press, 1991), n. 27.
2. Edward Said, 'Nationalism, Human Rights and Interpretation', *Raritan*, 12/3 (Winter 1993).
3. Bessie Head, *A Question of Power* (London: Davis-Poynter, 1973; Heinemann African Writers series, 1974). Bessie Head's other two novels are *When Rain Clouds Gather: A Novel* (New York: Simon and Schuster, London, Gollancz, 1969; Heinemann, 1972) and *Maru: A Novel* (London: Gollancz, New York: McCall, 1971; Heinemann African Writers series, 1972), and, posthumously published, *The Cardinals with Meditations and Short Stories*, ed. with an introduction by M. J. Daymond (Cape Town: David Phillip, Africasouth New Writing, 1993). For full details of all Bessie Head's writings and critical literature, see *Bessie Head:*

A Bibliography, ed. Susan Gardner and Patricia E. Scott (National English Literary Museum, 1, Grahamstown, 1976), and Supplement compiled by Craig Mackenzie (1990).

4. Charles Larson, 'The Singular Consciousness: R. K. Narayan's *Grateful to Life and Death*, Bessie Head's *A Question of Power*', in *The Novel in the Third World*, ed. Charles Larson (Washington: Inscape, 1976), 165; C. Larson, *English Round the World*, 10 (May 1974), 6, both cited in Gardner and Scott, *Bessie Head: A Bibliography*.

5. Bessie Head, 'Notes on Novel Writing', *A Woman Alone: Autobiographical Writings*, selected and ed. by Craig MacKenzie (London: Heinemann African Writers series, 1990), 62.

6. John Lonsdale, 'Mau Maus of the Mind: Making Mau Mau and Remaking Kenya', *Journal of African History*, 31 (1990).

7. Bessie Head, 'Dreamer and Storyteller', *Tales of Tenderness and Power* (Johannesburg: Donker, 1989; London: Heinemann African Writers series, 1990), 143.

8. Bessie Head, letter to Charles Sarvan, 25 Apr. 1980, publ. in Charles Sarvan, 'Bessie Head: Two Letters', *Wasifiri*, 12 (Autumn 1990), 15.

9. Head, *A Question of Power*, 104, 105.

10. Ibid., 193.

11. Victor Tausk, 'On the Origin of the "Influencing Machine" in Schizophrenia', in *The Psychoanalytic Reader*, ed. by Robert Fliess (New York: International Universities Press, 1948), 33.

12. Head, *A Question of Power*, 126, 36, 39.

13. Megan Vaughan, *Curing their Ills: Colonial Power and African Illness* (Cambridge: Polity Press, 1990), 22. As Lynette Jackson pointed out to me when I delivered this chapter at Columbia University, this belief should not be confused with the issue of the real incarceration of African women; see Lynette Jackson, 'Gendered Disorder in Colonial Zimbawbe: Case Analyses of African Female Inmates at the Ingutsheni Mental Hospital, 1932–57', *The Societies of Southern Africa in the 19th and 20th Centuries*, Collected Seminar Papers of the Institute of Commonwealth Studies, Univ. of London, ed. Shula Marks (1993), 45.

14. Sachs, *Black Hamlet*, 11.

15. Sachs, *Black Anger*, 3.

16. Ibid.

17. Elizabeth Evasdaughter, 'Bessie Head's *A Question of Power* read as a mariner's guide to paranoia', *Research in African Literatures*, 20/1 (1989).

18. This comparison is discussed by Susan Gardner and Patricia Scott in the introduction to their Bessie Head bibliography, 12, see n. 3 above.

19. Head, *A Question of Power*, 23.

20. Ibid., 22, 14.

21. I. Schapera, *The Tswana* (1953; revised edn. with John L. Comaroff, London: Kegan Paul International, 1991), 53.

22. Norman Rush, *Mating* (New York: Random House, London: Jonathan Cape, 1992), 363.

23. Ibid., 436.

24. Sarvan, 'Bessie Head: Two Letters', 26 June 1980, 14.

25. Sachs, *Black Hamlet*, 219.

26. Vaughan, *Curing their Ills*, 106.

27. Evasdaughter, 'A mariner's guide to paranoia', 74.

28. *Not Either An Experimental Doll: The Separate Worlds of Three South African Women*, ed. Shula Marks (London: The Women's Press, 1987).

29. *Not Either An Experimental Doll*, 200.

30. Sachs, *Black Hamlet*, 193.

31. Ibid., 190.

32. Head, *A Question of Power*, 15.

33. There has been some debate about the exact biographical details of Bessie Head's life and their relationship to *A Question of Power*; cf. Susan Gardner, '"Don't ask for the true story": A Memoir of Bessie Head', *Hecate*, 12/1–2 (1986), and reply by Teresa Dovey, '*A Question of Power*: Susan Gardner's Biography versus Bessie Head's Autobiography', *English in Africa*, 16/1 (May 1989).

34. Bessie Head, 'Notes from a Quiet Backwater I', *A Woman Alone*, 3.

35. Lewis Nkosi, *Mating Birds* (London: Constable, 1986). Gardner and Scott, in their introduction to the Bessie Head bibliography (n. 3 above), and Randolph Vigne (*Bessie Head: A Gesture of Belonging: Letters from Bessie Head, 1965–1979*, ed. Randolph Vigne (London: SA Writers, Portsmouth, NH: Heinemann, 1991), 224) make the point that Nkosi, a former colleague of Bessie Head's in South Africa before he was exiled by the government in the 1960s, has been one of the most important commentators on her writing: Nkosi, 'Women in Literature', *African Woman*, 6 (Sept.–Oct. 1976), and 'Southern Africa: Protest and Commitment', *Tasks and Masks: Themes and Styles of African Literature* (Essex: Longman), 1981.

36. Head, *A Question of Power*, 17.

37. Bessie Head, 'Social and political pressures that shape writing in South Africa', *A Woman Alone*, 66.

38. Head, *A Question of Power*, 131, 116.

39. Bessie Head, 'Notes from a Quiet Backwater II', *A Woman Alone*, 77.

40. Vigne (ed.) *A Gesture of Belonging*, 76.

41. On trans-generational haunting, see Abraham, 'Notes on the Phantom', and discussion in Introduction and Chs. 1 and 2 above.

42. Head, *A Question of Power*, 53.

43. Bessie Head, 'Writing Out of Southern Africa', *A Woman Alone*, 95.

44. See Introduction to Gardner and Scott, *Bessie Head: A Bibliography*, 9.

45. Head, *A Question of Power*, 44–5.

46. Ibid., 47–8.

47. Sachs, *Black Hamlet*, 62.

48. See Dubow, '*Black Hamlet*: A Case of "Psychic Vivisection"' and Dubow, introductory essay to *Black Hamlet*, 1996 edn.

49. Bessie Head, *Maru*, 109.

50. Sarvan, 'Bessie Head: Two Letters', 26 June 1980, 14.

51. Vigne (ed.), *A Gesture of Belonging*, 55.

52. Frantz Fanon, *The Wretched of the Earth* (1961), preface by Jean-Paul Sartre, trans. by Constance Farrington (London: Macgibbon and Kee, 1965; Harmondsworth: Penguin, 1967), 238.

53. N. Chabani Manganyi, 'The Violent Reverie', *Treachery and Innocence: Psychology and Racial Difference in South Africa* (Johannesburg: Ravan Press, 1991), 19.

54. Head, *A Question of Power*, 98.
55. Ibid., 35.
56. Vigne (ed.), *A Gesture of Belonging*, 55.
57. Ibid.
58. Bessie Head, 'Sorrow Food', *Tales of Tenderness and Power*.
59. Head, *A Question of Power*, 133.
60. Bessie Head, 'Some Notes on Novel-Writing', *A Woman Alone*, 63.
61. Vigne (ed.), *A Gesture of Belonging*, 182.
62. Ibid., 160.
63. Head, *A Question of Power*, 161.
64. Manganyi, 'The Body for Others', *Treachery and Innocence*, 50.
65. Head, *A Question of Power*, 24.
66. Julia Kristeva, 'What of Tomorrow's Nation', *Alphabet City*, 2 (1992), 34.
67. Caroline Rooney, 'Dangerous Knowledge', 111.
68. Head, *A Question of Power*, 22.
69. Sarvan, 'Bessie Head: Two Letters', 26 June 1980, 14.
70. Vigne (ed.), *A Gesture of Belonging*, 187.
71. Ibid., 168.
72. Joanna Chase, cited by Evasdaughter, 76.
73. D. S. Izevbaye, 'Criticism and Literature in Africa', in *Perspectives on African Literature*, selections from the proceedings of the Conference on African Literature held at the University of Ife, 1968, ed. Christopher Heywood (London: Ibadan, Nairobi: Heinemann, 1970), 28.
74. Megan Vaughan, 'Idioms of Madness: Zomba Lunatic Asylum, Nyasaland, in the Colonial Period', *Journal of Southern African Studies*, 9 (1983), 230; Wulf Sachs gives very similar examples in 'The Insane Native: An Introduction to a Psychological Study', *South African Journal of Science*, 30 (Oct. 1933).
75. Bessie Head, *A Woman Alone*, 67, *A Gesture of Belonging*, 64.
76. Bessie Head, *Serowe: Village of the Rain Wind* (London: Heinemann, 1981), 29, *Tales of Tenderness and Power*, 142, *A Woman Alone*, 20.
77. *Not Either An Experimental Doll*, 202, 204.
78. Manganyi, 'Crowds and their Vicissitudes: Psychology and Law in the South African Courtroom', in *Treachery and Innocence*, 99.
79. James Ngugi, 'The African Writer and his Past', in Heywood, *Perspectives on African Literature*, 5.
80. Vigne (ed.), *A Gesture of Belonging*, 60.
81. Head, *A Question of Power*, 200.
82. Bessie Head, *When Raid Clouds Gather*, 134.

Notes to Chapter Six

1. Arendt, *The Origins of Totalitarianism*, Part 1, 'Antisemitism'.
2. It was in relation to Dorothy Richardson that the expression 'stream-of-consciousness' was first coined, although Dorothy Richardson herself criticized the term. See May Sinclair, 'The Novels of Dorothy Richardson', for Sinclair's review of the first three volumes of *Pilgrimage*, *Egoist*, 5 Apr. 1918, and Diane F. Gillespie, introduction to Dorothy Richardson, both in *The Gender of*

Modernism: A Critical Anthology, ed. by Bonnie Kime Scott (Bloomington, Ind.: Indiana Univ. Press, 1990). Virginia Woolf said of Richardson: 'She has invented a sentence we might call the psychological sentence of the feminine gender', review of *Revolving Lights*, *Times Literary Supplement*, 19 May 1923, in Virginia Woolf, *Women and Writing*, introduced by Michele Barrett (London: The Women's Press, 1979).

3. Virginia Woolf, *Three Guineas*, 273, 313.

4. Henry James, *The Portrait of a Lady* (1881; Harmondsworth: Penguin, 1963), 196.

5. Dorothy Richardson, *Pilgrimage*, 13 vols. (J. M. Dent, 1915–67, repr. London: Virago, 1979).

6. See e.g. Robert Casillo, *The Genealogy of Demons: Anti-Semitism, Fascism and the Myths of Ezra Pound* (Evanston, 1988), Christopher Ricks, *T. S. Eliot and Prejudice* (London: Faber, 1988), Bryan Cheyette, *Constructions of 'the Jew' in English Literature and Society: Racial Representations, 1875–1945* (Cambridge: Cambridge Univ. Press, 1993).

7. Sinclair, *Mary Olivier: A Life* (1919; London: Virago, 1980), *Life and Death of Harriet Frean* (1922; London: Virago, 1980).

8. Sinclair, *Mary Olivier*, 374.

9. Virginia Woolf, *The Years*, 1937 (Oxford: Oxford Univ. Press, World's Classics, ed. Hermione Lee, 1992), 322, and see article by Phyllis Lassner in *Between 'Race' and Culture: Representations of 'the Jew' in English and American Literature*, ed. Bryan Cheyette (Stanford: Stanford Univ. Press, 1996); Stevie Smith, *Novel on Yellow Paper* (1936; London: Virago, 1980), 10–11, but see also 107; Djuna Barnes, *Ladies Almanack* (1928; Elmwood: Dalkey Archive Press, 1992), 15.

10. Cheyette, *Constructions of 'the Jew' in English Literature and Society*; the discussion that follows is indebted to Chapter 4, 'The "socialism of fools": George Bernard Shaw and H. G. Wells'.

11. Ibid., 144.

12. Ibid., 144–8.

13. This is the title of one chapter of Colin Holmes's study of English anti-Semitism, *Anti-Semitism in British Society 1876–1939* (London: Arnold, 1979), 'A nation within a nation?'.

14. Benjamin Kidd, 'Individualism and After', Herbert Spencer Lecture (Oxford: Clarendon Press, 1908), 10; Arnold White, *The Modern Jew* (London: Heinemann, 1899), 199.

15. White, *Modern Jew*, p. xvi.

16. James, *The Portrait of a Lady*, 196.

17. Kidd, 'Individualism and After', 20.

18. See Geoffrey Alderman, *The Jewish Community in British Politics* (Oxford: Clarendon Press, 1983), ch. 4, 'The Socialists Arrive', 53.

19. See Alderman, *The Jewish Community in British Politics* and Lloyd Gartner, *The Jewish Immigrant in England 1870–1914* (London: Simon, 1960; 1973).

20. Cited in Gartner, *The Jewish Immigrant in England*, 134.

21. Jean Radford, *Dorothy Richardson* (Hemel Hempstead: Harvester, 1991), ch. 2, 'A Form of Quest'.

22. Richardson, *Clear Horizon* (1935; 1979 Virago edn.), iv.
23. Josef Kastein, *Jews in Germany*, trans. by Dorothy Richardson, with a preface by James Stephens (London: Cresset, 1934), 121.
24. Ibid., 147.
25. Robert Neumann, *Mammon (die Macht)*, trans. by Dorothy Richardson (London: Peter Davies, 1933), 80. This second translation appears to have the most bizarre publishing history—rejected first by the English publishers, then by the author who objected to the pre-arranged cuts; described in Gloria Fromm's biography of Richardson as finally abandoned altogether, it is nonetheless listed in Fromm's bibliography and was published by Peter Davies in 1933 (even more oddly, inside the cover of the translation it lists the original as first published in 1931, and *Mammon*, i.e. the translation, as published in 1926; which would make this a novel, not impossibly, whose English translation preceded its German publication); see Gloria Fromm, *Dorothy Richardson: A Biography* (Urbana, Ill.: Univ. of Illinois Press, 1977), 266–8.
26. Neumann, *Mammon*, 30.
27. Richardson, *Deadlock* (1921; 1979 Virago edn.), iii.
28. Ibid., 150–2.
29. Ibid., 169.
30. Kastein, *Jews in Germany*, 61, 54–5.
31. Cited in Fromm, *Dorothy Richardson*, 222. Oscar Wilde gives these terms his own pro-decadent turn in *The Picture of Dorian Gray* (1891), in a conversation between Lord Henry Wotton and a Duchess: ' "I believe in the race," she cried. "It represents the survival of the pushing." "It has development." "Decay fascinates me more." ' (Oxford: Oxford Univ. Press, 1974), ed. by Isobel Murray, 195.
32. Sigmund Freud, 'Some Psychical Consequences of the Anatomical Distinction Between the Sexes' (1925), Standard Edition, xix. 257; *Three Essays on the Theory of Sexuality* (1905), Standard Edition, vii. 207.
33. Freud, *Beyond the Pleasure Principle* (1921), Standard Edition, xix.
34. Richardson, *Dawn's Left Hand* (1931; 1979 Virago edn.), iv. 155.
35. Ibid., 288.
36. Beatrix Potter, 'The Jewish Community', in Charles Booth, *Life and Labour of the People in London* (1st ser., London, 1902), vol. iii. 'Poverty', 192.
37. Cited by Brian Cheyette, 'Anglo-Jewish Fiction', in *The Making of Modern Anglo-Jewry*, ed. by David Cesarini (Oxford: Blackwell, 1990), 110.
38. White, *The Modern Jew*, 209.
39. Claire Buck, paper presented at Cambridge 'Modernism' Conference, July 1993.
40. Kastein, *Jews in Germany*, 78.
41. Otto Weininger, Viennese turn-of-the-century author of *Sex and Character* (1903) who killed himself shortly after completing this 'Jewish self-hating' and misogynistic text; see Sander Gilman, *The Jew's Body* (London and New York: Routledge, 1991), 131–7, and Jean Radford, paper presented at Cambridge 'Modernism' Conference, July 1993.
42. Potter, 'The Jewish Community', 190, 168.
43. Kastein, *Jews in Germany*, 61.

44. Fromm, *Dorothy Richardson*, 153.

45. Kidd, 'Individualism and After', 25.

46. Richardson, *Deadlock*, 150.

47. Gayatri Spivak, 'Three Women's Texts and a Critique of Imperialism', in *The Feminist Reader*, ed. by Catherine Belsey and Jane Moore (London: Macmillan, 1989).

48. Richardson, *Deadlock*, 166–8.

49. White, *The Modern Jew*, 193.

50. Potter, 'The Jewish Community', 182.

51. Gartner, *The Jewish Immigrant in England*, 264–5.

52. Alderman, *The Jewish Community in British Politics*, 65.

53. Richardson, *Deadlock*, 167.

54. Cited by John Rosenberg, *Dorothy Richardson: The Genius They Forgot: A Critical Biography* (London: Duckworth, 1973), 64.

55. Cited in Cheyette, *Constructions of 'the Jew' in English Literature and Society*, 144.

56. This analogy between woman and Jew, between racial and sexual oppression, has also taken the most concrete of forms; in June 1914, a demonstration at the Brighton synagogue on the part of Jewish suffragettes—particularly incensed at the role of established Jewish MPs such as Herbert Samuels and Rufus Isaacs in incarcerations and force-feedings—compared British treatment of suffragettes to the Russian treatment of Jews (Alderman, *The Jewish Community in British Politics*, 87).

57. Richardson, *The Quakers Past and Present* (London: Constable, 1914), 5.

58. Ibid., 6, 9.

59. Ibid., 11.

60. Richardson, *Deadlock*, 218.

61. Ibid., 171.

62. Richardson, *Dimple Hill* (1938; 1979 Virago edn.), iv. 427.

63. Ibid.

64. Ibid. Compare, too: 'We all live under a Metaphocrasy. Tell her I'm giving up thinking in words. She will understand. Will agree that thought is cessation, cutting one off from the central essence, bearing an element of calculation.' Richardson, *March Moonlight* (1967; 1979 Virago edn.), iv. 607.

65. Richardson, *Dimple Hill*, 429.

66. Richardson, *Clear Horizon*, 292.

67. Arendt, *The Origins of Totalitarianism*, Part 3, 'Totalitarianism', 438. Compare, however, Marx in 'Estranged Labour': 'Man is a species being, not only because in practice and in theory he adopts the species as his object', but 'also because he treats himself as the actual, living species; because he treats himself as a *universal* and therefore a free being.' *Economic and Philosophical Manuscripts of 1844* (London: Lawrence and Wishart, 1973), 112.

68. Arendt, *The Human Condition* (Chicago: Univ. of Chicago Press, 1958), 312, cited in Mary G. Dietz, 'Hannah Arendt and Feminist Politics', in *Feminist Interpretations and Political Theory*, ed. by Mary Lyndon Shanley and Carole Pateman (Cambridge: Polity, 1991), 244.

69. Elizabeth Young-Bruehl, *Hannah Arendt: For Love of the World* (New Haven: Yale Univ. Press, 1982). For a discussion of the way this difficulty traces itself

out in Arendt's own writing, see Gillian Rose, *The Broken Middle: Out of our Ancient Society* (Oxford: Blackwell, 1992), ch. 5, 'Love and the State: Varnhagen, Luxemburg and Arendt'.

70. For discussion of these criticisms, see Dietz, 'Hannah Arendt and Feminist Politics'.

Index

Torok, Maria 31
Toryism/Tories, *see* Conservatism
totalitarianism 92, 137
trade unionism 121
'trans-generational haunting' 5, 6, 31
translation 37, 122
　life 25, 144
　loss of complexity in 36
　problem of 22
trauma 44, 107
　always returns 11
　historic 32, 69
　Jewish history 41
　national indefinition 30
　of recognition 143
　theory of neurosis 11
Treurnicht, Andries 39, 50
tribalism 149
Trilling, Diana 139, 140, 146
Trilling, Lionel 133–48 *passim*
triumphalism 25, 27
Truro 61
truth 7–8, 114, 146
　'primitive' feminized 75
Tsepe, Joas 111
Tswana 104
Tutu, Desmond, archbishop of Cape
　Town 87
Twain, Mark 133, 139, 140

ukuthwaza 106
Umbro 90
UN (United Nations) 13, 44, 45, 82, 83, 84
uncertainty 29, 29, 31, 36, 63, 81
　national self-definition 30
　performatives of 27
unconscious 3, 10, 12, 21, 34, 92, 134
　bisexual 88
　black and white 80
　challenge to the dominant 115
　Conservative 149
　energies 9
　historical 51
　identification 71
　Jewish history in the image of 48
　let it have its say 30
　logic of dreams 31

making of political identities 26
more intractable determinants 33
one specific liberal tradition 93
partial autonomy 115
subject 'vanishes' or 'fades' into 88
superego and 90
thoughts 59
undercurrents 22
'universality' of 112
Western and African 'native'
　fundamentally the same 49
Unger, Roberto Mangabeira 82, 83, 85
United States of America 44, 46
unity 134
　psycho-cultural 62
universality 88, 99–116

values 145, 149
Vaughan, Megan 102–3, 106, 114, 115
Versailles 43
victims 110, 111, 112
Vienna 11, 49, 102
　Viennese Parliament 133, 135, 139
Vigne, Randolph 110, 111, 112, 114, 115
Vilna/Vilnius 44
violence 62, 82
　annihilated 91
　antidote to 59
　binding subjects to 10
　legitimate 8
　love against 91
　potential 64
　self-perpetuating 95
　sickened by 147
　vehement 108
virtue 76, 88, 92, 95
　ahistorical 73
　Aristotelian cultivation of 90
　becomes a must 68
　civic 66, 73, 74
　cultivation of 67
　dignity of 62
　for Iris Murdoch 74–5
　Jewish 127
　patriotic 61
　relative autonomy 67
　repository of 66